About This Book

Why is this topic important?

Organizational consulting generally has a broader focus than training. Whereas a trainer might develop people's understanding of team roles, a consultant might help a dysfunctional team function. Similarly, a trainer might deliver a workshop on developing good time management and productivity skills, whereas a consultant might be contracted to analyze and recognize work-flow through a team or through an entire division or operating unit. There are clearly similarities between training and consulting—and the terms are often used interchangeably—but each has a unique focus and requires divergent approaches, tools, and techniques.

What can you achieve with this book?

Offering entirely new content each year, *The Pfeiffer Annual: Consulting* show-cases the latest thinking and cutting-edge approaches to organization development and performance improvement contributed by practicing consultants, organizational systems experts, and academics. Designed for both the dedicated consultant and the training professional who straddles both roles, the *Annual* presents a unique source of new knowledge and ideas, as well as practical and proven applications for facilitating better work processes, implementing and sustaining change, and improving organizational effectiveness.

How is this book organized?

The book is divided into four sections: Experiential Learning Activities (ELAs); Editor's Choice; Inventories, Questionnaires, and Surveys; and Articles and Discussion Resources. All the material can be freely reproduced for training purposes. The ELAs are the mainstay of the *Annual* and cover a broad range of training topics. The activities are presented as complete and ready-to-use designs for working with groups; facilitator instructions and all necessary hand-outs and participant materials are included. Editor's Choice pieces allow us to select material that doesn't fit the other categories and take advantage of "hot topics." The instrument section introduces proven survey and assessment tools for gathering and sharing data on some aspect of performance. The articles section presents the best current thinking about workplace performance and organization development. Use these for your own professional development or as resources for working with others.

About Pfeiffer

Pfeiffer serves the professional development and hands-on resource needs of training and human resource practitioners and gives them products to do their jobs better. We deliver proven ideas and solutions from experts in HR development and HR management, and we offer effective and customizable tools to improve workplace performance. From novice to seasoned professional, Pfeiffer is the source you can trust to make yourself and your organization more successful.

Essential Knowledge Pfeiffer produces insightful, practical, and comprehensive materials on topics that matter the most to training and HR professionals. Our Essential Knowledge resources translate the expertise of seasoned professionals into practical, how-to guidance on critical workplace issues and problems. These resources are supported by case studies, worksheets, and job aids and are frequently supplemented with CD-ROMs, websites, and other means of making the content easier to read, understand, and use.

Essential Tools Pfeiffer's Essential Tools resources save time and expense by offering proven, ready-to-use materials—including exercises, activities, games, instruments, and assessments—for use during a training or team-learning event. These resources are frequently offered in looseleaf or CD-ROM format to facilitate copying and customization of the material.

Pfeiffer also recognizes the remarkable power of new technologies in expanding the reach and effectiveness of training. While e-hype has often created whizbang solutions in search of a problem, we are dedicated to bringing convenience and enhancements to proven training solutions. All our e-tools comply with rigorous functionality standards. The most appropriate technology wrapped around essential content yields the perfect solution for today's on-the-go trainers and human resource professionals.

Pfeiffer *Essential resources for training and HR professionals*
www.pfeiffer.com

The Pfeiffer Annual Series

The Pfeiffer Annuals present each year never-before-published materials contributed by learning professionals and academics and written for trainers, consultants, and human resource and performance-improvement practitioners. As a forum for the sharing of ideas, theories, models, instruments, experiential learning activities, and best and innovative practices, the *Annuals* are unique. Not least because only in the *Pfeiffer Annuals* will you find solutions from professionals like you who work in the field as trainers, consultants, facilitators, educators, and human resource and performance-improvement practitioners and whose contributions have been tried and perfected in real-life settings with actual participants and clients to meet real-world needs.

> *The Pfeiffer Annual: Consulting*
> Edited by Elaine Biech
>
> *The Pfeiffer Annual: Leadership Development*
> Edited by David L. Dotlich, Peter C. Cairo,
> Stephen H. Rhinesmith, and Ron Meeks
>
> *The Pfeiffer Annual: Training*
> Edited by Elaine Biech
>
> *Michael Allen's e-Learning Annual*
> Edited by Michael Allen

Call for Papers

How would you like to be published in the *Pfeiffer Training* or *Consulting Annual*? Possible topics for submissions include group and team building, organization development, leadership, problem solving, presentation and communication skills, consulting and facilitation, and training-the-trainer. Contributions may be in one of the following three formats:

- Experiential Learning Activities

- Inventories, Questionnaires, and Surveys

- Articles and Discussion Resources

To receive a copy of the submission packet, which explains the requirements and will help you determine format, language, and style to use, contact editor Elaine Biech at Pfeifferannual@aol.com or by calling (757) 588-3939.

Elaine Biech, EDITOR

The *2010*
Pfeiffer
ANNUAL

CONSULTING

Pfeiffer
A Wiley Imprint
www.pfeiffer.com

Contents

Experiential Learning Activities

**Communication Topics

Editor's Choice

Inventories, Questionnaires, and Surveys

**Communication Topics

Articles and Discussion Resources

**Communication Topics

Website Contents

Our readers are invited to download customizable materials from this book related to the experiential learning activities and the instruments, as well as a PDF of the book text. The following materials are available FREE with the purchase of this book at: www.pfeiffer.com/go/consulting2010. The following username and password are required for accessing these materials:

Username: consulting
Password: 2010

Experiential Learning Activities

Mirror Image: Reflecting on How Our Personal Pursuits Show in Our Professional Practice
Gary Wagenheim, Robert Clark, and Alexander Crispo

Words of Trust: Building Trust in the Workplace
David Piltz

Difficult Conversations: Making Them Easier
Beverly J. Bitterman

Unstructured Coaching Conversations: Coaching the Coach
Travis L. Russ

I'd Like You to Mee t . . . Introducing a New Hire
Lucille Maddalena

**Communication Topics

Editor's Choice

Inventories, Questionnaires, and Surveys

Team Effectiveness Assessment Measure (TEAM)
Udai Pareek

Corporate Social Responsibility: Determining Your Position
Homer H. Johnson

Scale of Intellectual Capital for Organizations (SICO)
Sacip Toker, James L. Moseley, and Ann T. Chow

PDF

The book text is available in PDF format.

Preface

If everyone in all organizations communicated perfectly, I'd be out of a job. As a consultant, much of the work I conduct addresses communication—the lack of communication, miscommunication, or poor communication. And all of the work I do is dependent on good communication for success. The 2010 Pfeiffer Training and Consulting *Annuals* focus on communication.

"Why communication?" you might ask. It seems so, well, commonplace. Yes, communication is ordinary and something we routinely do every day. We've all been communicating ever since we were born, so you would think with all that practice, we would get it right! The truth of the matter is that communication is hard work. Communication encompasses many elements. It includes basic word choice and tone of voice. Communication also includes more complex elements such as the infinite differences in the use and meaning of words to each individual and the perceived assumptions that filter a message to create a completely different meaning.

So in this simple yet complex action we call communication, is there something that we can change or address that assures improved communication? Is there one thing that we can identify that will truly make a difference? As I read through the submissions, I found a thread running through them that formed the fabric of trust. Trust and communication seem to work hand-in-glove to improve employee relations, enhance leadership skills, implement change more easily, and build personal relationships.

The submissions offer many ideas for both building trust and improving communication. Here are a few ideas I gleaned from the submissions.

Clearly articulate expectations. Setting expectations that identify not only what but also why is critical. Understanding the bigger picture and the rationale for the task takes the guesswork out of the job. Putting the "why" behind the "what" builds trust.

Provide complete information. Enable others by ensuring that they have all the information required to make good decisions. Communicate more than information. Include your thoughts and ideas, your half-baked ideas, and your feelings. Anyone on the receiving end will better understand the complete picture. Keep everyone in the loop. Share what you know, when you know it. Sharing knowledge builds trust.

Confront concerns and problems early. Sweeping difficulties under the rug means that they will pile up and you will eventually stumble over them. Avoiding difficult people or situations creates even more difficulties later. Addressing challenging issues builds trust.

Be genuine. Honesty, candor, openness—all define the kind of communicator who fosters a healthy environment. Letting people in on who you are, always telling the truth, being forthright with comments, and avoiding deception sets you apart as authentic. Honesty builds trust.

Follow through. Do what you say you are going to do. And if you can't, tell others quickly. Dependability builds trust.

Listen. Listen until it hurts. Demonstrate that you can deal with the truth. Whether the message is good, bad, or indifferent, listen and behave appropriately. Display behavior that says it's okay to tell all. I've always thought that every organization should have an official listener on staff. Listening builds trust.

Model what you say and say what you mean. People will rely on you if they know that your message is congruent with who you are and what you represent. Being yourself builds trust.

Excellent communication involves more than selecting the right words and sharing information. It is also about building trust. Ralph Waldo Emerson wrote, "What you are shouts so loudly, I can't hear a word you're saying." What are you? What are you shouting? Can people hear what you are saying? Are your words congruent with your actions? Are you building trust to ensure that others hear you? The 2010 *Pfeiffer Annuals* are sure to help you in your job and your personal life to ensure that what you are aligns with what you say—building trust and improving communication at the same time.

Although every submission is in some way related to communication, we have selected several that stand out above the rest. The *Training Annual* presents eleven communication submissions and the *Consulting Annual* provides you with twelve communication submissions. Both *Annuals* continue to present our other popular topics: team building, leadership, problem solving, and so forth. The communication theme is an added bonus to concentrate some of our great contributors' talents in one year.

The 2010 *Training Annual* includes a wonderful array of tools to help you with communication. You will, of course, want to check out the ELA by Deborah Laurel for building trust. The ELA by Noam Ebnor from Israel is a takeoff on the "prisoner's dilemma" style negotiation and is sure to help your teams understand some of the elements of trust when working with other groups. Building trust for better communication often relies on understanding the differences and finding similarities between individuals. Two ELA authors address this topic: Cher Holton and Karen Reed. Both are fun as well as functional. You'll also want to check out the excellent array of communication-focused articles. Start out with Bob Lucas' "Using Trust to Achieve Workplace Success."

The 2010 *Consulting Annual* also includes communication tools. Start with the building trust ELA by David Piltz. Repeat contributor Devora Zack presents a practical activity to demonstrate how well-formed questions redirect attention from problems to outcomes. I must admit, I have already used Travis Russ' activity for unstructured coaching conversations. It achieved its objectives and then some. New article contributors Mona Lee Pearl, Phil Van Horn, and Jody Shields provide us with valuable advice when communicating instrument results.

Page through the table of contents in each volume. I think you will be pleasantly surprised about the wide variety of practical contributions for 2010. You will be delighted with the exciting new ELAs, articles, and inventories you'll be able to use without asking permission.

What Are the Annuals?

The *Annual* series consists of practical materials written for trainers, consultants, and performance-improvement technologists. We know the materials are practical, because they are written by the same practitioners who use the materials.

The *Pfeiffer Annual: Training* focuses on skill building and knowledge enhancement and also includes articles that enhance the skills and professional development of workplace learning and performance (WLP) professionals, aka, trainers. The *Pfeiffer Annual: Consulting* focuses on intervention techniques and organizational systems. It also includes skill building for the professional consultant. You can read more about the differences between the two volumes in the section that follows this preface, "The Difference Between Training and Consulting: Which *Annual* to Use."

The *Annuals* have been an inspirational source for experiential learning activities, resource for instruments, and reference for cutting-edge for thirty-eight years. Whether you are a trainer, a consultant, a facilitator, or a bit of each, you will find tools and resources that provide you with the basics and challenge (and we hope inspire) you to use new techniques and models.

Annual Loyalty

The Pfeiffer *Annual* series has many loyal subscribers. There are several reasons for this loyalty. In addition to the wide variety of topics and implementation levels, the *Annuals* provide materials that are applicable to varying circumstances. You will find instruments for individuals, teams, and organizations; experiential learning activities to round out workshops, team building, or consulting assignments; ideas and contemporary solutions for managing human capital; and articles that increase your own knowledge base, to use as reference materials in your writing, or as a source of ideas for your training or consulting assignments.

Many of our readers have been loyal customers for a dozen or more years. If you are one of them, we thank you. And we encourage each of you to give back to the profession by submitting a sample of your work to share with your colleagues.

The *Annuals* owe most of their success, though, to the fact that they are immediately ready to use. All of the materials may be duplicated for educational and training purposes. If you need to adapt or modify the materials to tailor them for your audience's needs, go right ahead. We only request that the credit statement found on the copyright page (and on each reproducible page) be retained on all copies. Our liberal copyright policy makes it easy and fast for you to use the materials to do your job. However, if you intend to reproduce the materials in publications for sale or if you wish to reproduce more than one hundred copies of any one item, please contact us for prior written permission.

If you are a new *Annual* user, welcome! If you like what you see in the 2010 edition, you may want to consider subscribing to a standing order. By doing so, you are guaranteed to receive your copy each year straight off the press and receive a discount off the cover price. And if you want to go back and have the entire series for your use, then the *Pfeiffer Library*—which contains content from the very first edition to the present day—is available on CD-ROM. You can find information on the *Pfeiffer Library* at www.pfeiffer.com.

I often refer to many of my *Annuals* from the 1980s. They include several classic activities that have become a mainstay in my team-building designs. But most of all, the *Annuals* have been a valuable resource for nearly forty years because the materials come from professionals like you who work in the field as trainers, consultants, facilitators, educators, and performance-improvement technologists, whose contributions have been tried and perfected in real-life settings with actual participants and clients to meet real-world needs.

We encourage you to submit materials to be considered for publication. We are interested in receiving experiential learning activities; inventories, questionnaires, and surveys; and articles and discussion resources. Contact the Pfeiffer Editorial Department at the address listed on the copyright page for copies of our guidelines for contributors or contact me directly at Box 8249, Norfolk, VA 23503, or by email at pfeifferannual@aol.com. We welcome your comments, ideas, and contributions.

Acknowledgments

The Pfeiffer *Annuals* could not be a success without the diligent work of many. Thank you to the enthusiastic, responsive, attentive people at Pfeiffer who produced the *2010 Pfeiffer Annuals:* Kathleen Dolan Davies, Lisa Shannon, Marisa Kelley, Dawn Kilgore, Susan Rachmeler, and Rebecca Taff. Lorraine Kohart of ebb associates inc, who each year assists our authors with their submission details and who ensures that we meet the deadlines, is a godsend to all of us. Thank you.

Most important, thank you to our contributors, who have once again shared their ideas, techniques, and materials so that trainers and consultants everywhere may benefit. Won't you consider joining the ranks of these prestigious professionals?

Elaine Biech
Editor
September 2009

The Difference Between Training and Consulting

Which Annual to Use?

Two volumes of the *Pfeiffer Annuals*—training and consulting—are resources for two different but closely related professions. Each *Annual* serves as a collection of tools and support materials used by the professionals in their respective arenas. The volumes include activities, articles, and instruments used by individuals in the training and consulting fields. The training volume is written with the trainer in mind, and the consulting volume is written with the consultant in mind.

How can you differentiate between the two volumes? Let's begin by defining each profession.

A *trainer* can be defined as anyone who is responsible for designing and delivering knowledge to adult learners and may include an internal HRD professional employed by an organization or an external practitioner who contracts with an organization to design and conduct training programs. Generally, the trainer is a subject-matter expert who is expected to transfer knowledge so that the trainee can know or do something new. A *consultant* is someone who provides unique assistance or advice (based on what the consultant knows or has experienced) to someone else, usually known as "the client." The consultant may not necessarily be a subject-matter expert in all situations. Often the consultant is an expert at using specific tools to extract, coordinate, resolve, organize, expedite, or implement an organizational situation.

The lines between the consulting and training professions have blurred in the past few years. First, the names and titles have blurred. For example, some external trainers call themselves "training consultants" as a way of distinguishing themselves from internal trainers. Some organizations now have internal consultants who usually reside in the training department. Second, the roles have blurred. While a consultant has always been expected to deliver measurable results, now trainers are expected to do so as well. Both are expected to improve performance; both are expected to contribute to the bottom line. Facilitation was at one time thought to be a consultant skill; today trainers are expected to use facilitation skills to train. Training one-on-one was a trainer skill; today consultants train executives one-on-one and call it "coaching." The introduction of the "performance technologist," whose role is one of combined trainer and consultant, is a perfect example of a new profession that has evolved due to the need for trainers to use more "consulting" techniques in their work. The "performance consultant" is a new role supported by the American Society for Training and Development (ASTD). ASTD has shifted its focus from training to performance improvement.

As you can see, the roles and goals of training and consulting are not nearly as specific as they once may have been. However, when you step back and examine the two professions from a big-picture perspective, you can more easily differentiate between the two. Maintaining a big-picture focus will also help you determine which *Pfeiffer Annual* to turn to as your first resource.

Both volumes cover the same general topics: communication, teamwork, problem solving, and leadership. However, depending on your requirement and purpose—a training or consulting need—you will use each in different situations. You will select the *Annual* based on *how you will interact with the topic, not on what the topic might be*. Let's take a topic such as teamwork, for example. If you are searching for a lecturette that teaches the advantages of teamwork, a workshop activity that demonstrates the skill of making decisions in a team, or a handout that discusses team stages, look to the Training *Annual*. On the other hand, if you are conducting a team-building session for a dysfunctional team, helping to form a new team, or trying to understand the dynamics of an executive team, you will look to the Consulting *Annual*.

The Training Annual

The materials in the Training volume focus on skill building and knowledge enhancement as well as on the professional development of trainers. They generally focus on controlled events: a training program, a conference presentation, a classroom setting. Look to the Training *Annual* to find ways to improve a training session for 10 to 1,000 people and anything else that falls in the human resource development category:

- Specific experiential learning activities that can be built into a training program;

- Techniques to improve training: debriefing exercises, conducting role plays, managing time;

- Topical lecturettes;

- Ideas to improve a boring training program;

- Icebreakers and energizers for a training session;

- Surveys that can be used in a classroom;

- Ideas for moving an organization from training to performance; and

- Ways to improve your skills as a trainer.

The Consulting Annual

The materials in the Consulting volume focus on intervention techniques and organizational systems as well as the professional development of consultants. They generally focus on "tools" that you can have available just in case: concepts about organizations and their development (or demise) and about more global situations. Look to the Consulting *Annual* to find ways to improve consulting activities from team building and executive coaching to organization development and strategic planning:

- Skills for working with executives;

- Techniques for solving problems, effecting change, and gathering data;

- Team-building tools, techniques, and tactics;

- Facilitation ideas and methods;

- Processes to examine for improving an organization's effectiveness;

- Surveys that can be used organizationally; and

- Ways to improve your effectiveness as a consultant.

Summary

Even though the professions and the work are closely related and at times interchangeable, there is a difference. Use the following table to help you determine which *Annual* you should scan first for help. Remember, however, there is some blending of the two and either *Annual* may have your answer. It depends . . .

Element	Training	Consulting
Topics	Teams, Communication, Problem Solving	Teams, Communication, Problem Solving
Topic Focus	Individual, Department	Corporate, Global
Purpose	Skill Building, Knowledge Transfer	Coaching, Strategic Planning, Building Teams
Recipient	Individuals, Departments	Usually More Organizational
Organizational Level	All Workforce Members	Usually Closer to the Top
Delivery Profile	Workshops, Presentations	Intervention, Implementation
Atmosphere	Structured	Unstructured
Time Frame	Defined	Undefined
Organizational Cost	Moderate	High
Change Effort	Low to Moderate	Moderate to High
Setting	Usually a Classroom	Anywhere
Professional Experience	Entry Level, Novice	Proficient, Master Level
Risk Level	Low	High
Professional Needs	Activities, Resources	Tools, Theory
Application	Individual Skills	Usually Organizational System

When you get right down to it, we are all trainers and consultants. The skills may cross over. A great trainer is also a skilled consultant. And a great consultant is also a skilled trainer. The topics may be the same, but how you implement them may be vastly different. Which *Annual* to use? Remember to think about your purpose in terms of the big picture: consulting or training.

As you can see, we have both covered.

Introduction

to The 2010 Pfeiffer Annual: Consulting

The 2010 Pfeiffer Annual: Consulting is a collection of practical and useful materials for professionals in the broad area described as human resource development (HRD). The materials are written by and for professionals, including trainers, organization-development and organization-effectiveness consultants, performance-improvement technologists, facilitators, educators, instructional designers, and others.

Each *Annual* has three main sections: Experiential Learning Activities; Inventories, Questionnaires, and Surveys; and Articles and Discussion Resources. A fourth section, Editor's Choice, has been reserved for those unique contributions that do not fit neatly into one of the three main sections, but are valuable as identified by the editorial staff. Each published submission is classified in one of the following categories: Individual Development, Communication, Problem Solving, Groups, Teams, Consulting, Facilitating, Leadership, and Organizations. Within each category, pieces are further classified into logical subcategories, which are identified in the introductions to the three sections.

The Training *Annual* and the Consulting *Annual* for 2010 have a slightly different focus from past years. Both focus on communication, a topic that is always high on every organization's list of things to improve, and a topic that learning and consulting professionals address regularly.

The series continues to provide an opportunity for HRD professionals who wish to share their experiences, their viewpoints, and their processes with their colleagues. To that end, Pfeiffer publishes guidelines for potential authors. These guidelines are available from the Pfeiffer Editorial Department at Pfeiffer's offices in San Francisco, California.

Materials are selected for the *Annuals* based on the quality of the ideas, applicability to real-world concerns, relevance to current HRD issues, clarity of presentation, and ability to enhance our readers' professional development. In addition, we choose experiential learning activities that will create a high degree of enthusiasm among the participants and add enjoyment to the learning process. As in the past several years, the contents of each *Annual* span a wide range of subject matter, reflecting the range of interests of our readers.

Our contributor list includes a wide selection of experts in the field: in-house practitioners, consultants, and academically based professionals. A list of contributors to the *Annual* can be found at the end of the volume, including their names, affiliations, addresses, telephone numbers, facsimile numbers, and email addresses. Readers will find this list useful if they wish to locate the authors of specific pieces for feedback, comments, or questions. Further information on each contributor is presented in a brief biographical sketch that appears at the conclusion of each article. We publish this information to encourage "networking," which continues to be a valuable mainstay in the field of human resource development.

We are pleased with the high quality of material that is submitted for publication each year and often regret that we have page limitations. In addition, just as we cannot publish every manuscript we receive, you may find that not all published works are equally useful to you. Therefore, we encourage and invite ideas, materials, and suggestions that will help us to make subsequent *Annuals* as useful as possible to all of our readers.

Introduction
to the Experiential Learning Activsuits Section

Experiential learning activities ensure that lasting learning occurs. They should be selected with a specific learning objective in mind. These objectives are based on the participants' needs and the facilitator's skills. Although the experiential learning activities presented here all vary in goals, group size, time required, and process, they all incorporate one important element: questions that ensure learning has occurred. This discussion, led by the facilitator, assists participants to process the activity, to internalize the learning, and to relate it to their day-to-day situations. It is this element that creates the unique learning experience and learning opportunity that only an experiential learning activity can bring to the group process.

Readers have used the *Annuals'* experiential learning activities for years to enhance their training and consulting events. Each learning experience is complete and includes all lecturettes, handout content, and other written material necessary to facilitate the activity. In addition, many include variations of the design that the facilitator might find useful. If the activity does not fit perfectly with your objective, within your time frame, or to your group size, we encourage you to adapt the activity by adding your own variations. You will find additional experiential learning activities listed in the "Experiential Learning Activities Categories" chart that immediately follows this introduction.

The 2010 Pfeiffer Annual: Consulting includes thirteen activities, in the following categories:

Individual Development: Self-Disclosure

Mirror Image: Reflecting on How Our Personal Pursuits Show in Our Professional Practice, by Gary Wagenheim, Robert Clark, and Alexander Crispo

Communication: Building Trust

**Words of Trust: Building Trust in the Workplace, by David Piltz

---

**Communication Topic

Communication: Conflict

> **Difficult Conversations: Making Them Easier, by Beverly J. Bitterman

Communication: Feedback

> **Unstructured Coaching Conversations: Coaching the Coach, by Travis L. Russ

Communication: Listening

> **I'd Like You to Meet . . .: Introducing a New Hire, by Lucille Maddalena

Problem Solving: Generating Alternatives

> **Redirect: Achieving Positive Outcomes, by Devora Zack

Problem Solving: Action Planning

> **Team Extreme Challenge: Solving Difficult Tasks, by Amy Henderson

Teams: How Groups Work

> **Puzzling Behavior: Discovering How Teams Work, by Jo-Ann C. Byrne

Teams: Problem Solving/Decision Making

> Beyond the Olympics: Discussing Autocratic vs. Democratic Leadership, by Barbara Pate Glacel

Consulting, Training and Facilitating: Facilitating: Opening

> Signatures and Shoes: Breaking the Ice, by Mahaveer Jain

Consulting, Training and Facilitating: Facilitating: Skills

> Facilitation Tools: Using Spectrogram Analysis, by Elisabeth C. Ayres, Catherine Cable, and Sophia Zia

Leadership: Motivating

> Follow the Leader: Exploring Trust As a Leadership Requirement, by Harriet Rifkin

---

**Communication Topic

Organizations: Vision, Mission, Values, Strategy

A Bull's-Eye Every Time: Setting Short-Term Goals, by Linda S. Eck Mills

To further assist you in selecting appropriate ELAs, we provide the following grid that summarizes category, time required, group size, and risk factor for each ELA.

Category	ELA Title	Page	Time Required	Group Size	Risk Factor
Individual Development: Self-Disclosure	Mirror Image: Reflecting on How Our Personal Pursuits Show in Our Professional Practice	13	60 minutes	Any size	Moderate
Communication: Building Trust	Words of Trust: Building Trust in the Workplace	19	Approximately 2 hours	Unlimited, in groups of 4 or5	Moderate
Communication: Conflict	Difficult Conversations: Making Them Easier	23	1 to 2 weeks	8 to 16 members of an intact work group	Moderate to High
Communication: Feedback	Unstructured Coaching Conversations: Coaching the Coach	35	Approximately 2 hours	3 to 24 managers or supervisors	Moderate
Communication: Listening	I'd Like You to Meet . . .: Introducing a New Hire	45	60 to 90 minutes	10 or fewer	Moderate
Problem Solving: Generating Alternatives	Redirect: Achieving Positive Outcomes	51	70 minutes	3 to 100	Moderate
Problem Solving: Action Planning	Team Extreme Challenge: Solving Difficult Tasks	59	15 to 30 minutes	5 to 15 members of an intact group	Low to Moderate
Teams: How Groups Work	Puzzling Behavior: Discovering How Teams Work	63	40 to 50 minutes	8 to 12 members of a work team	Moderate
Teams: Problem Solving/Decision Making	Beyond the Olympics: Discussing Autocratic vs. Democratic Leadership	67	3 hours	Multiples of 4 or 8	Moderate to High
Consulting, Training and Facilitating: Facilitating: Opening	Signatures and Shoes: Breaking the Ice	77	45 to 60 minutes	15 to 30	High
Consulting, Training and Facilitating: Facilitating: Skills	Facilitation Tools: Using Spectrogram Analysis	81	45 minutes	Up to 30	Low
Leadership: Motivating	Follow the Leader: Exploring Trust As a Leadership Requirement	87	Approximately 90 minutes	8 to 30 managers	High
Organizations: Vision, Mission, Values, Strategy	A Bull's-Eye Every Time: Setting Short-Term Goals	93	1.5 to 4 hours	5 to 20 from the same organization	Low

Experiential Learning Activities Categories

Note that numbering system was discontinued beginning with the 2004 *Annuals*.

	Vol.	Page
INDIVIDUAL DEVELOPMENT		
Sensory Awareness		
Feelings & Defenses (56)	III	31
Lemons (71)	III	94
Growth & Name Fantasy (85)	'72	59
Group Exploration (119)	IV	92
Relaxation & Perceptual Awareness (136)	'74	84
T'ai Chi Chuan (199)	VI	10
Roles Impact Feelings (214)	VI	102
Projections (300)	VIII	30
Mastering the Deadline Demon (593)	'98–1	9
Learning Shifts (643)	'00–1	11
Secret Sponsors (657)	'00–2	11
Spirituality at Work (670)	'01–1	11
What You See (740)	'03–2	11
Highly Leveraged Moments	'04–T	11

	Vol.	Page
Z Fantasy	'04–C	11
Well-Being	'05–T	11
Picture Yourself	'05–C	11
Presuppositions	'06–C	11
The Serendipity Bowl	'07–T	11
Change Partners	'08–T	11
Empathy Walk	'08–C	11
Encouragement	'09–C	13
One Life, Many Roles	'10–T	13
Self-Disclosure		
Johari Window (13)	I	65
Graphics (20)	I	88
Personal Journal (74)	III	109
Make Your Own Bag (90)	'73	13
Growth Cards (109)	IV	30
Expressing Anger (122)	IV	104
Stretching (123)	IV	107
Forced-Choice Identity (129)	'74	20
Boasting (181)	'76	49

	Vol.	Page
The Other You (182)	'76	51
Praise (306)	VIII	61
Introjection (321)	'82	29
Personality Traits (349)	IX	158
Understanding the Need for Approval (438)	'88	21
The Golden Egg Award (448)	'88	89
Adventures at Work (521)	'95–1	9
That's Me (522)	'95–1	17
Knowledge Is Power (631)	'99–2	13
Spirituality at Work (658)	'00–2	15
The Imposter Syndrome (696)	'02–1	11
Internet Impressions (710)	'02–2	11
Purposeful Spot Game (723)	'03–1	11
Quotations	'04–T	19
Take a Risk	'05–C	17
Trait Trade	'07–C	11
Ten Things	'08–T	17
Triplets	'08–C	17

Mirror Image
Reflecting on How Our Personal Pursuits Show in Our Professional Practice

Activity Summary

Examines how our hobbies, activities, interests, or sports can serve as metaphors of who we are in our professional practice.

Goals

- To surface previously hidden assumptions about participants' professional practice.

- To examine, challenge, and change those assumptions.

- To inform self-awareness.

Group Size

Any size group.

Time Required

60 minutes.

Materials

- One Mirror Image Worksheet for each participant.

- Pencils or pens for participants.

Physical Setting

A room large enough for groups to work without disturbing one another. Writing surfaces and moveable chairs should be provided.

Facilitating Risk Rating

Moderate.

Process

1. Introduce the session by explaining that participants will be exploring the notion that their favorite personal pursuits may serve as "mirrors" to reflect deeper assumptions they hold about their professional practices. Say that choice of personal pursuits can serve to illuminate tacit assumptions about who we are in our professional practices.

2. Give each participant a writing utensil and a copy of the Mirror Image Worksheet. Ask them to reflect on and write responses, in whatever form feels appropriate to them, to the open-ended questions on the worksheet. Encourage participants to be creative and add their own questions or categories for later discussion.

3. Allow approximately 10 minutes for completing the worksheet, giving a 2-minute warning before calling time.
   (10 minutes.)

4. Ask the participants to form small groups of three to share their responses with one another. Encourage them to use answers to the questions only as a guide to inform their stories. Ask listeners to utilize active listening skills in probing for clarity and meaning and for providing support. All participants should take turns as storytellers and listeners.
   (20 minutes.)

5. After they have had time to rotate through all the stories, ask participants to discuss the common themes, assumptions, and insights that emerged. Also ask them to discuss differences among the various stories.
   (10 minutes.)

6. After the small group dialogue, debrief the entire session. First, ask a representative from each group to report common themes, assumptions, and insights. Ask about differences among stories. Finally, ask the entire group the following questions:

- What did you observe and hear in your session that was meaningful?

- What did you feel during the session, either when you were presenting or when others were presenting?

- What insights have you gained about yourself or others through this activity?

- How has this experience changed the way you think about your professional practice?

- How will you use this new information in your professional practice? (20 minutes.)

Variations

- Change the questions to reflect the particular workshop topic or professions represented.

- Assign the questions as pre-work for the workshop.

- Have participants design their own questions.

Resources

Brookfield, S. (1995). *Becoming a critically reflective teacher*. San Francisco: Jossey-Bass.

Johns, C. (1994). Guided reflection. In A. Palmer, A. Burns, & C. Bulman (Eds.), *Reflective practice in nursing: The growth of the professional practitioner* (pp. 110–130). Cornwall, UK: Blackwell Science Ltd.

Morgan, G. (1986). *Images of organizations*. Beverly Hills, CA: Sage.

Ortony, A. (1975). Why metaphors are necessary and not just nice. *Educational Theory, 25*, 45–53.

Palmer, P.J. (1998). *The courage to teach: Exploring the inner landscape of a teacher's life*. San Francisco: Jossey-Bass.

Schön, D.A. (1987). *Educating the reflective practitioner*. San Francisco: Jossey-Bass.

Spencer, L. (1989). *Winning through participation: Meeting the challenge of corporate change and technology of participation*. Dubuque, IA: Kendall/Hunt.

Submitted by Gary Wagenheim, Robert Clark, and Alexander Crispo.

Gary Wagenheim, Ph.D., *is an adjunct professor at Simon Fraser University and the Helsinki School of Economics. He teaches graduate courses in leadership and organizational behavior. He is a member of the*

Learning Strategies Group, which specializes in providing customized education programs for organizations, and an external faculty member for McKinsey & Company. In addition, he owns and operates Wagenheim Advisory Group, which provides corporate training, coaching, and organization development programs.

Robert Clark, Ed.D., *is an associate professor of educational administration at California State University–Dominguez Hills. He teaches graduate courses on educational leadership, with an emphasis in instructional leadership and servant leadership. He is a retired school superintendent and currently provides leadership coaching for several public school principals in southern California. Dr. Clark earned his doctorate at the University of Southern California. He is a member of several professional organizations.*

Alexander Crispo *is an associate professor in the Organizational Leadership Department in the College of Technology at Purdue University. He teaches graduate and undergraduate courses in leadership and change management. He earned his bachelor of science degree in industrial distribution and his master of science in industrial management from Clarkson University. He is past-president of the International Society for the Exploration of Teaching and Learning and a member of the Organizational Behavior Teaching Society.*

Mirror Image Worksheet

What is your favorite personal pursuit, for example, hobby, activity, interest, or sport?

What attracted you to this pursuit in the first place?

How did you learn the skills of this pursuit?

What assumptions do you hold about the skills, values, and actions associated with this pursuit?

How are assumptions in your personal pursuit like assumptions in your professional practice? In other words, how do assumptions you hold about skills, values, and actions in your personal pursuit manifest in assumptions you hold about skills, values, and actions in your professional practice?

What assumptions should you challenge, confirm, disconfirm, or change in your professional practice? How would you test these assumptions?

Words of Trust
Building Trust in the Workplace

Activity Summary

A critical thinking activity that allows participants to explore the concept of building trust in the workplace.

Goals

- To recognize different meanings that participants ascribe to trust.

- To explore the complexities and subtleties of building and maintaining trust.

Group Size

An unlimited number of groups of four or five.

Time Required

Approximately 2 hours.

Materials

- Blank paper for each participant.

- Flip-chart paper and felt-tipped markers for each small group.

- A pen or pencil for each participant.

- A way to keep time accurately.

- Masking tape.

Physical Setting

A room large enough for the groups to work without disturbing one another and enough wall space to post completed flip-chart pages.

Facilitating Risk Rating

Moderate.

Process

1. Explain to the participants that the activity is a chance to explore and experience what it takes to create a trusting relationship among co-workers.

2. Divide the participants into groups of four to five by traditional numbering of participants or by asking participants to form groups with those next to them. Give each group a flip chart and markers and every participant blank paper and a pen or pencil.

3. Say that the activity has five rounds plus a debriefing session and that you will enforce a strict time limit for each round.

4. Tell the groups that Round 1 will be 4 minutes long. Explain that, during Round 1, each person will *independently* create a list of all the words that describe what trust means to him or her personally. (You can choose to let people use trust to encompass all of life or to encompass the workplace only.) Start Round 1.
   (10 minutes.)

5. At the end of 4 minutes, call time and ask participants to share their lists within their groups and to create two new lists and record them on a flip-chart page. List 1 should have five words everyone agrees with, and List 2 should have five words that there was disagreement about. Say that they will have 15 minutes for Round 2. Start the round.
   (15 minutes.)

6. At the end of 15 minutes, call time and ask each group to trade their flip-chart sheet with the two lists on it with another group. (If there are only two groups, have them exchange papers.)

7. Tell the participants that Round 3 will be 15 minutes long and the task this time is to create one picture that illustrates each list of words on the flip-chart page they received. Clarify that each group needs to create *two* pictures—one for each list. Start Round 3.
   (20 minutes.)

8. At the end of 15 minutes, call time. Tell groups to trade their flip-chart pages with the two lists and two pictures with another group.

9. State that Round 4 will also last 15 minutes. The task this time is for each group to create a realistic, practical, and action-oriented tip that describes how to build, maintain, or enhance trust in the workplace. Say that the tip should integrate both lists of words and the pictures. Start Round 4. (15 minutes.)

10. Call time after 15 minutes and tell the groups they will now have a chance to share the tips they created, the pictures, and the lists of words on their flip-chart sheets.

11. Allow each group 1 to 2 minutes to share with the large group, depending on the number of groups you have. (10 to 20 minutes.)

12. Lead a processing discussion based on the following questions:

    - What was difficult about this activity? Are some of these difficulties a factor when you are building trust in the workplace? Why or why not?

    - What was easy about this activity? When is building trust easy for you?

    - What did you learn about trust in general?

    - How did the strict time limits mimic one challenge of building trust in the workplace? Describe one thing you can do to overcome that challenge.

    - How did the rounds and tasks help or hinder in building trust within the small groups? How is this similar or dissimilar to the workplace?

    - How did differences in opinion and perspectives or conflict among the small group members hinder building trust? How is this similar or dissimilar to the workplace?

    - Will you do anything differently as a result of what you learned during this activity?
    (20 minutes.)

Variation

Instead of beginning with what trust means to them, you can ask participants to create lists of all the words that describe:

- The kinds of things that keep trust from developing

- Things that help to build trust

- How conflict gets in the way of trust

- The emotions they feel when trust is broken and when trust is maintained

———————

Submitted by David Piltz.

David Piltz *is a managing partner of The Learning Key®, a company specializing in developing innovative learning solutions. He has been creating and offering programs in leadership, organizational and educational change, communication, teamwork, customer service, and personal and professional effectiveness for more than fourteen years. He developed* The House That Cards Built *and* Picture This, *available at www. thelearningkey.com.*

Difficult Conversations
Making Them Easier

Activity Summary

An activity that teaches participants how to prepare for a discussion that they feel could be conflict-laden.

Consultant's Note

The activity gives work teams better skills for the "storming" phase (see Bitterman, 2007) and also fits with the concept of holding each other accountable to team agreements. The activity can also be used by a manager dealing with two employees who are in conflict. The process fits well as a learning experience under a curriculum focused on improving communication and team work. Other topics might include team building using behavioral styles as a focus; dialogue and listening skills training; or teaching managers basic coaching skills.

Goals

- To learn techniques for constructive conflict required for high-performing teams.

- To provide a model for launching into a difficult conversation.

Group Size

8 to 16 participants who are members of an intact work group.

Time Required

Over a period of 1 to 2 weeks:

- 30-minute manager meeting to explain the steps.

- 1.5- to 2-hour experiential learning with the team to provide the concepts and opportunity to practice.

- Brief follow-up meeting with the team to review the concepts and discuss barriers to implementation.

Materials

- One copy of Difficult Conversations: Reflecting on Past Experience for each participant.

- One copy of the Difficult Conversations Planning Guide for a Successful Outcome for each participant.

- Pens for participants.

- Two flip charts and felt-tipped markers.

- Masking tape.

Physical Setting

A room large enough for each of the formal meetings. Chair arrangement that promotes a feeling of unity and gives some security. Tables arranged in a circle or U-shape work well.

Facilitating Risk Rating

Moderate to High.

Manager Preparation Meeting

Prior to the workshop, meet with the team's manager. Explain that most teams experience some workplace conflict stemming from team changes, role ambiguity within the team, lack of clear direction, or personality and background differences. Say that conflict that focuses on issues is to be encouraged, but that conflict that involves personal attacks and passive or aggressive behaviors is not healthy and needs to be channeled into more effective ways to communicate. Ask the manager to provide some history and examples of conflict within the team so that you can determine whether positive conflict occurs and what his or her opinion is regarding the source of any negative conflict. The following issues are examples of concerns you might hear that would suggest a need for training:

- People complaining to the manager about team/group members.

- Individuals refusing to work with one another.

- Projects/work falling behind schedule.

- Ineffective team agreements.

- Some members silent.

- Issue escalation to HR or up the management chain.

Explain the approach you propose to use:

- Team will be convened.

- In your opening remarks you will suggest that conflict between workmates is normal and healthy—unless it is destructive. The purpose of the session will be to give people the tools to keep conflict constructive.

- You will establish ground rules.

- You will deliver a mini-lecture/discussion on conflict.

- Teams will have an opportunity to practice.

Assure the manager that you will help to create a safe space for conversations among team members. Ask the manager to attend the meeting, but say that he or she should create a space for the team to do the majority of the work.

Process

1. Convene the team. Welcome them and thank them in advance for their participation. Let them know that you are happy to be talking with them about conflict. Say that all high-performing teams have conflict and that they too can deal with conflict in a positive way. Say that conflict within a team creates an opportunity to advance the team to a higher level of performance. Ask them to consider, for example, the national party system in the United States with the Democratic and Republican parties and the division of power among the Legislative, Executive, and Judicial branches of the government. Regardless of how effective the current system may be, they should recognize that the system was set up to encourage conflict so that all positions on an issue could be considered. Say: "Our founding fathers knew the difficulties of having only one source of power." (Or come up with another example from sports or current events to illustrate the fact that conflict is helpful to successful, well-thought-out initiatives.)

2. Tell them that they will be learning some ways to successfully negotiate when there is conflict. Let them know that ground rules will be set to make the environment safe.

3. Begin by asking the group what ground rules they would like to propose to create an effective meeting. Look for the following items and make a list on the flip chart. Suggest that they add items they may have missed. Reach agreement with the group that they will enforce the ground rules.

   • One person speaks at a time.

   • What is said in the room stays in the room.

   • Cell phones silenced.

   • All participate for best results.

   • It's OK to pass if you feel you do not want to contribute at a specific time.

   • We will end on time.

4. Give everyone copies of Difficult Conversations: Reflecting on Past Experience sheet. Ask them to reflect on a time when they had a disagreement with someone at work and the situation was successfully resolved and the relationship was as good if not better than it previously was. Then ask them to reflect on a time when the situation did not improve over a long period of time. Have them complete the chart individually. Tell them they will not need to tell who was involved in the conflicts they write about or tell what it was about.
   (10 minutes.)

5. After everyone has finished recording their conflicts, ask for and post the positive outcomes on one flip chart and the negative ones on the second. Ask only for general descriptors of the positive conflicts they have recalled.
   (10 minutes.)

6. When you have finished listing characteristics of the positive conflict outcomes, move to the negative, using the same approach, asking for general descriptors of the conflict only—no details.
   (15 minutes.)

7. When you are finished with both lists, ask the participants to form small groups to discuss the following questions:

   • What stands out for you on the negative list (for example, turf wars, operating in silos, a history of negative interactions, personality clashes, didn't really care about the other person, or perhaps attacking occurred)?

- What was different about the positive disagreements (for example, about issues, people generally respected each other, there was a history of working through issues, people cared about each other, and people avoided personal attacks)?
(15 minutes.)

8. Ask the small groups to share what they came up with and note their comments on a flip chart. Ask them to recall what the "big deal" was about the negative issues. Ask: "So what happened? Why did it trouble you so much?" Look for underlying feelings that created discomfort for them. For example:

   - It made me feel unimportant.

   - I felt like I had to do all the work.

   - I felt disrespected.
   (10 minutes.)

9. Tell them that it is often our interpretations of events that get us in trouble in relationships. Our perceptions may or may not be true. In order to work out a conflict situation, we have to be open to seeing issues from another point of view. The other critical piece is caring enough to be willing to work toward a more constructive relationship for personal satisfaction and the good of the team.

10. Say that you hope they are now willing to spend time discussing how to set up difficult conversations so that they have a greater potential to lead to positive outcomes.

11. Give everyone a copy of the Difficult Conversations Planning Guide for Successful Outcomes. Walk them through the handout.
(5 minutes.)

12. Ask them to pair up and, using one of the following issue sets (or make up other sets of moderate intensity relevant to the group), plan the difficult conversation up to Step 6 on the Planning Guide. Each partner is to take one side of the issue and do the planning for that side.

   - A.1: Co-worker is continuously late to project meetings.

   - A.2: Co-worker has been given another "choice" assignment and doesn't feel he or she needs to attend project meetings.

   - B.1: Co-worker tends to use language and a tone of voice that makes you feel inferior.

- B.2: Co-worker thinks you take too long to make decisions.

- C.1: Co-worker's staff do not follow agreed-on guidelines.

- C.2: Co-worker's staff do not think the guidelines are important.
  (10 minutes.)

13. Pull the group together to debrief the activity so far. This will keep them on the same page. Go through the first six steps and ask for a couple of examples for each step. If you feel someone didn't "get" the intent of a step, ask the group, "What is another way that could be said?"
    (10 minutes.)

14. Now they should be ready to have the practice conversations. Ask them, "What would be some productive attitudes to have going into the conversation?" You would like to hear "positive," "confident," "open," "caring," "upbeat."

15. Ask them: "What kinds of attitudes would likely get in the way of a good outcome?" You would like to hear "defensive," "confrontational," "closed-minded," "negative," "discouraged," "self-centered."

16. Tell them they are nearly ready to launch into the conversation; however, you'd like to review some listening skills. Ask someone to tell the group what you just said. Give kudos. Say that it's easier to listen when you aren't emotionally engaged. You have to try harder when emotions are up, and some of their comments can reflect back the emotion. For example, if your partner is yelling or speaking in a loud voice, you might say, "I get that you are angry." Indicate that a whole workshop could occur just around listening. And, if their intentions are in the right place, they don't have to be perfect in order to have a good outcome with their difficult conversations.

17. Tell them to go ahead and hold their difficult conversations. Allow 5 to 10 minutes for the practice.
    (10 minutes.)

18. Pull them back together and debrief the experience.

- How did it go?

- What happened that surprised you?

- What did you do that you wouldn't do next time?

- How did feelings change and shift?

- Did any agreements come out of your discussions?

- What questions do you have about the process?
(10 minutes.)

19. Let them know that difficult conversations become less stressful with practice and that they are not likely to ever be "easy." Remind them they now have tools for success. Review the tools with them, listing items on the flip chart. They know how to get clear about their own thoughts, prepare themselves to open their minds to others' ideas, get a meeting off to a good start, and be prepared to really listen to the other person's point of view. Let them know who in the organization can serve as a sounding board in planning a difficult conversation or in mediating a conversation between two people if the stakes are high and they need help in the future.

20. In closing the session, ask each participant to consider one benefit of the discussion and one thing he or she will do differently. Ask them to write these down. Then throw out a ball (or wad of paper) and ask the person who caught it to state a benefit and toss the ball to another group member. Keep going until all benefits are given. Then do the same for the one thing they are willing to do as a result of their learning in the session. (15 minutes.)

Follow-Up

Meet with the group a week or two after the workshop. Ask the group questions such as:

- Has any one had an opportunity to try out a difficult conversation? How did it go?

- Has any one found him- or herself needing to do such a conversation and then avoiding it still? What would it take to actually set up a conversation?

State whether or not you, yourself, have had an opportunity for such a conversation. Say that you too will be looking for opportunities in the future and you hope they will too.

Reference

Bitterman, B. (2007). Storming to norming: Clearing the way for team agreement. In E. Biech (Ed.), *The 2007 Pfeiffer annual: Consulting* (pp. 85–90). San Francisco: Pfeiffer.

Submitted by Beverly J. Bitterman, M.S.N.

Beverly J. Bitterman, *owner of Beverly Bitterman and Associates, is an organizational coach and team developer. She is an effective facilitator who creates environments in which groups are comfortable communicating about issues, uncovering and removing barriers to high performance, and taking concrete action to move forward on projects. Bitterman also delivers competency and behavioral style assessment instruments, teaches communication skills for the University of South Florida Continuing Education Department, and is president of the Suncoast Healthcare Executive Association.*

Difficult Conversations: Reflecting on Past Experience

Question	Positive Experience	Negative Experience
Briefly describe what, where, when, who was involved.		
What did you want that you weren't getting? What was your position?		
What did the other party want? What was his or her position?		
Was there "history" to the conflict, or was it a new issue?		
What was your intention for the relationship after the conflict? Were you clear that you did/did not want the relationship to be preserved?		
During the discussion, to what extent were you able to focus on the effect of the issue or behavior on you rather than making the other person out to be wrong?		
Did you learn something you didn't know as a result of the discussion you had?		
What was the emotional tone of the meeting: calm, loud, angry, sad, closed, or other?		

The 2010 Pfeiffer Annual: Consulting.

Difficult Conversations Planning Guide for a Successful Outcome

Planning

1. Be clear about your goal. What do you want to happen as a result of the conversation? Is there something you want another person to start, stop or change? Is this action tangible (show up on time, complete assignment) or is it intangible (perhaps something like respect, feeling heard or acknowledged)?

2. What is your intention for the relationship with the other person? Do you want the relationship to continue, improve, or dissolve?

3. What did the other person do that caused you difficulty?

4. What might your role have been in the way things are going/turned out?

5. What are the observable facts about the situation, e.g., what could be caught on videotape (stealing, walking into a meeting late, loud voice, etc.)?

6. What is your interpretation as to the motive of the other person/s involved?

7. What don't you know about the situation or the reason for the individual's behavior?

8. What about this situation makes it significant to you, something you don't want to let go? Perhaps it is how the situation makes you feel or the impact it is having on others.

9. What are three to five messages that you want to make sure the other person hears from you? Messages are assertive statements whereby you "own" your feelings and desires. They do not involve blame or shame. Examples include:

   • "I want us to work this out."

   • "I have been feeling (disrespected, let down, annoyed, disengaged, out of the loop, etc.)."

   • "I feel that we could be doing a better job of (communicating, working together, finding agreeable solutions, meeting targets)."

   • "I know that I have been (avoiding you, not pulling my weight, distant, not easy to work with lately)."

   • "What is troubling me is that (you aren't responding to my emails, you have been absent from meetings, you don't seem to think our meetings are important, you made xyz error that resulted in abc)."

Holding the Conversation

10. Invite the other party to have a discussion. This can be a hard step and it can set the tone for the discussion. You might say something as simple as "I'd like to arrange a time to meet with you and discuss (how we could work better together, our recent blowup, the project we're working on). Would tomorrow at 2 p.m. work for you? How about in the conference room (neutral spaces are good)?"

11. Once you have an agreement, plan to help yourself be as calm as possible and expect the meeting will work out for the best.

12. Open the discussion with a general statement about what has been going on. Keep it high-level, emotion-free and fact-based, for example: "You and I have been having a hard time working together." "I would like to see if we can figure out how to work better together." "I want to see what we can do to get our project done on schedule." (If you are in doubt about your ability to do that, enlist a trusted person to hear your opening.)

13. Use one to three of your pre planned messages from Step 9.

14. Invite the other party's perspective on the issue by saying something like: "I would like to hear your perspective on the issue."

15. Listen to what the other person has to say. This means being quiet and really listening for both the words said and the emotion behind them. This does not mean that you half-listen and plan your rebuttal statement while the person is talking.

16. Especially in conflict, the statement that happens after listening needs to be about what was just heard. Yes, it can sound stilted. However, it's a good idea to say (and mean) something like "I want to make sure I understand your position. What I hear you say is. . . . Is that right?" Continue trying to recap until the other party says "Yes."

17. Now you can either propose your idea for what would make the situation better or you can invite the other person to make a proposal.

18. Expect some discussion here. The goal is to come up with a plan that both can commit to giving a trial. Also, come up with an agreed-on time (like a week) to check in and see how it is going.

19. If you are new at this or the situation is particularly volatile, you may want some help with the conversation. Often a manager, HR professional, or coach could be made available to help ensure that both parties are listened to and have the opportunity to express their thoughts, feelings, and requests.

Unstructured Coaching Conversations
Coaching the Coach

Activity Summary

A way for participants to discover the value of using unstructured conversations to coach their employees.

Goals

- To identify appropriate situations for using unstructured coaching conversations.

- To learn and practice four unstructured facilitation strategies for having unstructured coaching conversations.

Group Size

From 3 to 24 managers or supervisors.

Time Required

Approximately 2 hours.

Materials

- One Unstructured Coaching Conversations Worksheet for each participant.

- One Unstructured Coaching Conversations Observer Feedback Form for each triad.

- One pen or pencil for each participant.

Physical Setting

A room in which participants can easily move their chairs to work in triads.

Facilitating Risk Rating

Moderate.

Process

1. To introduce the topic say: "When coaching their employees, managers often rely on 'structured conversations,' very planned and organized interactions designed to achieve concrete performance outcomes. For example, managers often use structured conversations to train a new employee to perform a job correctly. Also, structured conversations are often used to correct an employee's performance errors. By the same token, structured conversations can be used to praise an employee for exceptional performance and to encourage repetition of positive behaviors. Often linear in nature, structured coaching conversations are carefully planned to produce very specific, predictable, performance-based outcomes. On the downside, such tightly controlled conversations can bias what is discussed. Such one-sided conversations can suppress free exchange of thought, stifle innovation and creativity, and limit candid exchanges between employees and managers. Often employees' needs, feelings, and interests go overlooked. Consequently, structured conversations may not be the best coaching tool for every situation. It may be more appropriate, in some instances, to use *unstructured* coaching conversations."

2. Explain that the goal of this activity is to help participants learn how to use *unstructured* coaching conversations with their employees. (5 minutes.)

3. Distribute one copy of the Unstructured Coaching Conversations Worksheet and a pen or pencil to each participant. Explain that the first step is to define what an unstructured coaching conversation is. As you give the definition, have participants take notes in Part 1 of the worksheet. Say:

   "An unstructured coaching conversation is an *unplanned, free-flowing dialogue* between managers and employees. Using this technique, managers provide little direction. There is no standard formula or rigid sequencing of questions. Because of the fluid nature of these conversations, managers should not use them to coach employees to reach specific, predetermined, and nonnegotiable performance goals. Instead,

the overarching objective is to empower employees, listen to them, and ascertain their needs as individuals. Often, employees appreciate it when managers speak to them without having hidden agendas or ulterior motives. During unstructured conversations, managers let employees do most of the talking—about whatever they want. Managers do not lead the conversation. They simply ask open-ended questions and practice active listening. The only objective is simply to hear what employees are saying. Again, these conversations are not intended to achieve specific performance outcomes. Rather, the objective is to give employees a voice as well as the opportunity to express themselves and to openly disclose their thoughts, feelings, and ideas."
(10 minutes.)

4. Divide participants into pairs and ask them to work together to complete Part 2 of their worksheets. Explain that they will brainstorm the pros and cons of using unstructured coaching conversations. Allow approximately 8 minutes for this task, giving participants a 2-minute warning before calling time. After time expires, ask a few volunteers share what they wrote (sample pros: Fosters two-way communication; gives employees a voice; prevents coaching conversations from being biased by manager's agenda; fosters a greater sense of trust and openness; prevents front-line problems from being unchecked and unresolved; strengthens loyalty to company).

5. Next, ask a few volunteers to share what they listed as being the cons of using unstructured coaching conversations (sample cons: May cause confusion about manager's expectations; may produce unexpected and/or negative results; may waste time on irrelevant/non-work-related issues; may reduce manager's power/control in the workplace).
(15 minutes.)

6. Point out that these pros and cons underscore the importance of using unstructured conversations with the right employee, at the right time, and in the right situation. Ask: "Generally speaking, when might it be beneficial to use unstructured conversations to coach employees?" (sample responses: Discussing employees' career goals; discussing employees' reactions to new job experiences; soliciting employees' ideas for improving products or processes; discussing employees' personal problems that are limiting their job performance; discussing ways high performers could challenge themselves to elevate their performance to a higher level.) Ask:

"Generally speaking, in what coaching situations might using unstructured conversations backfire?" (sample responses: Training employees to follow a process or procedure; delegating a concrete task that must be completed in a specific way; explaining how job expectations are not being met; giving warnings to poor performing employees; explaining why an employee's relationship with the company is being terminated).

Stress that managers must carefully consider on a case-by-case basis when it is (and is not) appropriate to use unstructured coaching conversations. Point out that managers must weigh several factors when making these decisions (e.g., purpose of conversation, manager's comfort level, employee's comfort level, employee's maturity level, employee's professional needs, employee's personal needs, time constraints, nature and importance of work relationship, etc.).

7. Ask for examples of when others may have used an unstructured conversation to effectively coach someone. Have the group discuss why it was appropriate in that particular situation to have an unstructured conversation with this person.
(10 minutes.)

8. Have them review the facilitation strategies for having unstructured coaching conversations. First, point out that there are multiple conversation starters that participants can use to initiate unstructured conversations. Have participants review Part 3 on their worksheets and place a checkmark beside at least three conversation starters they will likely use in the future. Allow approximately 2 minutes for this task. After time expires, ask a few volunteers to share their selections. Acknowledge that employees may give abrupt answers, terminating the conversation prematurely. Stress that managers must continue the conversation by encouraging employees to open up through the use of four facilitation strategies. Point out these strategies were inspired by research conducted by scholars in several academic disciplines, including organizational psychology and communication (Lindlof & Taylor, 2002; Patton, 2001; Richardson, Dohrenwend, & Klein, 1965; Whyte & Whyte, 1984). Have participants review these strategies and discuss them in small groups.
(20 minutes.)

9. Ask participants to summarize their discussions about the four facilitation strategies. Ask how each technique might be helpful to the coaching situation.
(5 minutes.)

10. Divide participants into groups of three. Have one person in each triad play the coach, one play the employee, and the other play the observer. Explain that the coach and employee will engage in an unstructured coaching conversation. The topic of the conversation should be chosen by the employee (e.g., a recent organizational change, a new company-wide initiative, attitudes about job/department/company, etc.). Tell the "coach" to begin the discussion by asking one of the conversation starters listed in Part 3 of the worksheet. Emphasize that the coach should use *all four* facilitation strategies that were just reviewed. Distribute an Unstructured Coaching Conversations Observer Feedback Form to each observer. Tell them to use this form to tally the number of times the "coach" uses each facilitation strategy. Also ask them to record their feedback on the coach's strengths (highly effective coaching behaviors) and development areas (coaching behaviors that can be improved). Advise the observers that they should be prepared to give verbal feedback about their observations after the role play. Allow approximately 8 minutes for the role play, giving participants a 2-minute warning before calling time.
(15 minutes.)

11. After time expires, have observers and employees provide feedback to the coaches. Allow approximately 5 minutes for this task, giving participants a 2-minute warning before calling time.
(10 minutes.)

12. Ask participants to share key insights and learnings they acquired during the role play. Summarize the session by asking:

   - What is the greatest benefit for you to use unstructured coaching conversations?

   - What was the most important lessons learned during the role plays?

   - How can you implement your insights into action on the job?

   - What other times outside of work might you use these same techniques?

   - Based on all you learned during this activity, how might you use unstructured conversations to coach your employees in the future?"

13. Wrap up by challenging participants to use this new coaching tool within the next few weeks. Suggest that they contract with someone else in the group to check on their progress at a specified time.
(15 minutes.)

Variations

- Have participants switch roles so that each person in each triad has a chance to practice the different roles: coach, employee, and observer.

- Use this activity to help resolve strained manager/employee relationships. In these cases, have coaches and their actual employees complete this activity together, practicing the dynamics of unstructured conversations in real time to resolve interpersonal/workplace challenges. These experiences are usually perceived as highly valuable and practical, as coaches receive real-time feedback about their employees' perspectives as well as key strengths and development areas. Clearly, such situations are extremely risky and should only be supervised by experienced learning professionals.

Resources

Lindlof, T.R., & Taylor, B.C. (2002). *Qualitative communication research methods* (2nd ed.). Thousand Oaks, CA: Sage.

Patton, M.Q. (2001). *Qualitative research and evaluation methods* (3rd ed.). Thousand Oaks, CA: Sage.

Richardson, S.A., Dohrenwend, B.S., & Klein, D. (1965). *Interviewing: Its form and functions*. New York: Basic Books.

Whyte, W.F., & Whyte, K.K. (1984). *Learning from the field: A guide from experience*. Thousand Oaks, CA: Sage.

Submitted by Travis L. Russ.

Travis L. Russ, Ph.D., *is an assistant professor of communication in the School of Business Administration at Fordham University. He teaches undergraduate and graduate courses in organizational communication, intercultural communication, as well as learning and development. As a professional consultant, he designs and facilitates learning solutions for a wide variety of clients in the corporate, educational, and nonprofit sectors. His expertise includes organizational change, workplace communication, leadership, and diversity. He has published numerous development programs and academic articles.*

Unstructured Coaching Conversations Worksheet

Part 1

An unstructured coaching conversation is an unplanned, free-flowing dialogue between managers and employees.

Part 2

With a partner, brainstorm the pros and cons of using unstructured conversations to coach employees.

Pros	Cons

Part 3

Place a check mark beside at least three of the following conversation starters you will start using with your employees:

- ❏ Tell me what's on your mind.

- ❏ What do you think about . . .?

- ❏ I'd really like to hear your thoughts on. . . .

- ❏ How are you feeling about . . .?

- ❏ Tell me your ideas about. . . .

- ❏ I really want to know your insights about. . . .

- ❏ What are you thinking?

- ❏ [add your own]_____

Part 4

Use these facilitation strategies for effective unstructured coaching conversations.

Facilitation Strategy	How This Would Be Helpful

Facilitation Strategy

Encouraging. This refers to encouraging verbal statements such as "Uh-huh" or "That's interesting" and/or making positive nonverbal head nods. These responses prompt employees to continue talking, but do not bias the direction of the conversation. In other words, this strategy does not directly tell employees what to discuss but, rather, allows him or her to elaborate.

Calling Back. This technique involves a coach repeating an employee's last phrase or sentence. This should be done with a rising inflection to encourage the employee to continue discussing his or her last thought. This strategy communicates interest and an eagerness to explore the employee's comments.

Probing for Depth. This strategy is similar to the previous one, as attention is given to the last idea expressed. However, the coach doe not simply reflect the informant's last statement back, but asks a question or makes a comment to probe for additional information.

Injecting New Thoughts. In some cases, employees can become stuck on a topic, unable to move forward. This facilitation strategy involves carefully injecting new ideas into the conversation. This helps move the conversation along, minimizing redundancy and repetition. Of course, this technique is a great deal more directive than the previous three. In the spirit of unstructured coaching conversations, managers should use this strategy sparingly.

Unstructured Coaching Conversations Observer Feedback Form

Instructions: Carefully observe the unstructured coaching conversation. Tally the number of times the coach uses each facilitation strategy. Also, identify the coach's strengths (highly effective coaching behaviors) and development areas (coaching behaviors that can be improved). Be prepared to share your observations.

Facilitation Strategy	Tally
Encouraging	
Calling Back	
Probing for Depth	
Injecting New Thoughts	

Strengths	Development Areas

I'd Like You to Meet . . .
Introducing a New Hire

Activity Summary

An active way to learn ways to introduce new employees to the team.

Goals

- To practice listening to and retelling someone's story.

- To model methods to introduce new team members.

Group Size

Any even number of participants from 4 to 10.

Time Required

60 to 90 minutes, depending on group size.

Materials

- One I'd Like You to Meet . . .: Instruction Sheet for each participant.

- Writing utensils for participants.

- Flip chart and felt-tipped markers.

- Prepared flip-chart sheets with questions.

Physical Setting

Any meeting room.

Facilitating Risk Rating

Moderate.

Process

1. Tell participants that each of them will assume the role of a someone preparing to introduce a new hire to an existing work team. Request that each participant select someone to interview. Tell them that the person they choose to interview cannot in turn interview them and to be sure they do not interview someone who has already been interviewed. Say that they will have approximately 10 minutes per interview.

2. Give each participant a copy of the I'd Like You to Meet . . .: Instruction Sheet and a pen or pencil. Allow them a few minutes to read it and to write their notes.
   (5 minutes.)

3. Let them begin the interviewing process. Try not to interfere and let them figure out the configurations themselves, giving them 25 minutes. Announce the halfway point to reconfigure pairs.
   (25 minutes.)

4. Stop the interviews and ask for participants' attention. State that how well they listened to the other person's story is as important as how they present that story to the group.

5. Ask participants to take turns introducing teammates. Each presentation should last no longer than 2 minutes. During each presentation, listen and take notes for later discussion.
   (25 minutes.)

6. Following each presentation, ask the group to critique the quality of the introduction. Build on all statements and seek to emphasize different techniques to achieve an effective outcome. You might ask the following questions to initiate feedback:

   • What did you like best about the style and content of the presentation?

   • What makes someone's style easy to listen to and others less comfortable?

   • Explore what others found useful about the content and what seemed unimportant.

- From what you now know about the person being introduced, is there something that you found interesting and will probably discuss with the person privately later?
- What other ways could have been chosen to introduce this particular person?

(10 minutes.)

7. Initiate a discussion about listening by asking the group:

- What was omitted from the interview that you would have included about yourself?
- What made it easy to listen during this activity? Difficult?
- In what way did your planning and notes help or hinder your ability to listen?
- What lessons can we all take away from this activity regarding listening?

(10 minutes.)

8. Bring closure to the activity by asking:

- What makes an introduction memorable?
- What information should we provide to others for when we are being introduced?

(5 minutes.)

9. Review the strengths of the presentations and thank everyone for their participation. Ask what one thing they will remember and use when introducing new employees to their own groups.

Variation

When this activity is used as an icebreaker, it is recommended that the handouts be placed on the tables where participants will sit. The facilitator should then greet each participant and ask him or her to fill out the handout.

Trainer's Note

To maximize the effectiveness of this activity, it is recommended that you have several assessment tools and reference sources available for participants, as well as materials to distribute that discuss techniques to prepare a thorough and engaging self-introduction. One recommended assessment to identify personal descriptive words is *StrengthsFinder 2.0* by Tom Rath, available from Amazon.com.

Submitted by Lucille Maddalena.

Lucille Maddalena, Ed.D., *is an executive coach and management consultant providing management skill training, team building, meeting facilitation, conflict resolution processes, and group coaching programs. More than six thousand managers have successfully completed her popular Transitions to Management seminars. Her new workshop, Trail Setting and Story Telling, guides participants to achieve life and career goals while clearly defining their own legacies through storytelling.*

I'd Like you to Meet . . .: Instruction Sheet

Your task is to find someone in the room to greet. You will interview this person as if he or she were a new employee about to start a new job at your place of employment.

The person you interview will not interview you in turn, so you will need to form a new pairing to give your own information when asked. Be certain that you have both interviewed and been interviewed before the facilitator calls time.

Remember that, as the interviewer, you will pretend to be the manager of a newly hired employee; when you are interviewed, you will play the role of a new employee.

When asked to do so, you will introduce the person to the group, as if the group were the person's new work team.

Before the activity begins, take some time to consider what questions you want to ask and what information you want to obtain from your "new hire."

Write some notes to yourself here:

After you have interviewed someone, you will be asked to prepare a 2-minute introduction to present the person as a new team member. Describe the new hire's current job as his or her former position. Be sure to acknowledge the individual's skills, knowledge, and talent in your introduction.

Redirect
Achieving Positive Outcomes*

Activity Summary

A dynamic activity demonstrating how well-formed, intentional questions redirect attention from problems toward achievable outcomes.

Goals

- To demonstrate how to redirect attention from problems to possibilities.

- To practice outcome-based leadership skills.

Group Size

Suitable for groups of 3 to 100.

Time Required

90 minutes.

Materials

- One copy of Redirect Problem-Based and Outcome-Based Questions cut in half per group of three.

- One complete copy of Redirect Problem-Based and Outcome-Based Questions for each participant.

- Copies of Redirect Observer Notes for two-thirds of the participants.

- Two flip charts with markers at the front of room.

---

*This activity is an application with foundations in neuro-linguistic programming (NLP). Outcome thinking is referenced throughout NLP literature.

- A stopwatch or timer.

- Pens or pencils for participants.

- A bell, whistle, or chime (optional, recommended for large groups).

Physical Setting

Any space large enough to accommodate the group size. Ideally, participants should be able to sit comfortably in groups of three with some space between groups.

Facilitating Risk Rating

Moderate.

Preparation

1. Prior to the session, print copies of Redirect Problem-Based and Outcome-Based Questions (one set per team of three) on sturdy, colored paper. Cut the paper in half, with one set of questions on each half-page. Paper clip together pairs of "Problem" and "Outcome" questions for distribution among teams during the session. Also print copies of the Redirect Observer Notes for two-thirds of the participants and copies of the complete Questions sheet for everyone.

Process

1. Introduce the session with a general description of the goal of learning to turn problems into opportunities. Ask participants to form triads. If there is one extra person, that participant can serve as an observer. Two extra people can form their own team with one person serving dual roles as "Problem" and "Outcome" questioner and observer.
(5 minutes.)

2. When participants are settled into triads, explain that they are now to select roles. One person per group must volunteer to be the "problem" person. Explain that the person who agrees to be the problem person or "speaker" will later be telling teammates about a real-life personal or professional problem. This person will be telling the problem to teammates, but not to the entire group. Give some examples of problems, such as a decision that is difficult to make, an interpersonal challenge, a dilemma, a goal that has not been achieved, a resolution that is yet unreached, a professional challenge, etc. The person who agrees to share a problem should not reveal or discuss the problem at this point.

3. As participants determine who the problem person is for each triad, walk through the room, giving out pens or pencils to everyone who needs them and one Redirect Problem-Based Questions sheet and one copy of the Redirect Outcome-Based Questions sheet to the two members of each triad who will not be sharing a problem. It does not matter which of the remaining two team members on each triad receives which sheet, only that there is one of each per triad. Also distribute Redirect Observer Notes to all non-problem-sharers. (6 minutes.)

4. All triads should now have clear and parallel roles: one problem person one Problem-Based Questions person, one Outcome-Based Questions person, and two Observers (a dual role of the Questions people, as each will observe the other). Explain that there will be two rounds of this activity. Tell participants to look at what is written on the handouts. The person in each triad with "Problem" as the first word will be asking questions in the first round. The person with the "Outcome" paper will be an observer in the first round, observing and taking notes on his or her Redirect Observer Notes sheet. Say that observers will be asked to share observations with the group—including what was heard, seen, and intuited. If a team is finished with the first set of questions early, they should refrain from discussing the problem or asking questions extemporaneously. Be sure that everyone understands what to do and then begin Round 1. (7 minutes.)

5. Stop Round 1. If some groups are not finished with the entire set of questions, acknowledge that this is fine and say that enough information has been gathered to move forward. Tell them how to prepare for a second round. The person who just asked questions is now the observer, the previous observer is now asking questions, and the person with the problem remains in the same role. Tell them to assume the person asking questions has a basic knowledge of the problem and that this is a new conversation. Begin Round 2. Call time after 10 minutes. (10 minutes.)

6. Again, have all groups cease asking questions, even if they have not completed the full set of questions. Most groups will be ready for the next step. Ask observers from the first round what they observed about the speakers in Round 1. Encourage observations of behavior, word choice, attitude, tone, and nonverbal behavior. Post responses on the flip chart. Then ask observers from the second round what they observed about the speakers in Round 2. Summarize responses on a second flip-chart sheet. (20 minutes.)

7. Ask what differences participants noticed in what the speaker did in response to questions asked in the two rounds. Typically, Round 1 elicits responses that are negative, problem-focused, and dejected. The second set of questions usually brings out exploring possibilities, hopefulness, and reflection. Say that there is nothing wrong with the first set of questions; they gather information about the problem. However, the Outcomes questions move the person beyond the problem into possibilities and potential outcomes.
(10 minutes.)

8. State that outcome thinking is a practical, versatile approach to address and resolve challenges. *Outcome* questions redirect thinking, reframing challenges. Solutions emerge, replacing problems. *Problem* questions highlight past events, focusing on what has already occurred. By contrast, outcome questions place our attention on the future and potential and possibility. On a deeper level, these questions enable people to clarify what they *really* want.
(5 minutes.)

9. To continue participants' learning, pose some of the following questions to them:

   • What is achieved through problem questions? What is gained from outcome questions?

   • How can shifting focus from "What is wrong?" to "What do you want to achieve?" increase options and resources?

   • What ways can you apply outcome thinking to a professional or personal challenge in your life?

   • How can application of outcome thinking impact your performance and attitude?
   (15 minutes.)

10. Conclude by distributing uncut copies of the Redirect Problem and Outcome Questions. Say that they can learn to use outcome questions as challenges arise in their lives. Have them form small groups again to discuss how the problem questions limit their thinking about solutions. Have them brainstorm some more outcome questions they can ask themselves when problems come up in their own lives. If desired, they can discuss steps they can take to solve existing problems in their own lives now that they have seen the differences between the two approaches.
(10 minutes.)

Variation

This activity adapts easily to numerous circumstances, group sizes, and team compositions.

Submitted by Devora Zack.

Devora Zack *is president of Only Connect Consulting, Inc. (OCC), an award-winning leadership development firm celebrating ten years of exceeding expectations. She is a leadership development consultant, coach, and facilitator for over seventy-five clients, including Deloitte, IRS, America Online, Cornell, OPM, HBCU, DHS, IMF, the U.S. Treasury, and U.S. Department of Education. She has an MBA from Cornell University and a BA from the University of Pennsylvania (magna cum laude). Zack also holds certifications for neuro-linguistic programming and the MBTI. She is a member of Phi Beta Kappa and Mensa.*

Redirect: Problem-Based Questions

What's wrong?

What is the impact of your problem?

Why do you have this problem?

What or who caused it?

How has this problem limited your success?

What prevents you from fixing it?

Redirect: Outcome-Based Questions

What do you want?

What progress have you already made?

What can you try doing to change the situation?

What are some possible ways to resolve this challenge?

What resources can help you move forward?

What is a step you can take toward achieving your desired outcome?

Redirect: Observer Notes

What language, speaking style, and tone did you notice?

What did the speaker convey physically through nonverbal communication?

What was the speaker's attitude toward the problem?

How quickly did the speaker respond to the questions?

Does the speaker indicate the problem is solvable?

Other observations:

Team Extreme Challenge
Solving Difficult Tasks

Activity Summary

Teams use a Bop It Extreme 2 by Hasbro to experience the frustration of working on difficult tasks.

Goals

- To experience participants' reactions and resistance when faced with a seemingly impossible task.

- To work together as a team to reengineer a difficult task.

- To explore barriers to learning and development.

Group Size

Any intact group with 5 to 15 members; most effective with participants who already feel somewhat safe with each other and do not have reporting relationships.

Time Required

15 to 30 minutes per game; can be conducted multiple times throughout a training program to extend the experience.

Materials

- Bop It Extreme 2 by Hasbro, available at toy stores and online.

Physical Setting

Open area where participants can stand in a circle.

Facilitating Risk Rating

Low to Moderate.

Preparation

Prior to the session, become thoroughly familiar with the workings of Bop It Extreme 2, which you must purchase.

Process

1. Tell participants they will be involved in a challenge involving the game called Bop It Extreme 2.

2. Pull the handle to select the "Vox Bop" game option, which is for group play.

3. Explain and demonstrate to participants how the toy works. Bop It randomly shouts instructions for players to follow: Flick it, Bop it, Twist it, Pull it, or Spin it. These must be completed within a certain time frame that gets shorter the longer the game continues. Bop It also randomly shouts "Pass it," which means hand it over to the next player, who will continue responding to instructions. If the correct task is not completed in time, the game stops, shouts a negative comment, and must be started again.

4. Place all participants standing in a circle and allow each person to practice using the toy two or three times, passing it around until everyone has tried it. As some participants experience frustration or embarrassment about failing, provide encouragement and gently insist that the practice continue.

5. After all participants are somewhat comfortable with the game, announce that the challenge will begin and that the goal is to complete as many successful "passes" as possible before a game ends. Say that you will start the count over each time the game ends. Say that all participants must be involved. Give the group several tries at this. While they play, keep track of the number of "passes."

6. Periodically stop and debrief what participants are experiencing:

   - What do you notice about your personal reactions to this challenge?

   - Do some of you want to stop playing? Why?

   - How might your feelings during this game relate to real-life challenges you have faced on the job or in your personal life?

- Why do people often feel uncomfortable when they try something new and are not initially skilled at something?

- What impact does the game's negative feedback have on you personally?

- How can your reactions become a barrier to your growth and development?

7. Have the group play multiple rounds at intervals throughout the day. Gradually, participants will begin to problem solve and reengineer the process. Allow this to happen without giving feedback nor telling them the goal. Let their solution be the team's unique plan.

8. To encourage reengineering of the process when time is short, provide hints in the debriefings:

- How is the circle working for you?

- What is the exact goal again? (as many passes as possible)

- What restrictions do you have? (Everyone must participate; when the game says "Pass it," it must change hands.)

- What are some other ways to reach your goal?

- What if I told you that other groups have had over twenty-five completed passes? How do you think they accomplished that?

9. Conduct a final debriefing after they have succeeded in reengineering the process:

- What encouraged you to reengineer this challenge?

- When have you experienced this type of situation on the job?

- How were "errors" handled, and how did it impact those who made the errors?

- What did you learn about team dynamics from playing Bop It? What could you say about barriers to learning new things? About self-confidence and comfort zones? About constructive feedback?

- Who seemed to take a leadership role and why?

- How can you apply what happened to real life?

Consultant's Notes

- This can be a high-risk activity if participants are not comfortable with each other or if there are reporting relationships. This game requires that you be able to easily and calmly demonstrate the game, so read the instructions and practice, practice, practice!

- During the initial rounds when participants are failing and becoming frustrated, maintain a positive attitude and provide encouragement and congratulations with each small increase in the number of passes.

- The instructions can be hard to hear when shouted from the game, so participants will need to remain silent.

- I have conducted this activity over one hundred times, and each group handles it slightly differently. Use your judgment on whether to "bend" the rules or requirements a bit to give the team a sense of accomplishment and to experience the learning point(s).

- Battery replacement requires a Phillips screwdriver.

Variation

- This activity can be connected to key training content areas such as problem solving, creativity, performance feedback, teaching/training others, team dynamics, cooperation, and leadership.

Submitted by Amy Henderson.

Amy Henderson *has been involved in all facets of training and development since 1991. She has thousands of classroom hours facilitating training and has designed and implemented a wide range of programs. Her specialty is customizing programs to the needs of each client. She works effectively with construction foremen in the Arizona desert and also with insurance executives in Manhattan. Henderson does her homework and makes the content of her programs very practical and real-world. With her ability to quickly connect with people, she helps participants become involved and really learn.*

Puzzling Behavior
Discovering How Teams Work

Activity Summary

A puzzle construction activity that allows the facilitator to gain insight into the predominant behavior patterns exhibited by individuals placed in a "team" situation.

Goals

- To examine the behavioral dynamics of individuals on project teams.

- To discuss the impact certain behaviors have on the outcomes and success of project teams.

Group Size

Ideally, 8 to 12 people, either from the same organization or who are expected to work together as a team (all staff from one department, a divisional task force, etc.). Larger numbers can be accommodated as long as there is a puzzle for each group and people will be expected to work together in the future.

Time Required

40 to 50 minutes.

Materials

- One jigsaw puzzle (200 to 250 pieces) for each 8 to 12 people. Use puzzles that are a size that allows you to give each participant a section of twenty to thirty pieces. Prior to the session, each puzzle is put together by the facilitator, then broken up into as many sections as there are people in the group. Each section is then broken apart and placed in an individual bag. (Every small bag contains pieces that fit together to form one section of the puzzle.)

- A flip chart and markers.

- Masking tape for posting flip-chart sheets.

Physical Setting

A room large enough for all attendee to be seated at tables that are large enough to accommodate the completed puzzle(s). Wall space is required for posting flip-chart sheets.

Facilitating Risk Rating

Moderate.

Preparation

1. Prior to the session, put together each puzzle, then break it into as many sections [adjoining pieces] as there will be people in a small group. Then break each section apart again and place these smaller sections into plastic bags. (Every small bag should contain pieces that fit together to form one section of the puzzle.)

Process

1. Introduce the session by telling a story (with a current theme or that relates to the picture in the puzzle). For example, if the picture on the puzzle is of a pirate ship, the story could be about how the captain of a pirate ship may have no choice in selecting his "crew," the team with whom he is asked to work. He can, however, insist that everyone be committed to the common goal (plundering and sailing the high seas). Emphasize that, in the same way, they may not have a choice of members for project teams they are a part of, but each member must make an individual contribution to the effort. Say that knowing the behaviors that people are likely to display within the context of a task group can be very valuable. Permit a small amount of discussion before moving on.
   (5 minutes.)

2. Give a bag of puzzle pieces to each participant. (If more than one group is participating, ensure that all members of the same group receive pieces to

construct the same puzzle.) Make sure participants understand that each bag contains only the pieces to build one segment of the puzzle.

3. Tell the participants that their task is to complete the puzzle in fewer than 15 minutes. (Provide no picture of the completed puzzle as a reference.) Answer any questions, and then start the activity.

4. Observe the group dynamics as they work. If it seems necessary, give them a 2-minute warning before calling time.
   (15 minutes.)

5. Lead a discussion, recording their answers on flip-chart paper and posting them around the room. Use the following questions:

   • What did you notice as you worked? Was anyone reluctant to give up his or her puzzle pieces?

   • Did anyone try to take control of all the pieces?

   • What behaviors that others displayed helped you to discover where your section went?

   • Did anyone feel "steamrolled" or pressured—as if you HAD to give up your pieces? How did that make you feel?

   • What productive behaviors did you observe?

   • What counterproductive behaviors did you notice?

   • What positive effects resulted?

   • What negative effects resulted?
   (15 minutes.)

6. Lead a concluding discussion based on the following questions:

   • After participating in today's session, what would you say were some factors that positively or negatively impacted member behavior in past teams you have worked on?

   • Remembering that each member of a team should play a role and contribute to a final result, how might you assess and direct members of teams you were on for "best case" performance in the future?

   • What is the most valuable lesson you are taking away today? How will you implement it?
   (15 minutes.)

Variation

Especially when conducting this activity with multiple groups, you may find it helpful to have each group evaluate its performance prior to holding a discussion with all the groups. Provide each group with a flip chart and markers and, after they have put their puzzles together, ask them to discuss the experience, answering the following questions:

- What specific behaviors allowed you to complete the task effectively?

- What specific behaviors detracted from the task?

Once each group has had time to evaluate its individual performance, a debriefing can be held with the "larger" group to discuss the effects of certain behaviors on the work of the team.

———————

Submitted by Jo-Ann C. Byrne.

Jo-Ann C. Byrne *is the director of education and organizational development at St. Vincent's Healthcare in Jacksonville, Florida. She has been an educator for over thirty years, presenting at such conferences as the Florida Hospital Association and the National Nursing and Staff Development Organization. Byrne is co-author of the book* The Successful Leadership Development Program: How to Build It, How to Keep It Going.

Beyond the Olympics
Discussing Autocratic vs. Democratic Leadership

Summary

A team-building case study based on the XXIX Olympic games held in China in 2008.

Goals

- To discuss a variety of leadership styles.

- To consider the priorities of various issues of business, ethics, governance, profit, quality, and safety.

- To practice team skills of influence, speaking, listening, reaching consensus, and deciding.

Group Size

Multiples of 4 or 8.

Time Required

3 hours.

Materials

- One copy for each participant:

  - Beyond the Olympics Case Study and Instructions.

  - Beyond the Olympics Issues Worksheet.

The 2010 Pfeiffer Annual: Consulting.

- (Optional) Beyond the Olympics Impressions of Autocratic Leadership.

- Pencil or pen.

- Flip chart and paper and felt-tipped markers.

- (Optional) Videotaping equipment and monitor.

Physical Setting

A distinct area of a large room or a separate room if videotaping, with chairs and a table for the participants to put their handouts on. If videotaping, the room should be large enough for the camera to focus on all participants at one time.

Facilitating Risk Rating

Moderate to High.

Process

1. Seat participants in groups of 4 or 8 at tables. Explain that they will be working first individually and then within their groups to make some decisions.

2. Hand out the Beyond the Olympics Case Study and Instructions, the Issues Worksheet, and the Impressions of Autocratic Leadership article and pens or pencils. Ask that they not read the article until after the workshop. [Note: you may choose to leave this out, or explain that it expresses the opinion of one visitor only.]

3. Read the Case Study and Instructions aloud to the participants. Ask them to follow along as you read.
   (10 minutes.)

4. Ask them to individually rank order the fifteen issues on the Issues Worksheet in order of their importance for solving the problem. Tell them that they should not speak to one another during this activity.
   (15 minutes.)

5. When all participants have completed the individual ranking, ask them to decide on a group ranking in their table groups. Say that they must decide by consensus, not by voting or splitting the difference. This means that any member of the group should be able to present the group decision and support it as his or her own. If there are multiple groups using separate rooms, send them to the breakout rooms at this time. If there are a sufficient number of facilitators, one facilitator can go with each group as an observer and to operate the video equipment.
   (30 minutes.)

6. When a team has completed the rank ordering, they should work together to draft a 5-minute presentation they will give to the representative of the Chinese government to explain the first actions they will take to solve the problem and why they have chosen those actions. Each team should choose a spokesperson or persons to make the presentation after the draft is created.
   (10 minutes.)

7. Have each team, in turn, make its presentation to you (acting as the government representative).
   (20 minutes.)

8. After the presentations, tell participants to discuss the process that they used to rank order the issues. If the discussion was videotaped, review the video and discuss each team's conclusions.
   (60 to 90 minutes, depending on whether a video was made.)

9. Use the following questions to begin a whole-group discussion:

   • What did you do well?

   • What could you have done better?

   • Who had influence in your group? What influence tactics did he or she demonstrate?

   • Who took a leadership position? How did the person show leadership?

   • How well did you listen to one another? What evidence of leadership was there?

   • How well did you build on one another's ideas?

   • How well did you handle conflict? What techniques were employed?

   • How well did you resolve differences? What methods did you use?

   • What was your process like? Was it haphazard or planned?

   • How did you demonstrate when consensus had been reached?

   • What did you learn about yourself during this process?

   • What would you do differently next time in your group?
   (15 minutes.)

Variations

- If multiple facilitators are available, one facilitator can accompany each group to observe, operate the video equipment, and facilitate the process discussion after the activity. If no additional facilitators are available, the list of discussion questions may suffice for process learning in the group discussion.

- If multiple groups are completing the activity at one time, the groups can compete against one another in their presentations and decide which group of "consultants" wins the job. The criteria for winning could be based on long-term versus short-term solution or a predetermined criteria of what issues are more important than others among the issues of business, ethics, governance, profit, quality, and safety. For instance, ethics could trump profit or inspection could trump regulation (or whatever criteria you choose to emphasize).

Submitted by Barbara Pate Glacel.

Barbara Pate Glacel, Ph.D., *is principal of The Glacel Group of Virginia and Brussels, Belgium. She is author of three books and numerous articles, including a business bestseller on teams. She works with individuals, teams, and organizations in North America, Europe, Asia, and Africa. She has over thirty years' experience in executive coaching and leadership development at all levels of organizations. She is a well-known author and public speaker, working in multicultural environments with growing organizations.*

Beyond the Olympics: Case Study and Instructions

You are the leader of a team of consultants, hired by the Chinese government after the 2008 Olympic games held in Beijing. Your team consists of very experienced experts in leadership, strategy, change, and implementation. The team has consulted around the world, helping third-world countries in their transition to more participatory governments as they move into the 21st Century. The Chinese government, accustomed to strict control, is not comfortable with the messiness and unpredictability of democratic leadership. It is your job to use the Olympic success and the post-Olympic industrial scandals to influence the government to make some changes.

As part of your background reading, you were provided with the article entitled Impressions of Autocratic Leadership, written at the time of the 2008 Olympic games. It gives you a picture of some of the contradictions of government decisions within Chinese society. The public relations triumph of the government's decisions for the Olympics seemed, in some cases, contradictory to the welfare and development of the people.

After the excitement and the glamour of the Olympic games, the Chinese government was embarrassed because of the deaths of several infants due to melamine-laced milk products. Over 54,000 infants were affected, and products made from Chinese milk were pulled off shelves throughout Asia and as far away as Panama. The largest producer of milk products in China admitted to knowing about the melamine problem for many months, while purposely delaying any announcement in order not to embarrass the government during the Olympic games. The role of the government in this delay is unclear.

The problem of tainted products is not new in China. Over the previous year, revelations about toxic toothpaste, drugs, pet food, and toys have shaken trust in Chinese production. These scandals exposed evidence of corruption, influence-peddling, incompetence, and feuding bureaucracies whose only goals were to be low-cost producers to the world. In fact, it appears that the use of melamine to increase protein content of food products was well-known within the industry. Following the announcement of the melamine scandal, four brands of eggs were found to be contaminated because of melamine-laced feed given to hens. Next at risk are the cattle and hogs that ingested contaminated feed.

Chinese officials are known for covering up health scares. China's decision in 2008 to publicly address the melamine problem may be their admission that there is a wider issue for the Chinese food supply. However, even with that admission, the government has openly pressured lawyers to not represent the families of stricken children in seeking redress in court.

As the consulting team, you must first decide the most important issues to address. Then you must draft a statement that the government will present to its people providing the first steps it will take to resolve both the problem (short term) and the underlying causes (long term) that allowed the problem to happen.

Task One

Consider the fifteen issues on the Issues Worksheet and rank order their importance for resolving the problem for the Chinese government. Rank as number 1 the issue that is most important to resolve the problem and as number 15 the least important issue for resolving the problem.

First, work individually to determine your ranking of the fifteen items. When everyone in your group has completed his or her individual ranking, discuss the issues as a team and come to a consensus agreement on the rank order. Consensus means that there is no voting and that any member of the group could present the final rank order to the government representative and be in agreement with it.

Task Two

Spend 15 minutes and draft a 5-minute statement for the government representatives to present to the Chinese people giving the first steps the government will take to resolve both the short-term problem and the underlying causes (long term) that allowed the problem to happen.

Task Three

Make your presentation to the large group.

Task Four

Join in a group discussion of the process your team and others used to rank order the issues.

Beyond the Olympics Issues Worksheet

Your Rank	Team Rank	Issue
_____	_____	A. Integrity—behaving in a way that is holistic, upright, honest, and sincere; telling the complete truth about the product and its quality.
_____	_____	B. Ethical—conforming to high professional standards of conduct and exercising high moral judgment about what is right and wrong.
_____	_____	C. Government regulation—determining ethical standards by the government to benefit the welfare of the consumers.
_____	_____	D. Inspection—adhering to the standards set forth by the government and regularly examining all processes and product to determine adherence to those standards.
_____	_____	E. Transition from centralized planning to regulation—acknowledging the difficulty of that period of time when the government changes from direct involvement and scrutiny to a trusting mutual relationship in which the industry adheres to standards.
_____	_____	F. Safety concerns—attending to the ultimate use of a product and its impact on the consumer and the consumer's health and welfare.
_____	_____	G. Importance of brand—understanding of the choices in a capitalistic society between brands of the same product and the long-term implications of brand recognition and reputation.
_____	_____	H. Quality—producing the best and purest product that can be trusted by the consumer.
_____	_____	I. Exports—building capacity through those products that are exported to other countries and that impact the reputation of the industry, the economy, and the country where produced.
_____	_____	J. Profit—making money from the product through honest or dishonest measures.
_____	_____	K. Transparency—maintaining the truthfulness of the company, the industry, and the country to reveal the situation and its impact to all those involved.
_____	_____	L. Health costs—paying the related costs of business decisions when consumers fall ill from a tainted product and determining who pays those costs.
_____	_____	M. Culpability—deciding who is ultimately responsible for a business decision that results in illness, death, and decreased sales.
_____	_____	N. Management—making, revealing, or hiding the decisions that result in contaminated products by those in charge of the company.
_____	_____	O. Legal recourse—providing or not providing legal recourse for those who are impacted.

Beyond the Olympics: Impressions of Autocratic Leadership

Anyone who was in the vicinity of a television set during August 2008 knows that the games of the XXIX Olympiad were held in China. The Olympic motto of "Faster, Higher, Stronger" was played out on the world stage as China endeavored to present the best Olympics ever. In many ways, they succeeded in that goal.

Over the course of seven years, China spent in excess of $44 billion, the largest amount spent for any Olympics, to upgrade facilities for the Olympic games.

They set non-athletic records by awarding medals in 302 events, seating 91,000 people in the Olympic stadium (the "Bird's Nest"), utilizing 88,000 volunteers, and conducting the longest and highest-altitude torch race ever, with 21,880 torchbearers. China also led the gold medals race for all events with fifty-one.

However, observers from other parts of the world who visited China have noted some of their impressions of the results of autocratic leadership.

Roads

China added hundreds of miles of highways for the Olympic games, not only in Beijing, but in main tourist sites such as Xian, home to the Terra Cotta warriors. These are the most modern of highways, mostly toll roads, with multiple lanes and separated by beautifully planted median strips. Yet in Guilin, workers paved roads by hand using small hand-held cement trowels. In a land of 1.3 billion people, this sort of process keeps full employment.

Traffic

The new highways outside the city are high-capacity but have very little traffic on them. Even though traffic restrictions were in place to reduce pollution, the out-of-town roads could support ten times more traffic.

In the cities, even with the traffic restrictions, the wide avenues could hardly support the crush of vehicles and there seemed to be no laws governing traffic.

Subways

The main subway line from the heart of Beijing to the Olympic Green, home to the Bird's Nest and Water Cube, was new, modern, clean, and high-tech. A lighted system on the walls of the subway cars showed exactly where each car was and how far to the next stop. All signs were in both Chinese and Latin alphabets. Just one month before the games, the ticket process changed from a full-employment method of people selling individual paper tickets, people checking those tickets on entry, and more people checking on exit, to an automated plastic card system with machine readers. The local Chinese commuters on the subway were in awe over the technology and spent a lot of time reading their cards and trying to figure out how to use them.

Children

China's famous one-child policy was in clear evidence by the multitude of families who were also tourists in their own country. At Tiananmen Square, the three-member families were in great abundance. These only children are revered in the families. The young boys were dressed in NBA uniforms, complete with the basketball team names on the front and players' names on the back. The little girls were dressed in frilly dresses, many with flowery crowns on their heads. The result of imported fast food is also apparent in the growing girth of the children as compared to their parents.

Space

With 1.3 billion people in China, space is at a premium. Personal space and the rules of interpersonal engagement are very different from in the Western world. The subways and buses are so full of people that one literally sits on or leans into a complete stranger. Conversations are subdued and subjects are guarded. Mobile phone conversations are carried on behind hands covering one's mouth, and one's tone of voice and volume are low.

Friends

The Chinese people were ready for the world and were welcoming. A pair of eight-year-old girls on the subway sang a welcome song to Westerners that they had learned in school. The words were something like, "Hello, how are you? Welcome to China. We hope you have fun. When you leave, bye-bye." The volunteers at the games were friendly and gracious. Even when the Chinese team had lost an event to another country, they said "congratulations" as the victors left the venue. They were eager to talk and to trade pins.

Pin-Trading

Over the past twenty years, pin trading at the Olympics has become a big attraction. Typically, a corporate sponsor provides a pin-trading pavilion and pin collectors come from all over the world to display their wares and to trade. In Beijing, there was no such site. Crowd control was a big concern, even to the extent that there were few areas for sitting, very limited food court offerings, and sometimes oppressive security. The security guards were more concerned with crowd control than with allowing ticket holders to reach their events.

Security

Spectators went through metal detectors, and bags were checked both going into airports and even coming out of airports; going into subways—sometimes twice; and going into each Olympic venue. The rules seemed inconsistent. At one airport, they were most interested in one's magazines—to include a U.S. university alumni magazine. Who knows what subversive material it contained? At another site, they opened every item and unfolded every jacket, scarf, or flag. No liquids could be brought inside. And no pills could be brought inside. One person had brought Tylenol and was forced to take the pills at security, then was reprimanded for having the water bottle that the security guard had given her to take the pills. It wasn't comfortable.

What World?

One's first and last impression of China was of the brand new, modern, gleaming Beijing airport. It was highly efficient, very clean, and could rival any international airport in the world. Yet, in the city, the water is unfit to drink, even in Western hotels. The pollution is so extreme that there were days one could not see the buildings down the street from the hotel and the sunset with a cloudy neon orange color. China's race to the first world is coming at a price.

China did a fabulous job of putting on the biggest, most expensive, and most highly organized Olympics of the modern era. But it felt as though it had been done on the backs of the people—the people who were permanently displaced, the people whose rent was raised to pay for the facilities, and the people who were exiled from their Beijing homes during the time of the Olympics. Even now, as visitors nurse upper-respiratory infections caused by the pollution, it feels better to be back in a "messier" society that is less autocratic, even if less efficient and less productive.

Signatures and Shoes
Breaking the Ice

Activity Summary

An easy, effective, and non-intimidating icebreaker.

Goals

- To provide a way to develop more in-depth understanding among participants.

- To provide a different approach for introduction of participants before the opening of the training.

Group Size

15 to 30 participants.

Time Required

45 to 60 minutes, depending on number of participants.

Materials

- One whiteboard with five markers of different colors.

- Shoes or slippers of the participants.

Physical Setting

Any room large enough to accommodate all the participants. Participants must be able to see the whiteboard and have enough space for movement.

Facilitating Risk Rating

High.

Process

1. Ensure the whiteboard is clean and that markers are nearby.

2. Have participants sit comfortably on chairs. Say that the purpose of the activity is to get to know one another a bit better.

3. Once participants have settled in, ask them to stand to put their signatures on the whiteboard. Wait while everyone does this.
   (5 minutes.)

4. Invite the last two participants who signed the board to come forward. Tell them that they will act as representatives of the entire group by answering some questions. Ask everyone to pay attention.
   (5 minutes.)

5. Ask the two participants the following questions:

   - What happened to you when I asked you to put your signatures on the whiteboard?

   - How did you feel?

   - How do the signatures of participants look to you? Do they depict any kind of pattern?

   - How much risk is involved in putting your signatures on a whiteboard?

   - Are there any signatures of other participants similar to yours?

   - Which signatures are the most different from yours?

   - Did the activity energize the other participants? Why or why not?

   - How do you think the other participants are feeling right now?

   Thank the two participants and allow them to return to their seats.
   (10 minutes.)

6. Circle three to six signatures with each of the five different colored markers and then ask participants to form small groups on the basis of marker color. Have them move their chairs or sit on the floor.
   (5 minutes.)

7. When everyone is settled, ask participants to remove their shoes. During this instruction, observe the behavior of participants so that you can process it at the appropriate stage of the activity. Wait while everyone complies.

8. Ask participants in the small groups to create a shape using their shoes. Tell them they have 10 minutes.
   (10 minutes.)

9. Once the groups have created shapes with their shoes, use these questions to facilitate discussion:

   • What reactions did you have when you were asked to take your shoes off?

   • What shape did your group make with the shoes? Why did you choose that shape.

   • How much interaction occurred within your group? Who became an initiator? Who was less active?

   • Is there any similarity in the shapes chosen by groups?

   • Do you see any sense in doing this activity?

   • Was there any risk involved?

   • What impact did it have on your relationships with other participants?
   (10 minutes.)

10. Wrap up the icebreaker with some of your own observations on their behavior and then continue with the workshop.

Consultant's Note

This activity can invite participants to gain a more in-depth understanding of themselves and others—beyond any conventional introduction. Participants have a chance to share their feelings about themselves in relation to the others in the group. The participants' responses will give you a better picture of who is in the group and how you can relate with members of the group as a whole. It also provides participants an opportunity to become more open, informal, spontaneous, and energetic.

Variations

Use the activity for the following purposes:

• *Making small groups*: Create groups on the basis of colors of markers chosen for signatures or on the basis of signatures in columns or rows on the whiteboard.

• *Energizing*: This activity moves participants from passive to active mode, bringing them into the training not only physically but also psychologically and spiritually. They become more free from back-home baggage.

Submitted by Mahaveer Jain.

Mahaveer Jain, Ph.D., *is a dynamic and inspiring presenter, trainer, and consultant with over thirty years of experience in helping organizations find ways to create positive change results. He is a senior fellow with V.V Giri National Labour Institute, an autonomous body of the Government of India. He is an accredited T-group process trainer. He is founder of training of trainers programs on child labor and child rights in India. He has authored twenty books and twenty-nine training manuals and has contributed over one hundred papers to professional journals. Dr. Jain has been cited in a large number of national and international biographical reference books.*

Facilitation Tools
Using Spectrogram Analysis

Activity Summary

An exercise to practice using the spectrogram as a facilitation technique to increase participation.

Goal

- To introduce two process tools to increase participation and encourage diverse viewpoints from all participants.

Group Size

Up to 30 participants who are learning to facilitate groups.

Time Required

45 minutes.

Materials

- One copy of the Facilitation Tools Spectrogram handout for each participant.

- Colored masking tape.

- Labels for the spectrograms.

- A flip chart for each small group.

- Paper and markers for each participant.

- Post-it® Notes for participants' names.

Physical Setting

A room smaller than 15 by 20 yards with small tables and chairs for groups. Wall space to hang the flip-chart sheets.

Facilitating Risk Rating

Low.

Preparation

Lay three strips of colored masking tape on the floor from one end of the room to the other labeled "online," "local grocer," and "warehouse store." Make the lines far enough apart for participants to stand on them without crowding one another. Label each like a Likert scale with "strongly agree" at one end, "strongly disagree" at the other end and X's at the 25 percent, 50 percent, and 75 percent sections across the tape. Place one flip chart at the end of each line.

Process

1. Provide a session overview, explaining how participants will determine which method of grocery shopping is the most efficient and economic for *this group*.
   (5 minutes.)

2. Distribute paper, markers, and Spectrogram handouts. Ask participants to read through the handouts. Check to see whether there are any questions about using a spectrogram. Spend time discussing the tool as necessary.
   (10 minutes.)

3. Divide participants into three random groups by asking everyone to count off by threes. Assign Group 1 to online, Group 2 to local grocer, and Group 3 to warehouse.

4. Ask participants in each of the three groups to move along the line to show how strongly they feel about the grocery shopping method they have been assigned. Have them place Post-it Notes with their names at the positions they choose. Have them discuss within their small groups why they have chosen their specific positions.

5. Ask each group to use the flip chart and markers provided to list the pros and cons of the grocery shopping method they have been assigned. Provide a 2-minute and a 1-minute warning before calling an end to the discussion.
   (10 minutes.)

6. Ask each group to select one person to share the pros and cons they have listed. Allow approximately 5 minutes for each group to share.
    (15 minutes.)

7. After all three presentations, ask participants to think again about the best grocery shopping method *for single mothers* based on information they have heard from other groups.
    (5 minutes.)

8. Again, ask participants: "What would be the most efficient and economical grocery shopping method for you?" Have them stand next to their choices on any of the three masking tape strips.

9. Refer to the name tags on the masking tape and ask whether anyone would like to change his or her choice. Ask participants to return to their seats to have a final discussion on the tool they used. Summarize by asking.

    • In what kind of situation would you want to use a spectrogram?

    • What are the advantages of using one?

    • What are the disadvantages?

    • How might you change the process?

    • When might you use this tool in the future?
    (10 minutes.)

10. Close by giving them some sources for further information.

Reference

Facilitation: Spectrogram. (2008). Retrieved June 27, 2008, from facilitation.aspiration-tech.org/index.php/Facilitation:Spectrogram.

Submitted by Elisabeth C. Ayres, Catherine Cable, and Sophia Zia.

Elisabeth C. Ayres *is working at The Boeing Company as a leadership development specialist. She has been in the HR field for thirteen years and has experience with various aspects of HR, including workforce planning, organization development, staffing, compensation, and training. She holds a PHR and completed her master of arts degree in human resources and organization development certification from Marymount University in the summer of 2008.*

Catherine Cable *is currently the team leader/manager of the title department at Thomson Reuters. She has been in the managerial position for over six years and has extensive experience with training, team development, performance management, and team facilitation. She completed her master's degree in human resources and organization development certification from Marymount University in the spring of 2009.*

Sophia Zia *is a human resources manager for AECOM Technology Corporation. She has been in the HR field for eleven years and has experience with various aspects of HR, including training and team facilitation. She received her master's degree in human resources management from Marymount University.*

Facilitation Tools Spectrogram

A spectrogram is a group facilitation technique that is effective for enabling group interaction. Although we used three different spectrograms in this activity, it can be just as effective to use one spectrogram with one question or a series of related questions asking participants to move after you ask each question.

To create a "spectrogram," colored tape is placed across an open floor stretching 15 by 20 yards. Using a Likert scale or a variation of it, one end is marked "Strongly Agree" and the other end is marked "Strongly Disagree." "X" marks are made at the 25 percent, 50 percent, and 75 percent sections across the line. Participants are then read a non-controversial statement. Participants are asked to stand at the point along the line that indicates how strongly they feel about an issue. Those who agree strongly with the statement move toward the "Strongly Agree" end, and those who agree only mildly with the statement move toward the middle. Once everyone is in position, the facilitator asks each person along the line why he or she is standing there. Enthusiasm and passion are expected when participants are asked to describe why, and other listeners are encouraged to change their positions if someone else's statement changes their initial perceptions of the question.

This type of tool brings out differing opinions from the group and encourages dialogue among participants and sharing of differing points of view. It allows participants to reflect on each other's statements. It should not be something everyone agrees on but friendly differences of opinion. It is important to find the right kind of statement. Do not use a statement that is overly controversial but something you know people will have an opinion on, such as the rain. Something as simple as the rain can be an icebreaker question, such as "I love the rain because it cleans the air" or "I dislike the rain because it ruins my hair." This tool can be used at the beginning of the day or after lunch to encourage engagement and movement. If participants are unfamiliar with the spectrogram and are recalcitrant about participating, an easy way to introduce the tool is by contracting with two people in the beginning to play along.

As a final step, at the end of the spectrogram, each person can look to see who is nearby and introduce him- or herself to someone he or she did not know had the same views.

The main purpose of the spectrogram is to allow everyone to play an interactive role. It shows that there is always diversity in views among a group of people and that those views can change. It also establishes a means of interacting among all participants, not just within groups who are familiar with one another.

Resources

http://facilitation.aspirationtech.org/index.php/Facilitation:Spectrogram
http://kaliyasblogs.net/unconference/?p=29
www.aspirationtech.org/files/AspirationCreatingParticipatoryEvents.pdf

Follow the Leader
Exploring Trust As a Leadership Requirement

Activity Summary

An experience that allows participants to discuss the factors involved in creating a trusting working relationship with others.

Goals

- To identify how a manager or leader establishes a trusting relationship with a direct report.

- To discuss the concept of trust as a tangible, learned skill.

Group Size

It is preferable to have 8 or more supervisors from different organizations, departments, etc., who do not know each other well or at all. If people do know one another, then a group of 16 or more will work best. Maximum: 30 participants.

Time Required

Approximately 90 minutes.

Materials

- Paper and a pencil or pen for each participant.

- Enough kerchiefs to blindfold half the group.

- A minimum of five flip-chart easels with paper.

- Masking tape for posting the flip-chart sheets.
- Felt-tipped markers.

Physical Setting

A room large enough for dyads to walk around safely for approximately 3 minutes. People can walk the perimeter of the room or another walking pattern. The dyads need enough room to maneuver safely. Writing surfaces are needed for making quick notes after the first part of the activity. Wall space is required to post the flip-chart sheets.

Facilitating Risk Rating

High.

Preparation

1. Prior to the activity prepare a flip-chart page with a line down the middle and title the first column "Blindfolded-20 Seconds" and the second column "Walker-20 Seconds." On a second easel, start another flip-chart sheet. Make two columns and over the first column put "Blindfolded-End" and over the second column "Walker-End."

Process

1. Introduce the activity by telling the participants that you are going to ask them to volunteer for one of two roles and you are unable at this time to tell them the objective of the activity.

2. Explain that you need half of them to volunteer to be blindfolded. Say also that those who are blindfolded can talk about anything they wish during this activity. Mention that other individuals from this group (not including you) will walk each blindfolded person around the room for about 2½ minutes. These people will pick them up at their chairs and at the end of the stated time period will return them to their chairs. The blindfolds will be removed after everyone is seated. Ask for any questions and clarify if necessary.
(5 minutes.)

3. Explain that the "walkers" will each select a blindfolded person to take for a 2½ minute walk around the room. *Walkers are not allowed to talk, sing,*

whisper, or communicate in any way during the exercise. They must be abso-lutely silent. Refer to them as "walkers" and not leaders or guides or any other title that will give away the objectives of the activity.

4. Explain that there are no tricks. Mention that everyone must stay in this room (you need to keep an eye on the traffic flow and then signal the people as to when to stop). Give participants time to think about which role they want.

5. Ask for the volunteers to be blindfolded first. Distribute the kerchiefs. Ask the volunteers to put on their blindfolds.
   (5 minutes.)

6. Ask the remaining participants to come to an open space in the room. If you have an extra person because of an uneven number of participants, ask for someone to volunteer to make sure that chairs, purses, and other items are out of the way. You can also quietly ask that person later to watch for people potentially bumping into one another and/or to observe behavior and prepare to mention it during the debriefing.

7. Speak to the walkers loudly enough that the blindfolded volunteers can hear. Tell them that they are each to select a blindfolded person (do not use the word "carefully" because this is part of what you want them to experience). Say that your preference is that they pair with someone they do not know at all or know as well as they know others in the group. Mention that they should keep an eye on you, especially for when you sig-nal them to take people back to their seats. Repeat that everyone should keep his or her blindfold on until directed to remove them.
   (5 minutes.)

8. Tell walkers to pick up their people. Have the dyads walk for approxi-mately 2 ½ minutes.
   (3 minutes.)

9. Signal them to start bringing people back to their seats. As they start the seating process and before the first blindfolded volunteer is seated, call out that all blindfolds are to remain in place. Ask the walkers to go back to the part of the room from which they all gathered earlier.
   (5 minutes.)

10. When all blindfolded volunteers are seated, tell everyone that at a later time they can find out who their walkers were. Now they can remove the blindfolds. Hand out paper and pens or pencils.

11. Ask both the walkers and previously blindfolded people to think about the *first 20 seconds* of the activity and to write down on a piece of paper the first thoughts or feelings that come to mind. When they have finished, ask them to jot down the thoughts and feelings they had at the *end* of the activity.

    (5 minutes.)

12. Ask participants to read you their written comments, one person at a time. Start with the volunteers who were blindfolded. Initially request comments from the first 20 seconds and then request comments from the end of the exercise. Write their comments in the blindfolded columns of the two flip charts. If any comment is unclear, ask the person to explain it. Do not make any comments at this point. Note that the "Blindfolded-20 Seconds" column will have words like "unsure," "scared," "thinking about what to say," "a little uncomfortable," "did I do the right thing," "nervous," etc. The words that may be on the lists for the "end" column may be "comfortable," "trusting," "reliable," "consistency," "tried to communicate with me," "secure," "relaxed," etc. For the walkers, the first column may have words like "responsibility," "I don't know how to do this," "safety," or "scared," and the end-column words may be "trusted," "responsible," "guide," "careful," "relief they didn't bump into anything," etc. There is no way of knowing which words or phrases will be mentioned, so follow the trend of the majority of the comments.

    (10 minutes.)

13. After you have written all the comments on the flip-chart sheets, take a marker of a different color, cross out the word "blindfolded" and write over it the word(s) "employee" or "new employee" and then cross out the word "walker" and over it write the word "manager" or "leader" or another term that relates to your overall goal and audience.

14. Turn the participants and say: "Okay, now let's look at your comments through a different lens and see just how many are applicable in our real world and why they are important. Almost immediately you should see some recognition of what has just happened.

15. Start a discussion by looking at the Blindfolded-20 Seconds list and linking at least two words to how an employee (new or not) may feel in the real world, that is, nervous on his or her first day of work or nervous about approaching a manager on certain topics. Then work with the Blindfolded-End comments to find one or two words that could

demonstrate whether or not a manager has been effective in building a relationship or has tried to take care of an employee by removing stumbling blocks at work or has found a way to communicate that is comfortable, etc.
(10 minutes.)

16. Use the Walker-20 Seconds words and link one or two of them to how people should manage or lead new people on a team or at any time they are in a new relationship. Ask the following questions and lead a discussion:

    • How should a manager take responsibility for a new person?

    • To what extent should he or she try to communicate effectively?
    (10 minutes.)

17. Work with the Walker-End comments and again link one or two of those words to the real world. Ask whether managers should be responsible for leading people carefully. Link the word "safety" to the manager or leader role. Link the comments to the real world and guide the discussion. Generally, there are fewer than four words or phrases that may not make sense to link and that is okay.
    (10 minutes.)

18. Now divide the room in half and have one side be responsible for developing more connections between the blindfold comments and the real world and the other half responsible for the walker comments. Depending on the number of participants and time available, you may wish to form smaller groups. The objective is for each group to make a list of at least four more connections between the words from the early and late columns of each role and to report out. Their comments should relate to effective management and leadership practices that will make others feel engaged and satisfied in the work environment.
    (10 to 15 minutes.)

19. Ask each group to report its list. Make a final comment about trust and how it is earned through different behaviors and does not come without some time and effort on the part of both parties, with the manager leading the effort to initially make every employee feel comfortable. Ask participants to state one thing they will do back in the workplace as a result of this activity.
    (10 minutes.)

Variations

- (For members of the same organization) Have the group make a new list of key things that can be done in their organization to make new employees feel more welcome.

- (For managers) Have the group make a checklist of behaviors for developing trust between themselves and others that they can use as a self-assessment.

- (For leadership training) Discuss how effective leaders need to be trusted and link the activity to that attribute.

Submitted by Harriet Rifkin.

Harriet Rifkin, *owner of Rifkin & Associates, LLC, has a background in human resource management and development. She specializes in leadership strategies for success with various organizations. Rifkin has published a guide for writing employee handbooks and policy manuals through PSMJ Resources as well as contributing to the Trainer's Warehouse book of games. She is a certified DiSC instructor and has been an adjunct faculty member of various colleges in the Capital District.*

A Bull's-Eye Every Time
Setting Short-Term Goals

Activity Summary

An activity that engages participants in establishing short-term goals and outcomes.

Goals

- To develop short-term goals expected within a work group.

- To determine measurable outcomes for when one has reached short-term team goals.

Group Size

From 5 to 20 members of the same organization or work group in subgroups of 5 or 6.

Time Required

1.5 to 4 hours, depending on the number and complexity of the short-term goals and outcomes.

Materials

- One copy of the Bull's-Eye Lecturette 1 for the facilitator.

- One copy of the Bull's-Eye Lecturette 2 for the facilitator.

- Archery target or dart board.

- Unpopped popcorn.

- One large bag of popped popcorn for each participant.

- Limeade pie ingredients (one pie for every six participants):

  - One pre-made graham cracker or cookie crust.

  - One 8-ounce can frozen limeade or lemonade.

  - One 14-ounce can sweetened condensed milk (*not* evaporated milk).

  - One 8-ounce carton frozen whipped topping.

    Note: These items will need to be kept cold, either in a cooler with ice or in a refrigerator, before use and after the pies are made.

- Equipment to make and serve each pie:

  - Can opener.

  - Large bowl.

  - Large spoon.

  - Rubber spatula.

  - Pie server.

  - Knife.

  - Plates.

  - Forks.

  - Napkins.

- A flip chart and colored felt-tipped markers for each subgroup.

- A flip chart and colored felt-tipped markers for the facilitator.

- Masking tape for posting flip-chart sheets.

- Light-bulb shaped Post-it Notes for each participant—the same number as the number of short-term goals that need to be set. (May substitute stars or other Post-its.)

Physical Setting

A room large enough for the participants to work in groups at tables. Wall space is required for posting flip-chart sheets.

Facilitating Risk Rating

Low.

Preparation

1. Purchase the ingredients for the pie(s) and gather supplies.

2. Set up an archery target or dartboard with "Long-Term Goals" written in the center.

3. Develop a visual (PowerPoint, handout, etc.) with the long-term goals of the department, team, or organization so that all participants can refer to them during the session.

Process

1. Use the Bull's-Eye Lecturette 1 to introduce the session. Then have participants form small groups of 5 or 6 and have each group make a pie with the ingredients you provide. While they are making the pies, provide each group with a flip chart and markers and Post-it Notes.
    (10 to 15 minutes.)

2. Store the pies in a cool place for later. Then provide the groups with the long-term goal(s) of the department, team, or organization. Tell the groups to take one long-term goal at a time and to brainstorm short-term goals to meet that long-term goal and to write their ideas on their flip charts.
    (20 to 60 minutes, depending on the number of long-term goals.)

3. Ask the groups to post their flip-chart sheets for each goal on the same wall and share their ideas one group at a time. After all the ideas for a long-term goal have been presented, have each participant vote for his or her top three short-term goals by placing a light bulb Post-it next to each of those ideas. Note the short-term goals with the most votes and list them on a new flip-chart sheet for the long-term goal. Repeat the process for each long-term goal.
    (25 to 60 minutes, depending on the number of long-term goals.)

4. Distribute the bags of popped corn for participants to snack on while you give Bull's-Eye Lecturette 2 to introduce the concept of applying energy to get the desired end result.
    (5 minutes.)

5. Divide the group according to the number of long-term goals. (If there are four long-term goals, there would be four groups.) Have groups develop two to five measurable outcomes for each short-term goal that was

selected in Step 3 for that long-term goal. Use flip-chart sheets to record the measurable outcomes and post them on the wall.
(15 to 50 minutes.)

6. Have a spokesperson from each group present the measurable outcomes for that long-term goal. Follow this with discussion and refinement of the goal if needed.
(10 to 45 minutes.)

7. End the session by adding the short-term goals to the outside of the target. Note that the goals will move toward the bull's-eye as progress is make to meet that goal.

8. Have groups eat the pie made earlier to celebrate the success of the session while you debrief with these questions:

    - How would you rate the success of today's activities?

    - What would you have done differently as a team? Personally?

    - What will you do in the future to ensure a "bull's-eye" every time?
    (15 minutes.)

Variations

- Instead of actually making pies, discuss how it would be done instead, which will cut 10 to 15 minutes from the session.

- Instead of using popped popcorn, distribute small candies to participants.

Resources

Eck Mills, L.S. (2005). *From mundane to ah ha! Effective training objects.* Bernville, PA: Dynamic Communication Services. There is plenty of space in this book to write ideas and turn it into a personal reference source. Also included is a CD containing ninety-six colored pictures of the objects in the book. To order go to "Products" at www.theconsultantsforum.com/eckmills.htm.

If you are looking for additional ideas, visit your local Dollar Store. They have some interesting items that may be just what you are looking for. All Dollar Stores do not carry the same items and the price may be more than $1 for an item. It's also good to check back frequently, as their inventories change. Or check out the following:

Trainer's Warehouse: trainerswarehouse.com or 800-299-3770
Oriental Trading Company: orientaltrading.com or 800-875-8480.

Submitted by Linda S. Eck Mills.

Linda S. Eck Mills, MBA, *owner of Dynamic Communication Services, is a career coach, professional speaker, and educator. Her passion and expertise in active training and presentations, communication skills, and time management result in high-energy workshops that guarantee audience involvement, provide a unique presentation approach, and create a memorable and powerful learning opportunity full of tips and techniques. She is the author of numerous articles and books, including* From Mundane to Ah Ha! Effective Training Objects.

Bull's-Eye Lecturette 1

Our goal is to make sure we hit the bull's-eye on our corporate planning target to reach the long-term goals that have been established. To do this, we have to first review the long-term goals for the department (team or organization).

Today we are going to start the process of setting short-term goals and outcomes for our department (team or organization) that will lead us toward reaching our long-term goals. This is a big project, and I'd like to make it is as easy as PIE for you. Before we get started I'd like to review the PIE principle—Planning, Implementing, Evaluating—and have you think about this in relation to actually making a lime pie. And yes, you will get to eat the pie later today.

P represents *planning*. We may take many of the decisions in the planning process for granted. But let's stop for a minute and look at the decisions that need to be made in the planning stage.

1. What ingredients do you need to make the pie?

2. Where will you buy the ingredients?

3. What equipment will you need to make the pie?

I represents *implementing*. This is where we actually make the pie. We're going to use a no-bake pie recipe today. We'll mix one can frozen limeade that has been thawed, a can of sweetened condensed milk, and one 8-ounce container of frozen whipped topping together and pour it into a graham cracker crust. Next, this will go into the refrigerator until later today.

E represents *evaluating*. Later today we will eat the pie and have an opportunity to discuss what you would change to make it better the next time.

How does making a pie relate to our project today of establishing the short-term outcomes and goals desired by your team? Today you will be doing the planning part. Later you will implement that plan and evaluate the outcomes and goals. But equally important is the need to work together as a team to accomplish this. Basketball Hall of Famer Kareem Abdul-Jabbar is quoted as saying, "One man can be a crucial ingredient on a team, but one man cannot make a team." What would the pie be like if we left out one of the three ingredients we mixed together? What would the outcomes and goals be missing if we didn't involve all of you in this process?

Bull's-Eye Lecturette 2

[*Show the participants the unpopped popcorn (picture or actual kernels) and ask them what they see. Take a few comments and then deliver the following lecturette.*]

You are actually seeing a product that needs heat to transform it into the product we are actually looking for—something to eat. In the case of our team goals, the unpopped popcorn represents the short-term goals. Once the group applies energy to their ideas, they will have what they are actually looking for—measurable outcomes for each goal.

We need to have Specific, Measureable, Attainable, Realistic, and Timely (SMART) goals. Let's review these terms.

Specific—For a goal to be specific you need to think of six questions: who, what, when, where, why, and how? For example: Who is going to be responsible for this goal? What do you want to accomplish? When does this goal need to be accomplished by? Where will this goal be accomplished? Why is accomplishing this goal important? How will the work to accomplish this goal be executed?

Measurable—You need to set criteria you can use to benchmark your progress. How will we know we are making progress and meeting deadlines? How will we know when a goal has been accomplished?

Attainable—How can you make this goal a reality? In order to be successful, the goal needs to stretch you, but not to the breaking point so that you give up. Do you have the resources—financial, human, time—to reach this goal? If not, how can you be creative and find those needed resources?

Realistic—The goal must be something you are willing and able to work on. Without this motivation, you will not accomplish the goal. The goal needs to be something you truly believe can be accomplished. The goal should stretch your abilities and skills, but not discourage you.

Timely—Every goal needs a timeframe: date and/or time of day. Without a deadline, most things never are accomplished.

Introduction
to the Editor's Choice Section

Unfortunately, in the past we have had to reject exceptional ideas that did not meet the criteria of one of the sections or did not fit into one of our categories. So we created an Editor's Choice Section that allows us to publish unique items that are useful to the profession rather than turn them down. This collection of contributions simply does not fit in one of the other three sections: Experiential Learning Activities; Inventories, Questionnaires, and Surveys; or Articles and Discussion Resources.

Based on the reason for creating this section, it is difficult to predict what you may find. You may anticipate a potpourri of topics, a variety of formats, and an assortment of categories. Some may be directly related to the training and consulting fields, and others may be related tangentially. Some may be obvious additions, and others may not. What you are sure to find is something you may not have expected but that will contribute to your growth and stretch your thinking. Suffice it to say that this section will provide you with a variety of useful ideas, practical strategies, and creative ways to look at the world. The material will add innovation to your training and consulting knowledge and skills. The contributions will challenge you to think differently, consider a new perspective, and add information you may not have considered before. The section will stretch your view of training and consulting topics.

The 2010 Pfeiffer Annual: Consulting includes two editor's choice selections. Keep in mind the purpose for this section—good ideas that don't fit in the other sections. The submissions from Dawn Mahoney and Karl Sharicz and Carol Ann Zulauf Sharicz are perfect examples of items that are valuable to the readers of the *Annual*, but simply do not fit in any of the other categories.

Activity

Credit Bureau Reporting: Solving the Mystery, by Dawn J. Mahoney

Article

Importance of Consulting Diagnosis, by Karl E. Sharicz and Carol Ann Zulauf Sharicz

Credit Bureau Reporting: Solving the Mystery

Activity Summary

A written scavenger hunt that allows participants to practice resolving credit bureau reporting issues.

Goals

- To ensure that associates know how to find the information in order to answer questions on credit more quickly and with greater accuracy.

Group Size

An entire client relations department, including supervisory and managerial staff, who have contact with a credit bureau—from 20 to 40 participants.

Time Required

2 hours.

Materials

- Computer screen prints of the Universal Data Form.

- Computer screen prints of request forms.

- One copy of the Credit Bureau Reporting Guide per participant.

- Sample Consumer Credit Reports (three are given at the end of this activity).

- Sample Internal Reports (three are given at the end of the activity).

- Sets of written questions on the sample reports created by the facilitator (or use the sample questions given here).

- One copy of the answer key, created by the facilitator (if the sample questions are not used).

- (Optional) Prizes for the participants.

Physical Setting

A room large enough to accommodate the number of participants scheduled to attend.

Facilitating Risk Rating

Moderate.

Preparation

1. Make screen prints and copies of any credit bureau data information request forms from the company's computer system.

2. Make screen prints and copies of some universal data forms from the company's computer system.

Process

1. Begin the session by discussing the three credit bureau companies and the reports they provide. Use the Credit Bureau Reporting Guide for general information and hand out copies for participants to keep.

2. Hand out copies of screen prints of data request reports from the company's computer system that are sent to the main credit bureau companies on clients' behalf.

3. Give an overview of the credit bureau reporting process and the relevant codes displayed on the consumer reports, using the samples and the Guide.

4. Have participants practice completing copies of the Universal Data Form (UDF) and the Information Request Form for a fictitious client.

5. Discuss relevant time frames for the process, specifically how often information is submitted to the bureau and when during a calendar month, as well as realistic expectations for return of updated reports.

6. State that considerations include which credit bureau companies the clients have contracted with to report on their behalf, contract considerations, pricing, control table fields, and values.

7. Discuss with the group how best to resolve client assertions that a mistake has occurred.

8. Wrap up with a fun game. Have participants work in small groups and use the three sample Credit Counseling Reports and two Internal Reports to answer the questions on the Question Sheet. Explain that the activity is like a scavenger hunt that uses key field values and codes found on the reports.

9. Say that the small groups need to find what information was sent from the company's computer to the credit bureaus that resulted in the various consumer credit situations. In other words, the participants take information they know and apply it to the reports they are not familiar with.

10. Give the groups an hour (or another reasonable timeline) to find the answers. Then go over the answers with everyone, awarding small prizes, if desired.

Submitted by Dawn J. Mahoney.

Dawn J. Mahoney *is presently a manager of training and development for Brookdale Senior Living and past president of her local ASTD chapter. Mahoney has been designing and delivering training sessions for many years and considers providing this activity her way of giving back to the profession and honoring the people who've been there to assist her over the years.*

Credit Bureau Reporting Guide

Consumer credit bureaus serve as houses, or libraries, of information. They store information collected from credit grantors—financial institutions, finance companies, and retailers. These credit grantors in turn contract with the credit bureau(s) to provide repayment information for use by other credit grantors. Additionally, credit grantors may pull a credit applicant's credit bureau report for analysis.

There are three major (nationwide) credit bureau companies:

- Equifax

- TransUnion

- Experian (formerly known as TRW)

Many communities also have smaller, local credit bureaus that contract with one or more of the major companies to provide consumer credit information to local retailers, financial institutions, mortgage brokers, finance companies, etc.

Consumer credit bureau companies enhance the process, making it possible for consumers to:

- Make on-the-spot credit decisions;

- Use credit history from where it was originally established;

- Open charge accounts at retail outlets and financial institutions; and

- Use pre-approval programs.

Credit Reports

A credit report is information compiled directly from reports supplied by lenders the consumer does business with. Credit grantors use the information to determine whether they should extend credit to applicants or not.

Note: Although most people hold the belief these reports contain only negative information, the reality is that most people pay their bills regularly with little or no problems, and this is shown by the reports.

Common Questions About Reading a Credit Report

Q. The date on the cardholder's credit bureau report shows 3/09 and today is May 12. Why isn't the information reported more recent than that?

Verify that the client financial institution was included in the most recent update submitted to the bureaus, using the CP798-01 report found in the report dispatch system. If they were included, then the next step would be to request a "file dump" from appropriate staff.

Keep in mind that updates are the responsibility of the individual credit bureaus. Discussion of reporting delays are best handled by the client's financial institution with their credit bureau representative.

Q. This cardholder's account appears twice on his credit bureau report. Why?

If a balance transfer went through recently, it is possible two account numbers would appear on the credit bureau report. However, one of them should show a $0 balance and/or indicate it is closed.

If there are two accounts appearing and neither shows a $0 balance and/or closed condition, first consider the timing. If the balance transfer happened concurrently with the information being pulled, ask the client's financial institution to view the report again after the next update has been submitted to the bureaus. (Two sets of updates should be adequate to reflect the account's condition.)

If this appears on one or two accounts and the financial institution has waited through two updates, then ask the client to submit a Universal Data Form to the credit bureau(s).

If duplication has occurred on a large number of accounts, contact the Help Desk for further information. The client financial institution should also consider contacting the credit bureau(s) directly for resolution of the problem.

Q. None of my accounts is reporting. Why?

Verify that the client's parameters are set to report to one or more of the credit bureaus. Did they only recently submit a parameter change to report to the credit bureau(s)? If so, the relations representative for the financial institution should be aware of any parameter change request submitted. The rep will also receive a copy of the request upon completion of programming. Log into the report dispatch system and verify whether the client financial institution was informed the last time tapes were created. The dispatch numbers are either CP503001 or CP503002. The report number is CP798-01 [fill in the appropriate numbers for your system] and is a listing by Corp ID, lowest to highest.

If the account was reported, then it is possible the financial institution hasn't established a contract with that particular credit bureau. Or there is another type of issue at the credit bureau level. Ask the client to contact the credit bureau directly.

Q. What are the procedures I should recommend when a financial institution changes its name or merges with another financial institution?

It is their responsibility to contact all of the credit bureau companies they have existing contracts with.

Note: The financial institution may elect to have a comment line print on reports that displays their previous name—have them contact their credit bureau representative directly for procedures.

Q. What if the information is a mistake or it is negative information that needs to be updated with more current account condition detail?

Note: Bankruptcies remain on credit reports for ten years; tax liens, lawsuits, and judgments are retained for seven years.

Q. How are corrections to a consumer's credit report done?

If a client financial institution wants to add information to a credit report that more accurately reflects the condition of the account, it may do so by submitting a Universal Data Form.

Q. Which block/reclass codes apply? What do they look like on a credit report?

The block/reclass codes, as we recognize them, don't actually appear on credit reports. These codes only communicate account condition to client financial institution personnel. Outside of the computer system, they determine approval, decline, and pickup through the authorization system and are not reported (as such) to the credit bureaus. However, when accounts are blocked as B5 (Chapter 13),B6 (Chapter 11), or B7 (Chapter 7), *special comments* will appear on the credit reports. If the financial institution wants to report something special about an account, it must submit a Universal Data Form that adds *special comments* to the cardholder's credit report.

Additionally, a "V" block will appear as a "closed" account and "S" will appear as a "lost/stolen" account. But, the reclass code is not transferred to the bureaus.

Q. How often does the company report to the credit bureau(s)?

Once a month.

Q. When is the information reported to the credit bureau(s)?

The company gathers together all of the data to be reported to the three major credit bureaus on the second to last Saturday of every month. This information is saved to magnetic tape and sent to the credit bureau companies via courier service.

Note: Visa regulation 2.2.E (1-1.c) (11/15/98 issue) states: "An Issuer must report all Visa credit card accounts to at least one credit-reporting bureau and comply with the following reporting requirements."

Q. What if there is a mistake on someone's credit report?

As stated earlier, a credit report is based solely on the data contributed by the credit grantors and will only be as accurate as the information provided *and* whether it has been updated or not. Considerations, with respect to errors and corrections:

- Was erroneous data supplied?

- Who supplied the latest information?

- Has the credit bureau had sufficient time to load the latest updates into its files?

- Is the condition of the account reported to the credit bureaus?

- Whose responsibility is it to update or make corrections to the credit bureau?

- Which credit bureau companies should receive the updated information?

A consumer credit report contains four types of information:

Identifying Information

- Consumer's Name—including nickname and/or generation information (Jr., Sr., III)

- Consumer's Current and Previous Addresses

- Social Security Number

- Year of Birth

- Current and Previous Employers

- Spouse's Name (if applicable)

Credit Information

- List of accounts held with various credit grantors, to contain:

  - Type of Loan (revolving credit, student loan, mortgage, etc.)

  - Date Account Was Opened

  - Total Amount of Loan or Credit Limit

  - Account Balance

  - Monthly Payment

  - 24 Months' of Payment History

  - High Balance

  - Date of Last Update

  - Status of the Account (open, closed, etc.)

  - Others Responsible for Repayment (if applicable/ECOA code)

Public Record Information

- Any state or count judgments, liens, or bankruptcies

- Back child support (depending on the state)

Inquiries

- List of parties who've obtained copies of this credit record during the past two years and the date requested

Q. Who is able to obtain this information?

Federal law restricts who may see and obtain copies of credit reports.

Credit grantors, insurance underwriters, and employers are able to obtain a report only if a legitimate business need is demonstrated. Examples of legitimate need include underwriting an insurance policy, requests relevant to securing employment, and granting credit. However, all are required to obtain a signed authorization from the credit applicant before pulling his or her credit report. Credit bureaus are also able to release information to comply with a court order or subpoena.

Here's What a Credit Bureau *Doesn't* Do

- Decide whether a consumer should be granted credit or not;

- Rate consumers' credit worthiness;

- Know the reason(s) why credit was denied;

- Allow just anyone to obtain a copy of a consumer's credit report; and/or

- Provide information about race, religious preference, medical history, personal lifestyle, irrelevant background information, political choice, or criminal record.

Sample Consumer Credit Report 1

```
LC01      BCP06M     INQUIRY SCREEN (PAGE ONE)        15:58:02 06/08/99 ASF:
CORP: 000000 ACCT: 414812 000XXXXXXX        PROD: VCL 01E ACCT CHARGED OFF 012599
BLK/RCLSS: B5 DT: 012599 TYP/PROC: 10 BUS IND:      L UPD: 15:59        012599
VIP:     SRCE: 000 SCRE:   0 BILLDY: 09    DTOPN: 062394 ASSOC:
NME1: MRS LADYBYRD PEACOCK        NME2:                     IN COL: 000000
W DERRINGER DR                    PRV1:                     CLECTR:
PCTY:                           CL CLS:
DT ADD CH: 000000 SSN 1: 546987077 2: 000000000
CITY: SACRAMENTO             - FIN CHG: Y BILL CD: NOFINCHG NO FINANCE CHARGE
ST..: CA ZIP:          RLTN ACCT:              LAN:   MEMO: 4308805770
PREV:                    ACT:   STAT: 8 CD FEE:    RENEWDT: 0999 LST REV: 000000
TYPE1: V ISSUED: 1 0 0 0 OUT: 01              ISSDT: 120897    CURR EXPDT: 0006
TYPE2:    ISSUED: 0 0 0 0 OUT: 00             ISSDT: 000000    PREV EXPDT: 9806
BBAL PUR_____241.48 CRED LIMIT.:                3500 PREV CYC F/C.:   0.00
CURR PUR                              0.00 CASH LIMIT.:
DEBT PUR ADJ:         0.00 AVAIL CRED.:
CRED PUR ADJ:         0.00 AUTH TOTAL.:
BBAL CSH                              2900.29 AUTH COUNT.:
CURR CSH                              0.00 AMT LST PAY:
DEBT CSH ADJ:        0.00 AMT DISPUTE:
CRED CSH ADJ:        0.00 PAST, DUE...:
PAYMENTS                  0.00 PAY DUE   3500 C/ADV FEE        0.00
0 UNPD ANN FEE.:          0.00 358.23       LATE CHARGE..:     0.00
0 MISC FEES               0.00 104.20   DT LST PYMT..: 111798 0.00
DATE LAST USE: 092497     3141.77 DT LST DELINQ: 051399 0.00 DT PYMT DUE..: 060799
END BAL       3141.77 PR YR INT..:   353.95 CREDIT LMT DT: 020597
```

Sample Consumer Credit Report 2

```
BCP06M   INQUIRY SCREEN (PAGE ONE)            15:45:43 06/08/99 ASF:
CORP: 000000 ACCT: 414812 000.XXXXXXX    PROD: VCL 01E
BLK/RCLSS: VT DT: 122997 TYP/PROC: 10 BUS IND:  L UPD: 07:54  122997
VIP:   SRCE: 000 SCRE:  0 BILLDY: 09   DTOPN: 102296 ASSOC:
NME1: MS ROSE SCARLETT       NME2:   IN COL: 000000
600 TWISTED ROPE RD          PRV1:   CLECTR:
PCTY:                      CL CLS:
DT ADD CH: 000000 SSN 1: 2: 000000000
CITY: CHICAGO                FIN CHG: Y BILL CD: 0101011N CONV BILLING CODE
ST..: IL ZIP: 551282912 RLTN ACCT: 0000000001038900 LAN: MEMO: DAUGHERTY
PREV: 414812 000XXXXXXX ACT:   STAT: 5 CD FEE:  RENEWDT: 0999 LST REV: 000000
TYPE1: V ISSUED: 1 0 0 0 OUT: 01        ISSDT: 051997   CURR EXPDT: 9810
TYPE2:   ISSUED: 0 0 0 0 OUT: 00        ISSDT: 000000   PREV EXPDT: 0000
BBAL PUR    •      0.00 CRED LIMIT.:      500 PREV CYC F/C.:    0.00
CURR PUR           0.00 CASH LIMIT.•      500 C/ADV FEEₛ •      0.00
DEBT PUR ADJ:      0.00 AVAIL CRED.:      500 UNPD ANN FEE.:    0.00
CRED PUR ADJ:      0.00 AUTH TOTAL.:     0.00 LATE CHARGE..:    0.00
BBAL CSH           0.00 AUTH COUNT.:        0 MISC FEES  -      0.00
CURR CSH....:      0.00 AMT LST PAY:   406.00 DT LST PYMT..: 122397
DEBT CSH ADJ:      0.00 AMT DISPUTE:     0.00 DATE LAST USE: 052897
CRED CSH ADJ:      0.00 PAST DUE...:     0.00 DT LST DELINQ: 121197
PAYMENTS           0.00 PAY DUE          0.00 DT PYMT DUE..: 060799
END BAL            0.00 PR YR TNT..:     0.00 CREDIT LMT DT: 102797
```

Sample Consumer Credit Report 3

```
VIP:    SRCE: 000 SCRE: 0 BILLDY: 09 DTOPN: 111798 ASSOC:
NME1: COL CLARENCE MUSTARD    NME2:                    IN COL: 000000
10161 DAGGER PL               PRV1:                 CLECTR:
PCTY:                     CL CLS:
DT ADD CH: 111798 SSN 1: 123456789 2:
CITY: ARLINGTON              FIN CHG: Y BILL CD: 0101011N CONV BILLING CODE
ST..: VA ZIP:                RLTN ACCT:          LAN:  MEMO:
PREY:              ACT: A STAT: 5 CD FEE: A RENEWDT: 1299 LST REV: 000000
TYPE1: V ISSUED: 1 1 0 0 OUT: 02        ISSDT: 111798   CURR EXPDT: 0011
TYPE2:   ISSUED: 0 0 0 0 OUT: 00        ISSDT: 000000   PREV EXPDT: 0000
BBAL PUR          515.73 CRED LIMIT.:      5000 PREV CYC F/C.:   51.69
CURR PUR           10.75 CASH LIMIT.:      5000 C/ADV FEE   •    0.00
DEBT PUR ADJ:       0.00 AVAIL CRED.:       126 UNPD ANN FEE.:   0.00
CRED FUR ADJ:       0.00 AUTH TOTAL.:      1.00 LATE CHARGE..:   0.00
BBAL CSH         4346.23 AUTH COUNT.:      1    MISC FEES        0.00
CURR CSH            0.00 AMT LST PAY:    185.00 DT LST PYMT..: 051499
DEBT CSH ADJ:       0.00 AMT DISPUTE:      0.00 DATE LAST USE: 061499
CRED CSH ADJ:       0.00 PAST DUE...:    147.00 DT LST"DELINO: 000000
PAYMENTS            0.00 PAY DUE         146.00 DT PYMT DUE..: 070699
END BAL      •  4872.71 PR YR INT..:      0.00 CREDIT LMT DT: 000000
```

Sample Computer-Generated Report 1

Mrs. Ladybyrd Peacock	SS: 123-45-6789	Tropical Pets
West Drive	DOB: 02/15/50	Westchester Place
Sacramento, CA		Sacramento, CA

-- PROFILE SUMMARY --

PUBLIC RECORDS- - - - 1	PAST DUE AMT - - - - - - - $0	INQUIRIES - - - - - 5	SATIS ACCTS - - - - -6
INSTALL BAL - - - - -$6,484	SCH/EST PAY - - - - - - - $153+	INQS/6 MO - - - - - 1	NOW DEL/DRG - - - -7
R ESTATE BAL - $67,395	R ESTATE PAY - - - - - -$595	TRADELINE - - - -28	WAS DEL/DRG - - - - 3
REVOLVING BAL - - - - $0	REVOLVNG AVAIL - - - 100%	PAID ACCT - - - - 6	OLD TRADE - - - - 2-98

-- SCORE SUMMARY --

NEW NATIONAL RISK SCORE   - 360   SCORE FACTORS: 08, 04, 03, 37

-- PUBLIC RECORDS--

'US BKPT CT CA LOS ANGELES EX,: 9834599000   10-28-00   BK-13 PETIT

-- TRADES --

SUBSCRIBER SUB* KOB TYP TRM ECOA ACCOUNT #	OPEN BALDTE LAST PD	AMT-TYP 1 BALANCE MONTH PY	AMT-TYP 2 PYMT LEVEL PAST DUE	ACCTCOND MOS REV MAXIMUM	PYMT STATUS PYMT HISTORY BY MONTH
'COMMUNITY CREDIT 2506050 FP ISC 48 2 3388980987	3-00 3—31-00 12-99	$15,669-0 $1773	$1773-C 12-99	CHARGOFF (6)	VOLU SURR 999888
'RNB-MERVYNS 339696 DC CHG REV 1 630008875425	1-97 4-16-04	$200-L	$580-C 11-99	BKADJPLN (29)	CHARGOFF 7777999995528 333222111CCCCC
'U S FCU 2720494 FC EDU UNK 1 4776894	6-94 2-19-04	$3,500-L	$3,632-H 2-99	BKADJPLN (58)	DELINQ 180 999998888887777 CCCCCCCCCCCCC
'BANK FIRST 0201470 BC CRC REV 1 5546799654432563	7-97 11-13-00	$350-L	$417-H 11-98	BKADJPLN (17)	DELINQ 150 7547547547547

+++++ MORE

Sample Internal Computer-Generated Report 2

MISS SCARLETT ROSE   SS: 123-45-6789   E: ROSE AMONG THORNS CLUB
600 TWISTED ROPE RD   DOB: 06/17/78   RPTD: 06/99
CHICAGO, IL
RPTD: 1-99 TO 02-05 U 1X
LAST SUB: 2720494

426 RUE DE LA PARIS
NEW ORLEANS LA
RPTD: 2-90 TO 12-96

--- PROFILE SUMMARY ---

PUBLIC RECORDS - - - - 0	PAST DUE AMT - - - - - - - $100	INQUIRIES - - - - - 7	SATIS ACCTS - - - - -1
INSTALL BAL - - - - -$2,964	SCH/EST PAY - - - - - - - -- $100	INQS/6 MO - - - - - 2	NOW DEL/DRG - - - -1
R ESTATE BAL - - - - - N/A	R ESTATE PAY - - - - - - - - - N/A	TRADELINE - - - - -3	WAS DEL/DRG - - - -1
REVOLVING BAL - - - - $0	REVOLVNG AVAIL - - - - - - 0%	PAID ACCT - - - - 1	OLD TRADE - - - -10-96

-- SCORE SUMMARY ---
NEW NATIONAL RISK SCORE   - 566   SCORE FACTORS: 08, 02, 09, 36
-- PUBLIC RECORDS ---

-- TRADES ---

SUBSCRIBER SUB* KOB TYP TRM ECOA ACCOUNT #	OPEN BALDTE LAST PD	AMT-TYP 1 BALANCE MONTH PY	AMT-TYP 2 PYMT LEVEL PAST DUE	ACCTCOND MOS REV MAXIMUM	PYMT STATUS PYMT HISTORY BY MONTH
'COMMUNITY CREDIT 2506050 FP ISC 48 2 3388980987	3-00 3—31-00 12-99	$15,669-0 $1773	$1773-C 12-99	CHARGOFF (6)	VOLU SURR 999888
'RNB-MERVYNS 339696 DC CHG REV 1 630008875425	1-97 4-16-04	$200-L	$580-C 11-99	BKADJPLN (29)	CHARGOFF 7777999995528 333222111CCCCC
'WE-US FCU 2720494 FC EDU UNK 1 4776894	6-94 2-19-04	$3,500-L	$3,632-H 2-99	BKADJPLN (58)	DELINQ 180 999998888887777 CCCCCCCCCCCCC
'BANK FIRST 0201470 BC CRC REV 1 5546799654432563	7-97 11-13-00	$350-L	$417-H 11-98	BKADJPLN (17)	DELINQ 150 7547547547547

--- INQUIRIES ---

MOTHER GOOSE CREDIT UNION   1-25-99   9809999 F/C
SPRINT   11-11-98   2405276 UW
MBNA   5-16-97   1230194 BC

END - - - - - - EXPERIAN

Sample Internal Computer-Generated Report 3

MR JACK GREEN
5628 CANDLESTICK LN
CIRCLE PINES MN 55014-3509
RPTD: 6-00 TO 11-07 U 3X
LAST SUB: 1209090

SS: 363-12-4567
DOB: 1/23/53

COLONIAL CANDLES
RPTD: +10YR

'2395 3" ST NW ALEXANDRIA, VA
RPTD: 4-89 to 5-00

-- PROFILE SUMMARY --

PUBLIC RECORDS- - - - 0	PAST DUE AMT - - - - - - - $0	INQUIRIES - - - - - 1	SATIS ACCTS - - - - -8
INSTALL BAL - - - - - - - N/A	SCH/EST PAY - - - - - - - -$93	INQS/6 MO - - - - - 0	NOW DEL/DRG - - - -0
R ESTATE BAL - - $78,854	R ESTATE PAY - - - - - -$750	TRADELINE - - - - -9	WAS DEL/DRG - - - - 1
REVOLVING BAL - -$3,015	REVOLVNG AVAIL - - - -75%	PAID ACCT - - - - - 3	OLD TRADE - - - - 2-05

-- SCORE SUMMARY --
NEW NATIONAL RISK SCORE   - 36   SCORE FACTORS: 08, 04, 27, 04
-- TRADES --

SUBSCRIBER SUB* KOB TYP TRM ECOA ACCOUNT #	OPEN BALDTE LAST PD	AMT-TYP 1 BALANCE MONTH PY	AMT-TYP 2 PYMT LEVEL PAST DUE	ACCTCOND MOS REV MAXIMUM	PYMT STATUS PYMT HISTORY BY MONTH
'COMMUNITY CREDIT 2506050 FP ISC 48 2 3388980987	3-00 3—31-00 12-99	$15,669-0 $1773	$1773-C 12-99	CHARGOFF (6)	VOLU SURR 999888
'RNB-MERVYNS 339696 DC CHG REV 1 630008875425	1-97 4-16-04	$200-L	$580-C 11-99	BKADJPLN (29)	CHARGOFF 7777999995528 333222111CCCCC
'U S FCU 2720494 FC EDU UNK 1 4776894	6-94 2-19-04	$3,500-L	$3,632-H 2-99	BKADJPLN (58)	DELINQ 999998888887777 CCCCCCCCCCCC
'BANK FIRST 0201470 BC CRC REV 1 5546799654432563	7-97 11-13-00	$350-L	$417-H 11-98	BKADJPLN (17)	DELINQ 150 7547547547547

Sample Research Questions

What is Colonel Mustard's Kohls account number?

How many accounts does Miss Scarlett have with WE-US FCU?

What is Mr. Green's previous address?

How much is Mrs. Peacock's monthly house payment?

Who is Colonel Mustard's employer?

What is the status of Mrs. Peacock's VISA account?

What is Mr. Green's revolving balance?

Have any of the suspects had accounts charged off?

What does "UNK" mean when it appears on a consumer's credit report?

When did Mrs. Peacock open a loan with Community Credit?

Explain what it means to have the abbreviation "REV" on an account.

What type of loan did Mrs. Peacock, have at RNB-Mervyns?

Per Mr. Green's credit report, how many of his accounts are "satisfied"?

Answer Key for Sample Questions

What is Colonel Mustard's KOHLS account number?

9998898798

How many accounts does Miss Scarlett have with WE-US FCU?

2

What is Mr. Green's previous address?

2395 3rd St NW; Alexandria, VA

How much is Mrs. Peacock's monthly house payment?

$595

Who is Colonel Mustard's employer?

Department of Defense

What is the status of Mrs. Peacock's VISA account?

BKADJPN—She's agreed to pay at least part of the amount due

What is Mr. Green's revolving balance?

$3,015

Have any of the suspects had accounts charged off?

Yes, Peacock and Mustard

What does "UNK" mean when it appears on a consumer's credit report?

Unknown

When did Mrs. Peacock open a loan with Community Credit?

3/95

Explain what it means to have the abbreviation "REV" on an account?

Revolving charge

What type of loan did Mrs. Peacock, have at RNB-Mervyns?

Dept Store Charge Account

Per Mr. Green's credit report, how many of his accounts are "satisfied"?

8

The Importance of Consulting Diagnosis

Karl E. Sharicz and Carol Ann Zulauf Sharicz

Summary

In this article, the authors stress the importance of accurately diagnosing organizational issues. They provide a tool, a systems archetype, that can assist consultants in studying and diagnosing the dynamics inherent in a problem or decision. They then offer three case studies as examples, providing "solutions" for two of the studies and allowing the reader to work through the third case on his or her own.

Everyone knows that in every organization there are problems that need to be addressed. Some of the problems inherent in an organization are chronic, that is, they have been there for a really long time. If you are an internal or an external consultant, these are the types of problems you are called in to solve—and solve quickly, if you can! This article will focus on adding a new tool to your toolkit, if you will. We will examine how to look at problems from a dynamic point of view rather than being immersed in the details of the problem. When any of us starts to look at organizational problems from the underlying dynamic, we start to get to the level at which real change can be made—change that will have significant impact on organizational performance.

We will present three actual case scenarios. In the first two, we will diagnose the problems, explaining the dynamic of what is going on. Then, once the dynamic is understood, we will talk about the best place to make an intervention that has the best chance to solve the problem successfully. At this point you may be saying to yourself, "That sounds too good to be true!" It is a little more challenging than this. Once an intervention point has been determined, there are ramifications. As we all know, once one tries to make an intervention, that usually means that something will need to change in that organization. This is where the real challenge lies—in implementing the intervention.

In the third case scenario, we present the actual case but will leave it open so that you can determine the dynamics going on and the intervention that should be made. This will give you the opportunity to apply the tool we present to an actual organizational issue.

Case Scenario Objectives

The objectives will be to:

- Discuss the dynamics inherent in each case;

- Recommend the interventions to be made; and

- Discuss how these interventions will impact the organization—what changes need to be made.

Case Scenario 1: "Global Growth vs. the Old Home Team"

Your organization is going global at a very fast rate. One strategy is to offshore some key operations. In order to have this offshore site become productive quickly, a lot of the managers' and directors' time, attention, and resources are going to support the new global team. The staff "back home" hardly ever receives any communication about what is going on. The expectation is that the "back home" team should just keep on going along as it always has. The home team is starting to feel neglected; the global team is getting a lot more resources, training, and support. The turnover rate is increasing back home. The managers and directors continue to focus more of their attention and support on the global team. This dynamic has been going on for almost a year now.

Diagnosis

What dynamic is going on in this situation? We will use a systems thinking tool called a *systems archetype* to capture the dynamic. (*Note:* Only two archetypes are presented in this article. For more information on system dynamics tools and applications, see www.pegasuscom.com, the website for Pegasus Communications.)

The archetype shown in Figure 1 is called a "Success to the Successful" dynamic, and it is read like a "figure 8," beginning on the left-hand side of the figure.

This archetype can also be thought of as a "self-fulfilling prophecy." If one person or group (A) is given more resources, it has a higher likelihood of succeeding than the other group or person (B). This initial success justifies devoting more

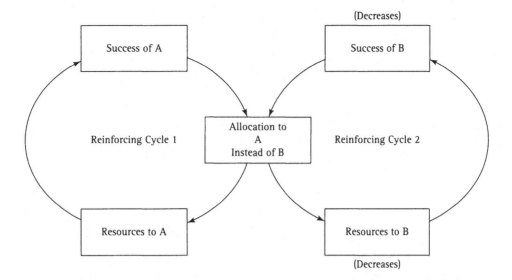

Figure 1. Success to the Successful Archetype

resources to A than to B (reinforcing Cycle 1). How many times have we seen this pattern in our organizations!

This is how we would read the dynamic:

1. (Starting with the left-hand side): As success of A increases, more allocation (of resources, attention, support) goes to A (our new global team) instead of B (our old home team).

2. As the allocation to A increases, the resources to B decrease.

3. As resources to B decrease, success of Team B decreases.

4. As success of Team B decreases, the allocation to A increases.

5. As allocation of resources, support, and attention continue to A, success of A continues.

Intervention to Be Made

Organizations that are in this type of a dynamic need to pay equal attention to both teams. Team B needs to be recognized with as much support and resources as its needs require, and communication needs to increase with this team so that they do not feel neglected.

How This Intervention Impacts the Organization

Pros to This Intervention

- It recognizes the contributions and needs of everyone.

- If people in Team B feel recognized and valued, the turnover rate should start to decrease.

- If Team B's needs are met, creativity and performance should also increase, leading to the success of all.

Cons to This Intervention

- Managers need to be made aware of the dynamic of what is going on, which is not an easy message to hear.

- This intervention does impact the already limited time and resources available; however, over time, the benefits gained should far outweigh the cons.

Case Scenario 2: "Boosting Revenues by Increasing Prices"

Your organization is losing market share, and revenues are also slipping. Senior managers have responded by devising a strategy to increase prices of products and services across the board. Marketing and sales agrees this is a good strategy. Historically, the customers have been price-conscious and the company plays in a highly competitive market. Your company has a spotty reputation of quality, and increasing prices will have to be justified. Customers moving to other vendors is believed to be part of the reason for losing market share. This is the end of the company's fiscal year and the price increase is effective immediately.

Diagnosis

The dynamic going on here is called "Shifting the Burden," as depicted in Figure 2. To read this dynamic:

1. Start with the problem symptom. In this case, the problem is *Losing Market Share*.

2. The symptomatic solution is *Increasing Prices*. The symptomatic solution is also known as the "Quick Fix" or "Band-Aid" solution.

3. There will always be side-effects any time there is a quick fix that addresses only a symptom. In this case, the side-effects are *impact on price-conscious customers, better positioning for the competition, the lack of value-added perceived by the customers with this price increase,* and *the possibility of continuing to lose market share over the long term based on this price increase.*

4. The Fundamental Solution is the focus the senior staff should have taken in making their decision. This would have had a longer-lasting impact on the problem.

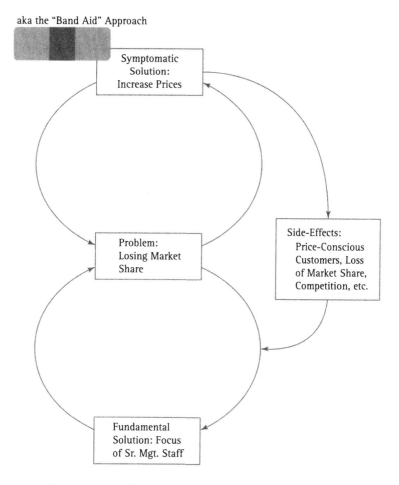

Figure 2. Shifting the Burden Systems Dynamic

Intervention to Be Made

Focus on asking "fundamental" questions, such as:

- If we raise our prices, how will that impact our customers?

- How will our customers perceive those price increases?

- How are we communicating this change to our customers?

- Are there other alternatives to a price increase?

- What are our competitors doing?

- What if we were to invest in augmenting our services and products instead of "just" increasing prices?

- What do we need to focus on, as an organization, to keep growing and thriving?

The fundamental solution usually takes a little more time, effort, and resources; however, in the long term, focusing on fundamental solutions reaps far greater benefits for any organization in terms of increased customer satisfaction, customer loyalty, employee satisfaction, and revenue and market share.

How This Intervention Impacts the Organization

Pros to This Intervention:

- When any organization focuses on customers and their needs, long-term benefits result, for example, increased customer loyalty.

- When senior staff focus on their internal processes and services/products, the emphasis shifts to the infrastructure of that organization rather then just a short-term strategy of "raising prices."

- Helps an organization remain in the game, that is, the organization remains competitive and is not priced out of the market without the added value being experienced by the customer.

Cons to This Intervention:

- It takes commitment by those in the organization to focus on sustaining yet growing the infrastructure.

- It is a longer-term solution; therefore, it takes more time and resources.

Your Turn: Experiential Application

This next case scenario highlights another dynamic in an organization. It may be either "Shifting the Burden" or "Success to the Successful." Read the following case and think about what dynamic it illustrates and what interventions need to be made to help address this issue. (The "solution" is provided in Exhibit 1 at the end of this article.)

Case Scenario 3: "Accelerating Billing Receivables"

Your organization is lagging in billing receivables, which is affecting quarterly revenue targets. Senior managers have devised a strategy of accelerating receivables by refusing services to some customers who have outstanding invoices. Furthermore, to encourage payments, some customers are being turned over to a collection agency that uses demanding tactics to secure payment of invoices. Some customers feel bound by their organization's payment terms and feel they have little control. Yet other customers have disputed their bills and are withholding payment until the dispute is resolved.

Diagnosis

What dynamic is being depicted in Case 3?

Intervention to Be Made

How This Intervention Impacts the Organization

Pros to This Intervention

-

-

-

Cons to This Intervention

-

-

-

Turn to Exhibit 1 at the end of the article for insights into this case.

Summary/Key Action Steps

Diagnosing issues in any organization is an ongoing process that helps to ensure that the organization is on track when making changes and is progressing in the right direction. A summary of the key steps in the process presented in this article includes the following:

1. Going past the "presenting" problem to determine the "fundamental" problem.

2. Diagnosing the problem by listening for the *dynamic* inherent in the problem.

3. Generating solid interventions based on that dynamic. Every dynamic has a high leverage point for making the most effective changes. The other option is referred to as "picking the low-hanging fruit." In some cases, that may be appropriate; however, as practitioners, striving for the highest leverage gives the most effective and longest-lasting points for change.

4. With any intervention, there are consequences, both pro and con. We need to discuss those consequences in order to make the most effective decisions and changes for the benefit of all.

Karl E. Sharicz *is a marketing manager with SimplexGrinnell, a Tyco International company, and focuses on customer loyalty measurement and management systems. His most recent career history includes training management roles within several high-tech manufacturing organizations. He holds a master's degree in adult and organization learning from Boston University. Sharicz spent several years in the applied biosciences, where he published many practical articles dealing with chemical analysis techniques and made numerous presentations to professional associations.*

Carol Ann Zulauf Sharicz *has her own consulting practice, specializing in leadership, systems thinking, and customer dynamics. Her clients span high-tech, federal and state governments, health care, education, financial, and consumer product organizations. Dr. Sharicz is also an associate professor at Suffolk University in Boston. Prior work experience includes being a senior training instructor for Motorola, Inc. She has many publications to her credit, including her book published by Linkage, Inc.,* The Big Picture: A Systems Thinking Story for Managers, *and is a frequent presenter at regional, national, and international conferences.*

Exhibit 1. Case Scenario 3 "Solution"

Diagnosis

The dynamic of Case Scenario 3 is "Shifting the Burden," as illustrated in Figure 3.

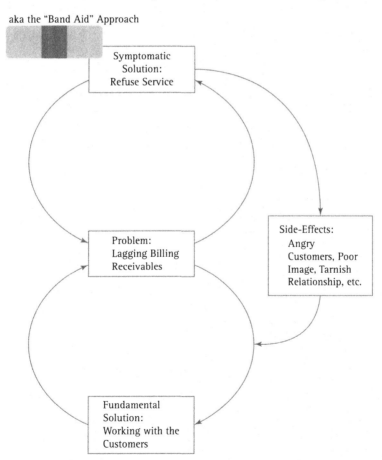

Figure 3. Dynamic of Case Scenario 3 Is "Shifting the Burden"

(Continued)

Exhibit 1. (*Continued*)

The problem is lagging billing receivables. The solution is to refuse service. The side-effects of this solution include angry customers, a poor company image, tarnished relationships, loss of business because the organization will not provide new services until old invoices are settled, and driving customers to the competition.

The fundamental solution is to work with the customers.

Intervention to Be Made

- Work with the customers to determine why bills are not being paid.
- Examine internal processes to make sure they are quality-driven and customer-focused.
- Offer incentives to customers to settle invoices early or by due date.
- Work toward sustaining really solid working relationships with customers.

How This Intervention Impacts the Organization

Pros to This Intervention

- Building relationships with customers as business partners is always a foundation to any business's success.
- It is a more positive and encouraging intervention.
- Incentives motivate people and give them choices in how they can pay.

Cons to This Intervention

- It takes time and skill to build relationships.
- Missing out on the quick revenue stream.
- Changing and systematically examining processes usually meets with resistance that would have to be addressed.

Introduction

to the Inventories, Questionnaires, and Surveys Section

Inventories, questionnaires, and surveys are valuable tools for the HRD professional. These feedback tools help respondents take an objective look at themselves and at their organizations. These tools also help to explain how a particular theory applies to them or to their situations.

Inventories, questionnaires, and surveys are useful in a number of training and consulting situations: privately for self-diagnosis; one-on-one to plan individual development; in a small group to open discussion; in a work team to help the team to focus on its highest priorities; or in an organization to gather data to achieve progress. You will find that the use of inventories, questionnaires, and surveys enriches, personalizes, and deepens training, development, and intervention designs. Many can be combined with other experiential learning activities or articles in this or other *Annuals* to design an exciting, involving, practical, and well-rounded intervention. Each instrument includes the background necessary for understanding, presenting, and using it. Interpretive information, scales, and scoring sheets are also provided. In addition, we include the reliability and validity data contributed by the authors. If you wish additional information on any of these instruments, contact the authors directly. You will find their addresses and telephone numbers in the "Contributors" listing near the end of this volume.

The 2010 Pfeiffer Annual: Consulting includes three assessment tools in the following categories:

Groups and Teams

Team Effectiveness Assessment Measure (TEAM), by Udai Pareek

Leadership

Corporate Social Responsibility: Determining Your Position, by Homer H. Johnson

Organizations

Scale of Intellectual Capital for Organizations (SICO), by Sacip Toker, James L. Moseley, and Ann T. Chow

Team Effectiveness Assessment Measure (TEAM)

Udai Pareek

Summary

Most of the work in organizations is being done in teams. Effectiveness of the individual as well as of the total organization, therefore, very much depends on the effectiveness of the various teams functioning in the organization. Team effectiveness deserves a great deal of attention.

A team is a collection of individuals with interdependent roles working for some goal(s) that are also congruent with the members' goals. A team has several characteristics: members are interdependent; it has common goal or goals; each member has a distinct role and his or her contribution is as important as that of any other member; and there is congruence between individual goals and the team goal.

Several types of teams function in an organization. The most common are composed of individuals who are assigned a particular task to be completed within a given timeframe. These are the natural teams of which an organization is composed, including departmental teams. Special teams that are constituted to work on some assignment to be completed within a time period are called "task forces." Groups that are ongoing or that are set up for a particular period of time to deal with certain issues are called "committees." Special teams may also be constituted to complete a particular task; these are called "project teams." Attention needs to be paid to ways to make all such teams effective in accomplishing their goals.

Attention also needs to be given when two or more teams are working together. Cross-functional or interdepartmental or inter-level teams have some special characteristics that go beyond those of the teams per se. Inter-team functioning is becoming more prevalent in most organizations.

Table 1. Characteristics of Effective Work Teams

Characteristics	McGregor	Likert
1. Commitment and Inspiring goals		8, 12, 13
2. Role Clarity	3, 9	23
3. Self-disclosure (including confrontation)	5, 7, 8, 11	17
4. Openness to feedback	4	18, 19
5. Competence		1
6. Creativity with constructive conformity		15, 16
7. Collaboration/support/trust	1	2, 4, 9, 14
8. Congruence between individual and group goals		3, 5, 6, 7, 11
9. Supportive leadership		10, 24
10. Management of power	2, 6, 10	20, 21, 22

The importance of feeling like a team for increased productivity was first studied at the GE Hawthorne plant in the early 1930s. McGregor (1960) also gave special attention to teams. Likert (1961) focused his attention on teams as important elements of the humanization of organizations. Both of them listed a large number of characteristics of effective work groups or teams. Dyer (1987) has described the ten characteristics of an effective work team suggested by McGregor and the twenty-four suggested by Likert. Table 1 lists Dyer's ten characteristics of effective teams in the order he used (Dyer, 1987, pp. 12–16). Both McGregor's and Likert's lists are also incorporated in the table.

Team effectiveness can be defined in several ways. To use the Johari Window terminology, an effective team is one in which people give their opinions and comments without hesitation; listen to and examine others' opinions, comments, and feedback at all levels; and are sensitive to the needs of others (perceptiveness). Team effectiveness can also be understood in terms of three main characteristics of *team functioning*: (1) clarity of roles and cohesion, trust, and closeness among members of the team; (2) confrontation, that is, solving problems as they arise rather than shying away from them; and (3) collaboration, that is, working together, giving and receiving help from one another. The four main characteristics of *team empowerment* are (1) clarity of rules of different members of the team; (2) autonomy of the team; (3) support provided to the team in terms of resources; and (4) accountability of the team members for achieving the goals set for the team.

An effective team can also be defined as one in which power is shared (widely distributed) and wherein the members use more persuasive than coercive power.

The Instrument and Its Administration

TEAM has been designed to measure the effectiveness of a team. The members of a team rate their own team on seven components, which are grouped into two main aspects of team effectiveness: *team functioning* (containing three dimensions) and *team empowerment* (having four dimensions). TEAM has twenty-eight items. The participants rate their team on a 5-point scale to indicate their experience with and perceptions of their own team. To create a group profile, first individuals find their own scores and then all scores are added together for each item. Raw scores can be used, or an average can be calculated. A scoring sheet is provided.

Reliability

The Alpha coefficient for one group was found to be .85. Equal and unequal length coefficients were both .88.

Using the Instrument for Team Building

After scoring the items individually, respondents can look at items for which ratings are low and prepare an action plan to increase those ratings. If there are sharp differences in the ratings from different respondents, the group may discuss why members experience the team differently.

The discussion can center around helping individuals to take risks and frankly expressing their opinions and reactions, helping them to accept feedback from others with enough opportunity to explore further, and increasing their sensitivity to or perceptiveness of others' needs and orientations.

Some other uses for the instrument in a training program are described below.

Role Negotiation

Team building can be done by using role negotiation (Harrison, 1976). With this approach the team members share their impressions of the team and then list what they would like the other group members to continue to do, stop or reduce, and start or increase doing in order to make the group more effective. If two teams are involved in a negotiation, more effective collaboration would result. A similar concept, using the Indian cultural context, has been proposed as "role contribution."

Team Roles

Belbin (1981) suggested eight team roles people take: chairman or coordinator, shaper, plant, monitor-evaluation, company worker, resource investigator, team worker, and completer-finisher. Team building can be done by discussing those or other roles on the team and how to improve the scores based on what each member brings to the team.

Behavior Modification

Behavior modification can also be used to help teams become more effective through individual members, after completing some assessments designed to determine individuals' orientation, style, and attitudes. The discussion can then center on what characteristics are missing or in excess on the team. Those whose characteristics do not match the needs of the team can be helped to change. For example, an instrument can be used to help team members examine their bases of power and to plan ways to increase their persuasive power.

Simulations

Artificial teams can be created in which people have an opportunity to experiment and learn from their behavior in a less threatening context. Various structured experiences can be used for this purpose, such as Broken Squares, Hollow Squares, Win As Much As You Can, Maximize Your Gains, and others (see the *Pfeiffer Library* for possibilities). After people participate in such activities, they discuss how similar dynamics operate in their back-home situations and how they can use their learnings from the simulation to make their own teams more effective.

Action Research

In this approach, team building is done through several steps that are generally used in action research or organization development. Dyer (1987) has used this approach in his elaborate discussion of team building through five stages: data strengthening, data analysis, action planning, implementation, and evaluation. Using this approach, diagnosis is done on the basis of questionnaires, interviews, or observations.

Appreciative Inquiry

In this approach, emphasis is given more on the positive aspects, including inspiring future dreams or goals and appreciating positive qualities in each other. Appreciative inquiry (Cooperrider & Whitney, 1999) has become quite popular as a method of increasing collaboration among people and for building strong teams.

Combining various approaches, the following are suggested for using the instrument for team building.

Future scenario: The team may work on a common understanding of the desirable future of the team. Members individually or in small groups prepare a picture of their team as they see it in the next five or seven years. Having a special future scenario will help to inspire individuals to move toward it. Envisioning the future is better than analysis of the past!

Linkage with individual goals: The future of the team should be linked with individual aspirations and goals. Individuals in small groups may discuss how their own aspirations and goals can be achieved through the ideal future of the team being developed by the group.

Force field analysis: The team may identify the forces that are positive and will help the team to move toward the desirable future and those forces that are likely to hinder its progress. Such analysis is helpful to move to the next step.

- Action: Strengthen positive forces The team may go into detail for reinforcing the positive aspects that may help the team to achieve its desirable future. They can take each positive force and work out plans to strengthen it further.

- Action: Reduce negative forces The team can take up all the restraining or inhibiting forces and plan specific action steps to reduce, if not eliminate them.

- Monitoring: After decisions are made to work on strengthening positive forces and reducing negative forces, a plan can be prepared to monitor the team over a period of time. Responsibility for monitoring can be assigned to one or two members of the team.

Whatever approaches are adopted for team building, emphasis should be placed on understanding team effectiveness and taking steps to increase it. A similar process can be used for building inter-team collaboration. Dyer (1987) also discusses ways of dealing with intra-team and inter-team conflicts. Many other resources are available that discuss other issues in team building.

References

Belbin, M. (1981). *Management teams: Why they succeed or fail.* London: Heinemann.

Cooperrider, D., & Whitney, D. (1999). *Appreciative inquiry.* Taos, NM: Corporation for Positive Change.

Dyer, W.G. (1987). *Team building* (2nd ed.). Reading, MA: Addison-Wesley.

Harrison, R. (1976). Role negotiation: A tough-minded approach to team development. In W.W. Burke & H.A. Hornstein, *The social technology of organization development.* San Diego: Pfeiffer & Company.

Likert, R. (1961). *New patterns of management.* New York: McGraw-Hill.

McGregor, D. (1966). *Leadership and motivation.* Cambridge, MA: MIT Press.

The Pfeiffer library. (2008). San Francisco: Pfeiffer.

Udai Pareek, Ph.D., *is chairman of the HR Labs of EMPI, New Delhi, and distinguished visiting professor at the Indian Institute of Health Management Research, Jaipur, India. He is chairman of the Governing Board of the Institute of Developmental Research and Statistics, Jaipur. He is an advisory member for Asia and the Middle East of Human Resource Development International. He is also a member of the Academic Advisory Board of the Global Committee on the Future of Organization Development. He has been chairman of the governing boards of numerous academies and organizations and he was the only Asian to become Fellow of the National Training Laboratories (NTL). He is also the editor of the* Journal of Health Management.

Team Effectiveness Assessment Measure (TEAM)

Udai Pareek

Your Name: ————————————— **Your Team:** —————————————

Instructions: Rate your team/group on the items below according to the following scale. Circle the numbers that apply in each case.

4 = This is highly characteristic of my team, and/or this always happens.

3 = This is fairly characteristic of my team, and/or this frequently happens.

2 = This is slightly characteristic of my team, and/or this sometimes happens.

1 = This is not very true about my team, and/or occasionally happens.

0 = This is not at all true about my team, and/or it almost never happens.

1. The goals of this team are well defined.

     4   3   2   1   0

2. Members of this team generally feel that their concerns and views are ignored by the other members.

     4   3   2   1   0

3. The team has enough freedom to decide its way of working.

     4   3   2   1   0

4. Members generally avoid discussing the problems facing the team.

     4   3   2   1   0

5. The team is given adequate resources to carry out its functions.

     4   3   2   1   0

6. Members do not volunteer to help others or to take responsibility.

     4   3   2   1   0

7. The sense of responsibility and accountability is pretty high among the team members.

     4   3   2   1   0

8. There is confusion among members of the team about its main tasks.

    4   3   2   1   0

9. Members support each other when required.

    4   3   2   1   0

10. The team only carries out the tasks given to it; it cannot decide its own priorities.

    4   3   2   1   0

11. The team generates alternative solutions for a problem.

    4   3   2   1   0

12. The team does not receive adequate support needed to perform its tasks.

    4   3   2   1   0

13. In the group the task is divided among small teams.

    4   3   2   1   0

14. No one cares to assess the true extent of achievement of the goals of the team.

    4   3   2   1   0

15. Each member knows what his or her role in the team is.

    4   3   2   1   0

16. This team does not function as a strong team.

    4   3   2   1   0

17. The members of the team have enough freedom in their own areas.

    4   3   2   1   0

18. There is a lot of hesitation in taking hard decisions in this team.

    4   3   2   1   0

19. The team has enough competent persons needed for its work.

    4   3   2   1   0

20. Members of this team hesitate to ask for others' help when they need it.

    4   3   2   1   0

21. The team uses appropriate ways of assessing its accountability.

    4   3   2   1   0

22. Members of the team are not clear how to work toward the team goals.

    4   3   2   1   0

23. Members back the decisions taken by the group.

    4   3   2   1   0

24. The team does not have autonomy in vital aspects of its working.

    4   3   2   1   0

25. Group members do not hesitate to express their differences with each other.

    4   3   2   1   0

26. There is lack of resources (human and financial) required by the team.

    4   3   2   1   0

27. Members respond positively to the help requested.

    4   3   2   1   0

28. The team does not have an internal mechanism for assessing its progress in achieving its tasks.

    4   3   2   1   0

TEAM Scoring Sheet

Instructions: To create a group profile, first calculate all individual scores for each item, using the following scoring instructions:

1. Reverse Items 2, 4, 6, 8, 10, 12, 14, 16, 18, 20, 22, 24, 26, 28 (0 becomes 4, 1 becomes 3, 3 becomes 1, 4 becomes 0) on the assessment.

2. Add together the ratings of items mentioned below for each of the seven components:

Task clarity	1, 8, 15, 22	
Cohesion	2, 9, 16, 23	
Autonomy	3, 10, 17, 24	
Confrontation	4, 11, 18, 25	
Support	5, 12, 19, 26	
Collaboration	6, 13, 20, 27	
Accountability	7, 14, 21, 28	

3. Next, determine the mean ratings of all the respondents for each item by dividing the total score of that item by the number of respondents.

4. Then calculate the Team Functioning score, Team Empowerment score, and Total Team Effectiveness score, using the following formulas. Each result ranges from 0 to 100.

Components	Items	Team Score
A. Team Functioning	B. Team Empowerment	Team Effectiveness　(A + B)/2

A. Team Functioning

Cohesion [　　　　]
(2 + 9 + 16 + 23) × 6.25

Confrontation [　　　　]
4 + 11 + 17 + 25 × 6.25

Collaboration [　　　　]
6 + 13 + 19 + 27 × 6.25

Total (A)/3 [　　　　]

B. Team Empowerment

Task clarity [　　　　]
(1 + 8 + 15 + 22) × 6.25

Autonomy [　　　　]
(3 + 10 + 17 + 24) × 6.25

Support [　　　　]
(5 + 12 + 19 + 26) × 6.25

Accountability [　　　　]
(7 + 14 + 21 + 28) × 6.25

Total (B)/4 [　　　　]

Team Effectiveness　(A + B)/2 [　　　　]

Corporate Social Responsibility
Determining Your Position
Homer H. Johnson

Summary

The questionnaire presented here is intended as a discussion starter for determining an organization's interest in taking corporate responsibility for social issues.

Prior to the late 1940s or 1950s the term "corporate social responsibility" was rarely or never discussed. However, beginning in the 1950s corporate social responsibility (CSR) became a very hot topic. In fact, there was a serious attempt to require all publicly held companies to submit to (and make public) an annual corporate social audit, much like they are required to submit to and make public an annual financial audit now. The CSR debate became very intense, with numerous advocates on both sides of the issue. As part of that debate, Milton Friedman published "The Social Responsibility of Business Is to Increase Its Profits" in 1970.

However, interest in corporate social audits waned in the 1970s, particularly after the U.S. Congress enacted several pieces of legislation that formed the Environmental Protection Agency, the Consumer Product Safety Commission, the Occupational Safety and Health Commission, and the Equal Employment Opportunity Commission. The enactment of this legislation seemed to cool the debate, at least temporarily. The advocates of CSR could point to the legislation as steps in moving companies to becoming more socially and environmentally responsible. While the business world was not thrilled with the legislation, it was something they could learn to live with, and perhaps even revoke if the membership of Congress became more conservative and more pro-business (Johnson, 2001).

In the last decade, the CSR debate has again come to the forefront. Greenhouse gases; global warming; U.S. companies who own or purchase from foreign sweatshop suppliers; polluted streams; very low wages paid to U.S. workers, plus lack of health benefits; and many other issues have fueled the debate. While no one has (seriously) suggested that an annual social audit be required of all public corporations, many companies are publishing annual reports of their CSR activities (for example, Procter & Gamble and The Gap); some companies have set up a separate organization, which they fund, to address social and environmental issues (Google .org); and several highly respected organizations (Aspen Institute) and business schools (Stanford) have emerged as strong advocates of CSR. Furthermore, there is evidence to suggest that at least some degree of corporate social responsibility beyond mere compliance with the law is good business practice (Heal, 2008; Johnson, 2003).

What Is Corporate Social Responsibility?

Corporate social responsibility has many versions. For some companies, obeying state and federal laws and making annual donations to a local charity is their definition of being good corporate citizens. However, most would agree that mere compliance with laws is *not* CSR; rather, the term refers to voluntary activities that go beyond compliance. For example, many U.S. companies, particularly in the clothing industry, are dependent on suppliers in third-world companies. Should a U.S. company require its suppliers to comply with U.S. regulations? Should the foreign supplier comply with U.S. child labor laws or with U.S. safety and health standards or U.S. environment standards? Or consider a U.S. manufacturing company that emits some form of air or water pollution? Is it enough that this company meets minimum U.S. standards, or should it go beyond the standards and attempt to eliminate all pollutants?

Those leaders or companies that are strong advocates of CSR argue that companies have a moral responsibility to impose higher standards, rather than just complying with U.S. laws or the laws in other countries. This means imposing high standards on foreign suppliers or going beyond federal standards to eliminate pollution.

Those companies that disagree with this position would argue that the responsibility of business is to provide the customer with a good product, to comply with all laws, and to provide jobs and pay taxes. A company that does all of this will contribute to the common good in that jobs and taxes will provide schools, city services, roads, and many more contributions to the nation and community.

CSR covers a wide array of topics and issues, and there are no "right" or "wrong" answers to many of the questions raised in this area. One purpose of the questionnaire presented here is to assist in clarifying one's position on this important topic.

About the Corporate Social Responsibility Questionnaire

Although there has been considerable recent interest in CSR, there was been little effort to develop a questionnaire to assess attitudes toward the topic.

The questionnaire presented here consists of ten statements from the CSR literature and debates. Each briefly describes a general position on CSR, pro or con. Five of the statements are against a more active CSR position, for example, "If a U.S. company has facilities in a foreign country, it should follow whatever labor and environmental policies are permitted in that country and not try to impose U.S. or any outside standards." Five of the statements are pro-CSR, for example, "Companies should pick their suppliers not only on cost and quality, but also on the supplier's commitment to high social and environmental standards."

The respondents indicate their degree of agreement or disagreement with each statement by using a 4-point scale ranging from "strongly agree" to "strongly disagree." The completed questionnaire yields a total score between 10 and 40, with the higher scores indicating a more pro-CSR position. It should be emphasized that the intent of the questionnaire is only to help clarify one's thinking on CSR and that each person's score is only an approximation of the direction and strength of that respondent's thinking.

Using the CSR Questionnaire

The purpose of the questionnaire is to begin a discussion about a business organization's social responsibility. Because of this limited purpose, the questionnaire covers only general CSR topics and does not cover specific issues, such as greenhouse gases or child labor. When using the questionnaire in workshops and business classes, some introductory material is needed to help the respondents begin thinking about CSR, because we find that people are rarely asked about their positions on CSR or have their positions challenged. Thus, they need some time to think about the topic.

One approach is to ask the respondents to define CSR and to give some examples of how one might see CSR in action. Ask: What does it mean to practice CSR? What would we see a company doing if it practiced CSR? Do you know of any companies that are strong advocates of CSR? What do these companies do that distinguishes them as CSR advocates?

Another facilitation approach would be to contrast two extreme CSR positions. For example, discuss Milton Friedman's position cited above and contrast that with Anita Roddick's, (The Body Shop) or Yvon Chouinard's (Patagonia). Several (usually brief) videos can be found on YouTube that advocate differing opinions on CSR. Recent YouTube postings include several videos by Anita Roddick, as well as a recent speech by Fred Smith (FedEx) on the "irresponsibility of corporate social responsibility." Seeing the contrasting viewpoints forces respondents to think about which approach they favor on the subject.

After introducing the topic as suggested above, administer and score the CSR questionnaire. Following the scoring, one useful activity is to have the respondents explain their positions. Particularly educational is to have persons with contrasting viewpoints explain their positions, including why they arrived at those positions. Discuss the pros and cons of each position in the group.

If the purpose of the workshop is to formulate a CSR policy for a company or discuss what might be part of such a policy, the next step might be for a company to begin applying CSR practices. Many employees have difficulty seeing how the general principles apply to their own company. However, if they focus on one or two CSR activities at the beginning, down the line they will begin to see other opportunities. Andrew Savitz has provided a step-by-step process for developing a CSR program in a company in his book *The Triple Bottom Line*, critical reading for those who are beginning the process as well as those who are further along.

References

Friedman, M. (1970, September 12). The social responsibility of business is to increase its profits, *The New York Times Magazine* p. 32.

Heal, G. (2008). *When principles pay: Corporate responsibility and the bottom line.* New York: Columbia University Press.

Johnson, H.H. (2001). Corporate social audits—this time around. *Business Horizons,* 44(3), 29–36.

Johnson, H.H. (2003). Does it pay to be good? Social responsibility and financial performance. *Business Horizons, 46*(6), 34–40.

Savitz, A. (2006). *The triple bottom line.* San Francisco: Jossey-Bass.

Homer H. Johnson, Ph.D., *is a professor in the School of Business Administration at Loyola University in Chicago. He is the author of numerous books and articles and is the case editor of the* Organization Development Practitioner. *His most recent book (with Linda Stroh) is* Basic Essentials of Effective Consulting.

Corporate Social Responsibility Questionnaire

Homer H. Johnson

Instructions: Indicate your degree of agreement or disagreement with each of the statements below by putting a number in front of each, using the following scale:

1 = strongly disagree

2 = somewhat disagree

3 = somewhat agree

4 = strongly agree

____ 1. Because conditions change so quickly and global rules are so relative, it doesn't make much sense for a company to have a tough and rigid ethics policy.

____ 2. If a U.S. company has facilities in a foreign country, it should follow whatever labor and environmental policies are permitted in that country and not try to impose U.S. or any other outside standards.

____ 3. Companies that comply with federal and local laws and make some charitable donations have contributed their fair share to social and environmental responsibility.

____ 4. Companies have no business spending stockholders' money on social causes such as campaigning for a ban on nuclear testing, saving the rainforests, or planned parenthood, no matter how important those issues are.

____ 5. The best way a company can contribute to the social good is to focus on making profits, which in turn will create good jobs, good products, and a healthy economy.

____ 6. The government should impose many more social and environmental requirements on companies and their operations to force them to become more socially and environmentally responsible.

____ 7. Managers have a moral obligation to go beyond local and federal requirements to make their operations environmentally safe and their procedures and policies socially responsible.

_____ 8. Companies should pick their suppliers not only on cost and quality, but also on the supplier's commitment to high social and environmental standards.

_____ 9. Companies have an obligation to the communities in which they are located and should be actively involved in improving the quality of life in the community.

_____10. Companies now are required to submit to an annual financial audit. All companies should also be required to submit to an annual social audit that assesses their commitment to social and environmental betterment.

Corporate Social Responsibility Questionnaire Scoring Sheet

Note that the scoring results are for discussion purposes only, in order to show differences among respondents.

Scoring

1. Add your scores for statements 1 through 5 _____; then subtract this total from 25 _____ (a).

2. Add your scores from statements 6 through 10 _____ (b).

3. Add your (a) and (b) scores _____.

Scores can range from 10 to 40. Higher scores indicate a belief that companies should have a high level of commitment to improving social and environmental conditions.

Scale of Intellectual Capital for Organizations (SICO)

Sacip Toker, James L. Moseley, and Ann T. Chow

Summary

The Scale of Intellectual Capital for Organizations (SICO) provides a diagnostic tool for determining how organizations and their leaders capture internal potential. It is based on an intellectual capital model consisting of human capital, structural capital, relationship capital, and renewable capital. The authors have added cultural capital and global capital to complete the organization's value chain. The tool also identifies the competencies that increase organizational readiness in leveraging the benefits from the six capitals: expanding intelligence, encouraging innovation, ensuring creativity, exercising integrity, envisioning awareness, and embracing differences. SICO consists of a forty-two-statement Likert-scale questionnaire, a scoring sheet, a profile chart, and a diagnostic sheet. Employee work groups or teams will find the instrument useful. Because the instrument has not been subjected to robust validity and reliability checks, it serves only as a diagnostic reflection and discussion tool.

Intellectual capital (IC) can be defined as collective knowledge (whether or not documented) of the individuals in an organization or society. IC can be used to produce wealth, multiply output of physical assets, gain competitive advantage, and/or enhance value of other types of capital. Intellectual capital is an undiscovered treasure in helping organizations maintain high performance. Organizations face a dilemma, however, when measuring their intangible assets or IC. The last two decades show an increase in the gap between real market value and all the intangible assets of an organization (Brinker, 2000). Intellectual capital, when measured and managed effectively, helps organizations maintain their competitive edge.

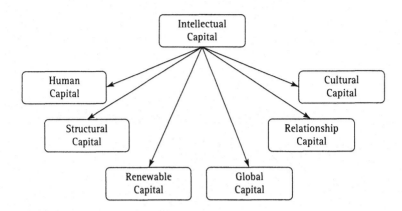

Figure 1. The Subcomponents of Intellectual Capital

In order to understand intellectual capital more closely, the authors developed the Scale of Intellectual Capital for Organizations (SICO). In format and structure it models the Mind Aptitude Scale for Organizations (MASO) by Moseley, Toker, and Chow (2009). SICO aims to measure the intellectual capital subcomponents identified in William Miller's Intellectual Capital model (1999). These include human capital (HC), structural capital (SC), renewable capital (RS), and relationship capital (ReC). In addition to four sub-capitals, the authors add cultural capital (CC) and global capital (GC) because they recognize the importance of organization culture on organizations' value chain processes and the criticality of globalization issues worldwide. SICO has six sub-capitals, as illustrated in Figure 1.

SICO provides a systematic approach in determining how organizations and their leadership use the six sub-capitals to capture internal potential and position themselves for future impact. It is possible that organizations that lack one or more capitals may still be profitable and gain market share, since market share is dependent on many factors. It is the authors' opinion, however, that organizations that possess and exhibit greater explicit intellectual capital add substantial value to their bottom lines. Each of the sub-capitals, adapted from Miller's work, is defined in Table 1.

In Miller's Intellectual Capital Model, the competencies that help organizations leverage the benefits of capitals are identified as well. Human capital is associated with *expanding intelligence*. Structural capital and renewable capital are associated with *encouraging innovation*.(The authors separated renewable capital from this competency and associated it with *ensuring creativity*). Relationship capital is associated with *exercising integrity*. To these the authors add *cultural capital*, associated with *envisioning awareness*, and *global capital*, associated with *embracing differences*. The core competencies associated with IC sub-capitals are illustrated in Table 2.

Table 1. Defining the Sub-Capitals of Intellectual Capital

Human Capital	One's ability to transform knowledge, expertise, and experience into new knowledge that can be shared and communicated with other people.
Structural Capital	Institutionalized knowledge in the form of procedures and policies, process, technologies, and knowledge documents that are databases and records of various forms.
Renewable Capital	Patents, licenses, products, services, and technologies that are produced by an organization in a controlled and planned pattern.
Relationship Capital	Networks providing resources for information and how they influence the most innovative customers in their industries.
Cultural Capital	The collection of unique behaviors that are strongly owned by employees and associated with the value chain and strategic direction of the organization.
Global Capital	The knowledge and ability to think and act quickly, flexibly, and contextually and to transcend local and regional geographic boundaries.

Table 2. Intellectual Capital Core Competencies

Capital	Core Competency
Human Capital (HC)	Expanding Intelligence
Structural Capital (SC)	Encouraging Innovation
Renewable Capital (RC)	Ensuring Creativity
Relationship Capital (ReC)	Exercising Integrity
Cultural Capital (CC)	Envisioning Awareness
Global Capital (GC)	Embracing Differences

Description of the Instrument

The Intellectual Capital Scale for Organizations (SICO) consists of forty-two statements, seven for each sub-capital, a Scoring Sheet, a Profile Chart, and a Diagnostic Sheet. The Likert "extent" scale is used. Table 3 provides a listing of the Likert responses and their corresponding meanings and numeric values. The intended audience for SICO is a work group or a team in an organization. Each employee in a work group or team is asked to complete the inventory by reading each statement carefully, reflecting on the current workplace setting and organizational practices, and choosing one of the five responses which best describes the organization's application, implementation, or belief.

Table 3. The Likert "Extent" Scale

1	**My organization does to a very little extent.** (My organization almost never does this successfully and then only with a great deal of effort.)
2	**My organization does to a little extent.** (My organization does this only poorly and with a great deal of concentration.)
3	**My organization does this to some extent.** (My organization does this at an average level.)
4	**My organization does this to a great extent.** (My organization does this well.)
5	**My organization does this to a very great extent.** (My organization does this at an exemplary level.)

Administration of the Instrument

SICO can be administered at tactical, organizational, or strategic levels of the organization. It can be administered either individually or team-wide. In team-wide usage, the results reflect the collective level of individuals' intellectual capital and associated competencies.

The instrument should be administered and scored using the SICO Scoring Sheet and Diagnostic Sheet. The results obtained from these tools can be used for further goal generation, discussions, personal or group-wise performance evaluation, or branding improvements.

We have aligned the six competencies with each of the six sub-capitals. The one-to-one correlation not only simplifies the diagnostic process but also provides a glimpse of organizational competencies and capitals at the completion of each diagnostic process.

Presentation of Theory

Intellectual capital is "the sum and synergy of a company's knowledge, experience, relationships, processes, discoveries, innovations, market presence, and community influence. It is also the source of inspired innovation and wealth production—the precursor for the growth of financial capital" (Miller, 1999, p. 42). Intellectual capital and sub-capital and their corresponding core competencies position the fabric of organizations to gain a leading edge on competitors.

Best practices or the most successful projects, however, are not always a foundational base for intellectual capital. Intellectual capital is the accumulation of many factors, so an organization must be capable of taking advantage of worst practices and failed initiations as well. Intellectual capital covers both positive and negative intentions. While the positives provide "best" examples, the negatives provide lessons learned. Organizations thus must consider both the best and the worst scenarios.

The importance of intellectual capital is very clear in terms of intangible assets organizations cannot channel into their bottom lines. The discrepancy between current market value and real market value that includes intellectual capital rises drastically every year (Brinker, 2000). It has been found that organizations must gauge and utilize intellectual capital to increase their value.

Miller (1999) challenges corporate managers to initiate and build their IC core competencies in the workplace. He cautions management to have a strategy that starts with dialoguing with employees. He notes, "Without a coordinated strategy, intellectual capital may become a flavor-of-the-month program that leads to a greater Dilbert Effect—the mass cynicism of employees to any management initiative" (p. 45).

The authors expand Miller's three core competencies (expanding intelligence, encouraging innovation, and exercising integrity) to six core competencies (as shown in Table 2). The authors believe that the expanded model of competencies provide detailed and clearer diagnostic results for individuals and work groups in an organization. A more detailed discussion of core competencies associated with intellectual capital is presented in the next section.

Core Competencies of Intellectual Capital

In the 1990s, many corporations decentralized their organizations and operations in responding to tremendous growth. Today, many corporations resort to outsourcing due to cost reduction and global competition. Regardless of the organizational structure, the challenge is quite the same: *How to manage, grow, and maintain the intellectual capital.*

Just as a homeowner makes her monthly mortgage payment to pay her loans and to build up her home's capital, an organization increases its intellectual capital by employing competent workers. A homeowner has the money to pay the mortgage; workers possess IC competencies of an organizational nature. Mortgage payments increase a home's capital; core competencies bolster capital of an organization. Moreover, an organization must manage and expand its organizational intellectual capital to stay competitive in its market space. Prahalad and Hamel (1990) note that an organization must also mobilize its core competencies across its infrastructure when needed. When core competencies are recognized, an organization can spread and distribute those core competencies widely and quickly among business units and product lines.

A Call to Leadership

To sustain the intellectual capital of an organization, leadership must take an inventory of its organizational competencies. In this section, we will briefly explain and provide ideas for identifying and nurturing organizational competencies, which will, in turn, reciprocate by increasing organizational intellectual capital. We believe that the process of identifying and assessing intellectual capital and competencies is indeed a cyclical diagnostic process. Whether or not one starts with the process of identifying intellectual capital or with the assessment process of identifying organizational competencies is unimportant. The point is that the diagnostic process begins.

Thus far, our discussion has been focusing on human competencies. The other organizational competencies are the company's product and production. Human competencies are intangible and in flux, whereas production and products are tangible. Although it is beyond the scope of this discussion, knowing one's product and production competencies is equally important. Once human competencies have been identified, core products and production will follow. Armed with knowledge and data of both competencies, individuals are empowered by (1) identifying core product sets based on market share and competition and (2) assigning and aligning the workforce to various production teams or business units quickly and efficiently. Let us look more closely at the six competencies.

Expanding Intelligence

To maintain the organization's competitive edge, the intelligence among employees must be expanded. As suggested by Miller, this can be done through dialogue, taking an inventory of intelligence. The intelligence can be as mundane as planning, more systematically organizing data, or accessing information more concisely. Dialogue will also uncover tacit knowledge such as undocumented procedures and shortcuts that are stored in the brains of employees.

Encouraging Innovation

The subtle difference between being innovative and being creative is that being *innovative* applies to the process and operation of an organization and being *creative* applies to product creation. Training employees and discussing ways and methods of optimizing processes and various operational procedures is to encourage innovation. Helping employees to add knowledge to existing knowledge, explaining new territories, and identifying new marketplaces encourage employees to be innovative.

Ensuring Creativity

In the same vein, employees must listen hard to customers and encourage thinking "outside the box" when designing and creating new products and services. An organization ought to foster a working environment that ensures creativity. An organization should allow its employees to make mistakes and provide resources, exercise rewards, and praise exceptional performance generously.

Exercising Integrity

An organization must abide to its code of conduct and its moral responsibility to its employees, to its customers, and to society at large. An organization must document and publish its code of conduct, accessible and retrievable by stakeholders, employees, and customers. An organization should foster integrity. Reward systems must be executed fairly.

Envisioning Awareness

One of the biggest challenges in any organization is communication, which bolster awareness. An organization should capitalize on its technology network to widely disseminate information and data. Rumors and hearsay are inevitable; however, clear and honest communiqués can defuse misunderstanding and bad feelings.

Embracing Differences

Like it or not, our world economy is deeply interconnected. We interact with people from all over the world, even if we stay in our own homes. For example, computer technical support most likely is generated by some computer troubleshooters in India or in The Philippines. The bottom line is that the computer problem is solved regardless of the language, culture, individual bias, race, time zone, or geographic barriers. Transcending these barriers means embracing all differences and focusing on the results.

Our collective ability to embrace differences elevates not only our global presence but our competitiveness in the world economy.

Suggested Uses for the Instrument

There are myriad uses for SICO:

- It can be used as a diagnostic instrument to identify a possible cause of a potential problem.

- It can be a tool to help organizations make decisions for strategic planning and forecasting.

- When used in conjunction with other available data, it can guide allocation of a variety of resources.

- If it were more rigorously validated and rendered reliable, it could be used as a research instrument for further study and investigation.

- Finally, it is both a reflection and discussion piece for individuals and team members to measure organizational value.

Validity and Reliability

Items in the SICO were developed on the basis of Miller's intellectual capital conceptualization. Each sub-capital was scrutinized by the authors, and individual items were generated. The items accepted by all three authors were placed in the scale. The items not initially agreed on were revisited and revised. This process leveraged the authors' expertise, experiences, and their intuitive sense.

The instrument can be accepted as content valid. However, there are no available empirical data nor data to support reliability.

References

Brinker, B. (2000). *Intellectual capital: Tomorrow's asset, today's challenge.* Retrieved on August 3, 2008, from www.cpavision.org/vision/wpaper05b.cfm

Hafeez, K., & Essmail, E.A. (2007). Evaluating organization core competences and associated personal competencies using analytical hierarchy process. *Management Research News, 30*(8), 530–547.

Miller, W. (1999). Building the ultimate resource. *Management Review, 88*(1), 42–45.

Moseley, J.L., Toker, S., & Chow, A.T. (2009). Mind aptitude scale for organizations (MASO). In E. Biech (Ed.), *The 2009 annual: Volume 2, consulting* (pp. 137–151). San Francisco: Pfeiffer.

Prahalad, C.K., & Hamel, G. (1990, May/June). The core competence of the corporation. *Harvard Business Review,* pp. 275–291.

Rosen, R., Digh, P., Singer, M., & Phillips, C. (2000). *Global literacies: Lessons on business leadership and national cultures.* New York: Simon & Schuster.

Sirkin, H.L., Hemerling, J.W., & Bhattacharya, A.K. (2008). *Globality: Competing with everyone from everywhere for everything.* New York: Business Plus.

Sacip Toker, BSc, MSc, *is an instructional technology doctoral candidate and graduate research assistant in the College of Education at Wayne State University, Detroit, Michigan. In his native Turkey, he was involved in several online training programs and provided instructional technology support to the faculties at Middle East Technical University. He also taught information technology and instructional planning courses at Suleyman Demirel University. He is a member of AECT.*

James L. Moseley, Ed.D., LPC, CHES, CPT, *is an associate professor of instructional technology in the College of Education at Wayne State University, Detroit, Michigan. He teaches performance technology, performance consulting, strategic planning, and program evaluation courses and directs dissertations and projects. He consults with all levels of management. Moseley is the recipient of teaching awards and service awards, the co-author of six books, numerous articles, and book chapters. He is a member of both ISPI and ASTD.*

Ann T. Chow, BA, MS, *is a full-time doctoral student in instructional technology in the College of Education at Wayne State University, Detroit, Michigan. Chow received her formal education in Taiwan, Vietnam, Italy, and America. Her business and managerial experiences are as diverse as her academic credentials. She has worked as manager and consultant in companies in Asia and corporations in the United States. Currently, she is the associate director of The Metro Bureau Inc., an organization for superintendents and K-12 school districts that supports school systems in Southeastern Michigan.*

Intellectual Capital Scale for Organizations (SICO)

Sacip Toker, James L. Mosley, and Ann T. Chow

Instructions: Read each numbered statement in the instrument and circle the number that best describes your response. Your immediate response is usually the most accurate.

My organization does this:

> 1 = To a very little extent
>
> 2 = To a little extent
>
> 3 = To some extent
>
> 4 = To a great extent
>
> 5 = To a very great extent

1. The culture of the organization is an important determinant of strategic values.

   1   2   3   4   5

2. "Globality," "manyness," and "multinational" are key terms that transform the business of today into the corporate success of tomorrow.

   1   2   3   4   5

3. All relationships in the fabric of the organization are based on strategic policies and goals.

   1   2   3   4   5

4. Cooperatively and collaboratively generated new knowledge are highly prized within the organization.

   1   2   3   4   5

5. As trends change and as the organization's marketing position adjusts, policies are periodically reviewed, reflected upon, and revised accordingly.

   1   2   3   4   5

6. Employees are encouraged to network both inside and outside the organization.

   1   2   3   4   5

7. Employees in the organization can transform their expertise and experience into new knowledge.

      1   2   3   4   5

8. Employees in the organization see the world's business challenges as distinct opportunities and think with an international mindset.

      1   2   3   4   5

9. In the organization, past and present heroes are main creators of cultural traditions, values, and mores.

      1   2   3   4   5

10. The organization frequently applies for patents and licenses.

      1   2   3   4   5

11. Information captured from innovative customers creates value that increases exponentially when shared across entire buying communities.

      1   2   3   4   5

12. Information, planning, process, and technical knowledge are associated with strategic value-creation processes.

      1   2   3   4   5

13. The organization capitalizes on value exhibited by its employees' work output and role modeling.

      1   2   3   4   5

14. An organization that shifts its perspective in light of new global realities positions itself for branding and market share.

      1   2   3   4   5

15. Innovation and research are highly prized in the organization.

      1   2   3   4   5

16. The culture of the organization is independent of fears and hidden agendas.

      1   2   3   4   5

17. The infrastructure of the organization processes data to obtain critical information.

      1   2   3   4   5

18. An organization that thinks globally and has sensitivity to market needs and demands enjoys a unique competitive advantage.

    1   2   3   4   5

19. The more the organization brings customers and partners into its value chain, the more energy the organization must put into the relationship.

    1   2   3   4   5

20. The new knowledge generated in the organization transfers and disseminates to all stakeholders and sponsors.

    1   2   3   4   5

21. Global talent planning is necessary for strategic growth in a global business environment.

    1   2   3   4   5

22. Employees within the organization feel a sense of belonging in contributing to the culture.

    1   2   3   4   5

23. The organization competes with itself in trying to surpass its previous goals and services.

    1   2   3   4   5

24. The organization encourages the personal and professional development of its employees.

    1   2   3   4   5

25. The business in the organization flows in every direction, creating a mindset that embraces profit, competition, sustainability, and collaboration.

    1   2   3   4   5

26. The organization enjoys a rich tradition of stories that are passed down from generation to generation.

    1   2   3   4   5

27. The organization focuses on lessons learned when mistakes occur.

    1   2   3   4   5

28. The organization gathers and stores data and knowledge that are beneficial for innovation and change.

    1   2   3   4   5

29. The organization identifies and sticks to those activities that add the most value for its customers and bring the greatest return on investment.

    1   2   3   4   5

30. The organization is experiencing a new economic order by competing with everyone from everywhere for everything.

    1   2   3   4   5

31. The organization listens to its employees to capitalize on their personal expertise and experience.

    1   2   3   4   5

32. The organization optimizes its value proposition around customers' purchases and uses their preferences and behaviors.

    1   2   3   4   5

33. The organization prides itself in fostering exemplary human values (honesty, commitment, integrity, etc).

    1   2   3   4   5

34. The organization's policies, procedures, and practices are well-documented and easily accessible for dissemination, consultation, and review.

    1   2   3   4   5

35. The organization's products and services are innovative in the marketplace.

    1   2   3   4   5

36. The rituals and practices in the organization are frequently celebrated.

    1   2   3   4   5

37. The structure of the relationship network in the organization is conducive to effective and efficient communication.

    1   2   3   4   5

38. The value proposition within our organization is shifting from products to the services that make a product more useful.

    1   2   3   4   5

39. The wealth embedded in client relationships are rich assets in the organization.

    1   2   3   4   5

40. The organizational culture embodied in the organization is composed of a variety of subcultures complementing each other.

    1   2   3   4   5

41. The organization encourages its employees to think outside the box and to take educated risks.

    1   2   3   4   5

42. Work processes are consistent with industry best practices.

    1   2   3   4   5

SICO Scoring Sheet

Instructions: In each of the Intellectual Capital charts below, find the question numbers from the survey and place the number score you assigned for that item in the box beneath the item number. Once you have done this for all six capitals, sum the values you gave to come up with a score for each IC. See the sample chart as an illustration.

Sample Chart

Item Number	3	13	16	18	22	30	35
Value Given	3	2	2	3	3	3	2
						Total Score	18

Cultural Capital

Item Number	1	9	16	22	26	36	40
Value Given							
						Total Score	

Global Capital

Item Number	2	8	14	18	21	25	30
Value Given							
						Total Score	

Human Capital

Item Number	4	7	13	20	24	27	31
Value Given							
						Total Score	

Relationship Capital

Item Number	3	6	11	19	33	37	39
Value Given							
						Total Score	

Renewable Capital

Item Number	10	15	17	23	28	35	41
Value Given							
						Total Score	

Structural Capital

Item Number	5	12	29	32	34	38	42
Value Given							
						Total Score	

SICO Profile Sheet

Instructions: To obtain a group profile for all the group for each of the six sub-capitals, the process is as follows.

Step 1: Add the scores all of the respondents for each sub-capital, divide the total by the number of respondents (rounding applies), then circle the quotient of each sub-capital on the SICO Profile Chart. For example, in a work group of ten, add the scores for Human Capital for each of the ten respondents, divide by 10 (rounding applies), and circle the result on the SICO Profile Chart. Complete the chart for all six sub-capitals.

Step 2: Next, calculate the placement number for your organization by adding all the circled numbers on the chart; then dividing by 6 (rounding applies). When you obtain the placement number, then use the SICO Diagnostic Sheet to check the meaning of your organization's score.

SICO Profile Chart

	My organization does this:				
	To a very great extent	**To a great extent**	**To some extent**	**To a little extent**	**To a very little extent**
Cultural Capital	35 34 33 32 31 30 29	28 27 26 25 24 23 22	21 20 19 18 17 16 15	14 13 12 11 10 9 8	7 6 5 4 3 2 1
Global Capital	35 34 33 32 31 30 29	28 27 26 25 24 23 22	21 20 19 18 17 16 15	14 13 12 11 10 9 8	7 6 5 4 3 2 1
Human Capital	35 34 33 32 31 30 29	28 27 26 25 24 23 22	21 20 19 18 17 16 15	14 13 12 11 10 9 8	7 6 5 4 3 2 1
Relationship Capital	35 34 33 32 31 30 29	28 27 26 25 24 23 22	21 20 19 18 17 16 15	14 13 12 11 10 9 8	7 6 5 4 3 2 1
Renewable Capital	35 34 33 32 31 30 29	28 27 26 25 24 23 22	21 20 19 18 17 16 15	14 13 12 11 10 9 8	7 6 5 4 3 2 1
Structural Capital	35 34 33 32 31 30 29	28 27 26 25 24 23 22	21 20 19 18 17 16 15	14 13 12 11 10 9 8	7 6 5 4 3 2 1
				SICO Placement	

SICO Diagnostic Sheet

30 to 35   Scores in this range mean that your organization has an excellent knowledge base system (competency and knowledge support system). The organization recognizes and inventories both formal and tacit knowledge of employees. Hence, the organization can respond to market shifts quickly because intellectual capital is managed and utilized effectively. The organization perhaps has a superior position in the industry. The organization is likely producing excellent products and services as a result of enthusiastic employees and management teams. The organization should continue to form project/program teams with workers who complement each other with their strong competencies. The organization should be actively investing in growing its employee competencies, so that it continues to expand and retain its intellectual capital.

24 to 29   Scores in this range mean that the organization is in tune with employee competencies and intellectual capital. The organization recognizes and inventories most of its employees' formal and tacit knowledge. The organization might have a strong presence in its industry. The organization probably is producing high-quality products and services as a result of fine employees and management teams. The organization should continue its good job in expanding and building employee competencies. The organization needs to perfect its knowledge base system (competency and knowledge support system). The organization should aim at 100 percent recognition and inventory of its workforce.

17 to 23   Scores in this range mean that the organization might be complacent. Perhaps due to lack of leadership in recognizing and inventorying employee competencies, many work groups are not aware of where to locate internal competencies and resources when needed. This results in a waste of organizational resources and a higher cost structure. Managers and employees might be saying and using the right words, yet acting indifferently. The organization might be profitable. However, to sustain and grow the business in today's global economy, the organization must implement or reconfigure its competencies and knowledge base system. Strengthening and expanding intellectual capital could offer the competitive edge the organization needs to excel in the marketplace.

12 to 16   Scores in this range mean that the organization should think critically of the future. The organization might not have the brain power, resources, and know-how to recognize and inventory employee competencies. The organization and the employees might be just "going through the motions." The organization might be doing well; however, the real question is whether or not its market position is diminishing quickly. Most importantly, would the organization be able to retain knowledgeable and competent workers for the long run. Also, the organization's products and services might not be viewed as competitively as they should be.

7 to 11   Red alert! Scores in this range mean that the organization might be losing knowledgeable and competent workers to its competitors. Perhaps it is replacing those workers with less-competent or inexperienced workers. Worker skills and competencies are not aligned with work and service productions. Therefore, the organization's products and services might be less desirable to consumers and customers. The organization might have difficulty responding to market demands and may be pressured by lower prices and suffer lower margins in return.

Introduction
to the Articles and Discussion
Resources Section

The Articles and Discussion Resources Section is a collection of materials useful to every facilitator. The theories, background information, models, and methods will challenge facilitators' thinking, enrich their professional development, and assist their internal and external clients with productive change. These articles may be used as a basis for lecturettes, as handouts in training sessions, or as background reading material. This section will provide you with a variety of useful ideas, theoretical opinions, teachable models, practical strategies, and proven intervention methods. The articles will add richness and depth to your training and consulting knowledge and skills. They will challenge you to think differently, explore new concepts, and experiment with new interventions. The articles will continue to add a fresh perspective to your work.

The 2010 Pfeiffer Annual: Consulting includes fourteen articles, in the following categories:

Communication: Communication Styles, Modes, and Patterns

> **Don't Let Your Clients Be Defined by Instrument Results, by Mona Lee Pearl with Phil Van Horn and Jody L. Shields

Communication: Feedback

> **Evaluating the Manager-Subordinate Dyad, by Mohandas Nair

> **360-Degree Tool Kit: Everything You Ever Wanted to Know About 360-Degree Feedback, But Were Afraid to Ask, by Jan M. Schmuckler, Ann M. Gormley, and Bruce Alan Kimbrew

---

**Communication Topic

Communication: Technology

> **Building Support and Engagement for Technology Initiatives, by Kris Taylor

Problem Solving: Change and Change Agents

> Consulting Opportunities in the Nonprofit Sector, by Phil Van Horn

Groups and Teams: Group Development

> **Forming TIGERS®-Hearted Teams, by Dianne Crampton

Consulting/Training: Strategies and Techniques

> Effective Executive Coaching: An Illustrative Case Study, by Leonard D. Goodstein

Consulting/Training: Interface with Clients

> Assessments and Coaching: An Incongruent Pair, by Teri-E Belf and Rafael Rivera

> Communicating with Professional Savvy, by Karen A. Travis

Facilitating: Theories and Models

> Successful Organization Development and Growing Pains, by Eric G. Flamholtz and Yvonne Randle

Facilitating: Techniques and Strategies

> Team Building Without Time Wasting, by Marshall Goldsmith and Howard Morgan

Leadership: Theories and Models

> Effective Leader-Employee Relationships in the 21st Century, by Edwin L. Mouriño-Ruiz

Leadership: Strategies and Techniques

> How Can You Develop Leaders? Let Me Count The Ways! by Lois B. Hart

Leadership: Top-Management Issues and Concerns

> Leveraging Business Data to Develop Strategic Learning Solutions, by Ajay M. Pangarkar and Teresa Kirkwood

---

**Communication Topic

As with previous *Annuals*, this volume covers a wide variety of topics. The range of articles presented encourages thought-provoking discussion about the present and future of HRD. We have done our best to categorize the articles for easy reference; however, many of the articles encompass a range of topics, disciplines, and applications. If you do not find what you are looking for under one category, check a related category. In some cases we may place an article in the "Training" *Annual* that also has implications for "Consulting" and vice versa. As the field of HRD continues to grow and develop, there is more and more crossover between training and consulting. Explore all the contents of both volumes of the *Annual* in order to realize the full potential for learning and development that each offers.

Don't Let Your Clients Be Defined by Instrument Results

Mona Lee Pearl, with Phil Van Horn and Jody L. Shields

Summary

As consultants engage in helping organizations attain ever-greater success, we benefit from the use of psychological profile assessment instruments. When used correctly by certified professionals, instruments such as the Myers-Briggs Type Indicator (MBTI), Keirsey Temperament Sorter, and even the relatively simple DiSC Profile (which doesn't require certification for delivery or scoring) provide insight for individuals and the organizations that employ them with regard to organizational fit, aptitudes, and preferences for such things as work environment and learning style. This helps employers and employees optimize all their resources.

However, when results are taken too literally, the individual and the organization can inappropriately use results to detrimentally "pigeonhole" the individual and thereby inadvertently curtail the potential for growth and change in the organization as well as the individual.

To guard against this unintended consequence, consultants must fully understand the intent and purpose of profiling instruments and learn to use language with the client that ensures the client also understands both the benefits and potential pitfalls.

The History of the Individual in the American Workplace

The contemporary employer knows that the best way to maximize human resources is to make reasonable efforts to accommodate the individual. Those good employers take into account, to the greatest extent possible, employees' personal preferences—how they like to learn new information, whether they enjoy working

The 2010 Pfeiffer Annual: Consulting.
Copyright © 2010 by John Wiley & Sons, Inc. Reprinted by permission of Pfeiffer, an Imprint of Wiley. www.pfeiffer.com

in teams or on their own, and even what kind of lighting and other ergonomic factors work best for each person. This attention to individual preferences is a relatively new development.

Looking back to the Industrial Revolution in America—which roughly coincided with the end of the War of 1812—we see workers treated as a means (labor) to an end (a product to sell). These hungry masses looking for work were certainly in no position to demand better wages or better working conditions; and because the employers learned how to run a business by looking back just a few years to feudal systems run by monarchs and aristocrats, they had no notion that humane treatment might yield more profitable results.

By the late 19th Century, educated social reformers and workers began to realize that their work had value beyond the meager monetary compensation they received. From the factories and mines across the country, people spoke up and acted to attain better pay and working conditions. While they were successful to a degree, they certainly did not begin to receive individualized attention to the specific needs of any one worker.

During and after World War II, the workplace took another dramatic turn as women began to work outside the home, technology began to develop, and higher education became affordable to the middle classes. At the same time, "the workplace" expanded. With increased household incomes, demand for goods and services grew, escalating the creation of new and different types of businesses. More workers, better-educated workers, workers with a greater sense of personal independence—all of this resulted in a workforce that was not content to be told what to do and how to do it without an opportunity to contribute to the processes that took up at least forty hours of their lives each week. Look back at management writing from 1900 to 1975 and one will find a change in how employers were encouraged to use human resources to maximize outcomes—from "tell them what to do and make sure they aren't allowed to vary" to "listen to your employees and they'll help you find better ways to do business." Look again from 1975 to 1995 to find new management theories on how to incorporate women into leadership and management positions. And look one more time from 1995 to today to see business writers proposing ever-more-elaborate plans for how to organize business around this diverse, educated, sophisticated, and creative workforce that has grown up in America.

As employers in the mid- to late-20th Century increasingly understood that retaining employees meant listening to their needs and ideas, industrial psychology (a new branch of a field of study that began gaining ground during World War II) earned a reputation as a positive means to understanding the motivations and needs of workers. The "personnel office" became used for more than hiring, firing, and payroll. Psychologists were added to the staff of large corporations and their theories became popularized through modern writings, available to even the smallest "mom and pop" shop owners. "Personality tests," such as the General Aptitude Test Battery (GATB—first used with military recruits toward the end of World War II), were designed and adapted specifically to determine whether an applicant was a good fit for an organization and how employees could most effectively be motivated and taught to give their best.

Personality Assessments in Today's Workplace

As an example of how employers adopted psychology into the workplace by the late 20th Century, many people in the workforce had a Myers-Briggs Type Indicator (MBTI) sign on their desks. Those seemingly innocuous cardboard tents were, and in some workplaces still are, as prominent as the workers' nameplates. Going through the MBTI exercise is fun and, *when well debriefed*, provides great insight about why individuals behave as they do. When the instrument is administered throughout an organization, those "type cards" become part of the shared language of the corporate culture and provide a common language among employees as well as between employees and their supervisors.

While the upsides to personality inventories are many, it is unfortunate that too often people are allowed to don their profiles as they would put on body armor. They make such declarations as, "I am an 'I' [an introvert in MBTI parlance], so don't try to get me to think out loud. I have to do my processing inside my head— and it could take weeks. I'll get back to you." Such behavior can have the opposite of the desired effect of providing individual insight to aid in personal development, which in turn provides the organization with a more mature, well-rounded, and productive staff member.

Personality Assessments Can Make a Positive Difference

A consultant—whether internal to the organization or as a third-party contractor— recommending and using personality assessments as a means to improve organizational effectiveness and agility can be one of the best ways to achieve positive results. Whether an organization is facing challenges to its overall growth, overhauling and aligning processes, or developing employees into the critical thinkers and problems solvers that are often desired and required in today's workplace, incorporating tools that assist individuals in identifying strengths and potential areas for growth provides a number of benefits.

Individuals gain *personal insight*. Regardless of the level of formal education an employee has attained, it is possible that no part of the course of study encouraged and assisted in learning about one's personal style and preferences. Completing an assessment and reviewing the analyzed results with a professional can provide genuine "aha!" moments that may catapult an individual to the next level of development.

The *employer gains tools for guiding development and finding best fit*. If an employee and an employer both better understand the employee's aptitudes; preferences for processing information, learning information, and making decisions; as well as the employee's strengths and/or areas of growth, through use of *appropriate* tools (not all tools measure each or any of these elements), they are better prepared to work together to build a strong development path for the employee. By understanding the data provided by proper assessments, the supervisor (in conjunction with the employer's organization development or human resources personnel) can work with the employee. Employee development might include ways to increase job value, possible job changes that better fit the employee, or general personal growth. The key to these conversations and the employee's development is choosing the *correct* assessment and having it administered by credentialed professionals.

In addition to aiding the individual, using an instrument for an entire team can greatly *aid team building by creating a common language*. If team members share the experience of participating in an assessment and being debriefed on what the results may mean, they have shared a meaningful experience and they exit the experience with "insider information" about one another. They also gain a non-threatening means of discussing differences among team members. For example, suppose an individual has a strong preference for "introvert" behaviors as measured by the MBTI and that this individual needs to persuade an employee with a strong preference for "extrovert" behaviors at the next desk to speak more softly. The "I" might say to the "E," "Listen, I know that as an 'E' you think out loud; however, my 'I' would appreciate it if your 'E' turned down the volume just a hair." This type of conversation is easier on both of them because it is not confrontational, but rather informational. And the information has been delivered in terms they both understand and respect. It is important to note again that MBTI is only one example. There are numerous alternatives, each of which assesses and measures a variety of components in different ways.

Avoiding Misuse of Personality Assessments

In an age when workers want to grow up quickly and take over the world, allowing them to inappropriately "typecast" themselves and their co-workers based on the results provided by any instrument may be detrimental to their personal and professional growth and to the organization's success. Avoiding this pitfall is simple, but requires vigilance.

Personality assessments, or type indicators, are not parlor games. They must never be used simply to amuse and entertain. While a goal of administering the instrument may be team building among staff members, it must never be a goal that is met solely by shared laughter. Once we start to laugh at the results, it is difficult at best to return to serious consideration of what the results can do to inform our choices and behaviors.

Discuss and define in writing what the client hopes to achieve through the assessment. It is your job as the consultant to ensure that the client understands the importance of the assessment process and the analysis of the results. Once the instrument is administered and the results are delivered to each employee, the employer cannot "unring the bell." Employees will react to the results, for good or ill, and hence the workplace will change.

If you are not certified to administer and analyze an instrument, either gain certification or find a certified administrator to provide the service. Even if an instrument is touted as not requiring certification, the administrator must be fully schooled in how the instrument was developed, what it is intended to measure, how it is intended to be delivered, and how to talk with the participants about the results.

Before choosing to become certified in one or more instruments, thoroughly research their credibility. Determine how long the instrument has been in use and what is said about it by its champions and its detractors. Once convinced it is a viable possibility, research the statistical validity of the results over time.

Once certified, you must never mislead a client about your experience in administering and assessing the results of the instrument. Whether delivering and scoring the assessment for the first time or the four-hundredth time, your experience has a bearing on the ability to thoroughly and objectively score and deliver the results. (After four hundred deliveries, a consultant may, in fact, be less effective than when he or she began because he or she will have begun to anticipate results.)

Understand and accurately describe to the client and anyone who is participating the limitations of what can be learned from the results. This may be the most important element of preventing people from putting on the results like armor. Once people understand that any psychological assessment has limitations, they are less likely to lean so heavily on the results that they stop dead in the growth process.

In addition, making sure that the client and the participants in the assessment understand its limitations can help circumvent typecasting or pigeonholing of *others* on the team. While the shared experience and common language resulting from taking and learning about the instrument can result in improved teamwork, there is also the risk that individuals will take others' results so seriously that they quit trying to "play nice" with certain team members. Learning that a teammate who is not a favorite on the team is also a very different type from the rest of the group can be taken as license to fully ostracize the "errant" member unless you emphasize that people can adapt to circumstances and surroundings. (Note that the theory on which the MBTI assessment is based posits that a person's "true type" does not change, but rather develops over time.)

Make sure the client agrees that, as the leader of the assessment process, you will be encouraging employees to use the results as part of a growth plan and not as a way to define themselves once and for all. As part of the overall contract with the employer, you will develop a variety of means to help this employee cadre grow into what the organization needs it to be. The instrument will be just one way of assisting in development of personal insight as a means to growth. The astute consultant will always talk about the results in that light—as insight aimed toward positive growth where needed.

Conclusion

To compete in today's global economy, employers must attend to the individual needs, strengths, and weaknesses of each employee. Psychological instruments administered by certified professionals are a relatively inexpensive and informative means to learn about employees. When a consultant uses an instrument correctly and debriefs it fully—using language that reminds those participating not to become stagnant based on the results—the assessment process results in employees with greater personal insight and employers who can maximize the aptitudes and strengths of the workforce.

Mona Lee Pearl *is executive vice president and chief operating officer, Western States Learning Corporation, and principal consultant, Align Organizational Development and Training (a division of Western States Learning Corporation). In addition to corporate executive duties, Ms. Pearl works as an organizational assessor, strategic planner, group facilitator, and trainer with employers, employee groups, and community nonprofit organizations. Ms. Pearl has developed and presented seminars on topics including gender communication, decision making, change management, and leadership. She earned a bachelor's degree with distinction in communication studies at the University of Missouri at Kansas City and a master's degree in management from Lesley University.*

Phil Van Horn *is president and CEO of Western States Learning Corporation, a non-profit corporation that provides life-long learning opportunities through a variety of consulting and training services. Throughout his professional career of more than thirty years, Mr. Van Horn has developed and delivered adult leadership and team-building courses for numerous organizations. He has served on numerous local, state, and national boards of directors. Mr. Van Horn received his M.Ed. from the University of Missouri-Columbia.*

Jody L. Shields *is a consultant with Align. She has more than sixteen years of experience in leadership, organizational planning, and marketing in the nonprofit and healthcare fields. Ms. Shields holds a bachelor of science degree from Arizona State University and is a Qualified Administrator for the Myers-Briggs Type Indicator. She is currently serving as a commissioner for a statewide nonprofit board and is the co-chair for the local United Way Women's Leadership Council.*

Evaluating the Manager-Subordinate Dyad

Mohandas Nair

Summary

Getting the best out of human resources is the most challenging task for a manager. Because each individual is unique, the manager can achieve better success if he or she manages each person uniquely. This article discusses a form of evaluation—appraising the manager-subordinate dyad—that can offer useful information and lead to more effective operations.

Managing the performance of human resources is the ultimate focus of any manager. Of the resources at the manager's command, the human resources are the most difficult to manage. No two people put in the same role will perform the same. Hence, a manager must manage each person differently.

To do so, the manager has to uniquely understand the person, the role the person plays, the difficulty of the assignment, the resources used, and the competencies brought to the work, both in terms of functional and people skills. The manager has to be there to observe, coach, and help the person in the performance of his or her assignment. The manager must provide an open environment and a climate of mutual trust and respect so that the subordinate feels free to communicate any problems.

Managers Need to Empower

Although today's organizations do tend to encourage their employees to take more initiative, there are still many organizations in which "supervisors" and not "coaches" are in control. In today's fast-changing world, however, a manager cannot possibly have all the information required to be in control. Also, because flattened organizational structures lead to a larger span of control, managers have no option but to empower subordinates. Direct supervision is not always possible; to be, effective, managers must be mentors or coaches.

This new role forces managers to change their mindsets and look at subordinates as valuable resources waiting to be tapped so that the organization achieves a better result than if the manager alone took charge. Empowering employees is also likely to increase employee commitment and retention and to create an environment of openness and mutuality.

Enlightened managers are aware that it is not their responsibility to actually do a job, but rather to ensure that the job is done. They also know that their subordinates want to be respected for their knowledge and experience and would like to be empowered to put in the best effort. After all, subordinates know their processes better than anyone else does.

The Manager–Subordinate Dyad

The manager-subordinate dyad is the fundamental pillar in an organizational structure. The performance of this dyad has a direct effect on the performance of the organization. Each dyad is unique. A manager with four subordinates will be involved in four dyads, each having unique processes dictated by each member's expectations and unique characteristics (personality, ability, attitude, and so forth).

In any organization, roles come with expectations. An individual plays a role or roles expected by the manager. That manager, in turn, plays roles expected by his or her manager. As situations change, the organization adapts by modifying the roles to meet the challenges of new situations. Understanding new expectations quickly and dealing with them effectively helps them deliver results.

The performance of a dyad is a function of the effectiveness of both players. Because of the different competences of the individuals in the dyad, the dyad's performance will vary. Thus, performance evaluations should be undertaken by the organization to focus on the performance of each dyad in the system and how the dyad could be improved over time.

To enable this to happen, the process should be mutual. As the manager is evaluating the subordinate on how he or she is performing in the role given to him or her, the subordinate is evaluating the manager as to whether the support and guidance provided are sufficient for the subordinate to perform his or her role to the manager's expectations. As the manager recommends a development plan for the subordinate, the subordinate could point out where the support expected from the manager was lacking and the consequences. The manager's management of the subordinate's work processes could also be commented on.

Real-Time Performance Evaluation

Fundamental for this system to be effective is a continuous real-time evaluation of the performance process. An ideal would be for the manager and subordinate, after every meeting of any kind, to set aside a moment to evaluate what has gone right or wrong between their last meeting and this one. They can adjust their action plans going forward, given that the information needed is fresh in their minds. They could discuss the need for a change in the process, a course correction, a need for the subordinate to take up a learning program or skill development, and so on.

The dyad could also focus on the plans set for the current period and work toward achieving milestones, taking into account any changes since their last meeting. The manager could share how the processes fit into his or her larger plans with other subordinates. Occasionally, the manager could have a joint discussion with all of his or her subordinates to cover issues involving all of them simultaneously, such as role overlap, authority, responsibility, and so forth.

The manager's feedback both to individuals and to the group should be frank to ensure that clear expectations are set. The subordinates could also provide feedback on shortcomings of the support received, clarity of role expectations, and their feelings on rewards and punishments.

An aid in this process could be a notebook maintained by the subordinate and manager to jot down thoughts and information culled from the meeting. The date of the meeting always should precede any notes about it. The manager could have a book for each subordinate or reserve pages for each subordinate in one notebook, which would be an essential guide to recollect discussions and follow up on action plans.

Although the process could seem time-consuming, the possible payback is too big to ignore. The subordinate is working on the manager's assignments. If the manager can get the best out of the subordinate, that will reflect well on the manager. Besides, this is really just a part of the normal process of management, which managers are doing on a day-to-day basis. The one added factor is the creation of an open, trusting environment. Is this too much to ask?

In organizations in which the processes are still dated and openness still a way off, dyad evaluation could be initiated with the assistance of facilitators. Managers should be made to realize that the process can lead to their own success—they can improve their effectiveness only when subordinates improve theirs.

The Periodic Appraisal

It is also necessary to have "formal" appraisals periodically to provide data for the other HR processes such as rewards or promotions. Formal appraisals provide a way to knit together the various dyad processes and give the organization a consolidated picture. Through a formal appraisal process, common training needs could be determined and valuable resources could be allotted across the organization. With a dyad real-time evaluation system in place, this process could be fairly routine and stress-free. It could be just one of the many meetings between manager and subordinate, but one in which some paperwork would be mandatory.

Written paperwork would provide higher management with information to reach decisions. If the process is administered uniformly and fairly, more credibility will attach to the decisions taken about rewards, promotions, transfers, and so forth.

The forms normally used in the self-appraisal processes could be modified to incorporate the additional features needed for the dyad appraisal. The focus of the form would be on the subordinate, but with space to capture data on the manager's behavior too. Forms could be filled in by the subordinate or jointly in the dyad, depending on the information to be captured.

The additional information could include:

- When planning for the period ahead, what will be the support provided by the manager? The subordinate could first describe his or her needs and a final decision could be captured.

- When setting goals and targets for the subordinate's future, the manager could share his or her own targets vis-à-vis the subordinate. The manager should also mention the frequency of meetings, areas in which support will be provided, training provided by the manager, and so forth.

- When writing about performance observed, the subordinate could mention his or her perceptions of the support provided by the manager and discussed with the manager.

- If appropriate, the subordinate could grade the manager on some scale. If openness is high in the dyad, the manager could obtain an idea of how he or she is perceived, ask for clarification, and use the information to constructively change behavior.

- There could also be a provision for the subordinate to note certain desired behavior from the manager.

- The form could be sent to the manager's manager for review and he or she could have a brief meeting with the manager or with the dyad, as desired.

Comparison with 360-Degree Appraisals

It would be interesting to compare the process with a 360-degree appraisal, whereby feedback is collected from other levels and from peers. Here the feedback is frequently given as an average of all responses about the positives and negatives of the manager's behavior. When the manager needs to interact with a particular individual in the future, the manager does not have specific information about the individual's feedback. Thus, the manager may not be able to improve his or her interaction with that individual.

One advantage of 360-degree feedback is confidentiality. However, if trust has been developed in the dyad, confidentiality would not be an issue.

Conclusion

For the successful implementation of a manager-subordinate dyad system, there has to be an open culture, especially in the dyad. The initiative should come from the manager. Considering that the subordinate is performing the manager's assignments and the subordinate's effectiveness impacts on the manager, the manager has the most at stake in a successful process.

New organizations could use the process from the beginning to implant the right culture and climate for dyad effectiveness. Remember, if there is a lack of openness in the dyad relationship, the process cannot be used as intended.

Mohandas Nair *is a management educator, teacher, trainer, writer, and a facilitator of learning. He earned a B.Tech (Mech.) from IIT Kharagpur, India, has a diploma in training and development, and has thirty-plus years of experience in industry and consultancy in the fields of industrial engineering and human resources development. He has published two books, written numerous articles, and facilitated management development programs.*

360-Degree Tool Kit
Everything You Ever Wanted to Know About 360-Degree Feedback, But Were Afraid to Ask

Jan M. Schmuckler, Ann M. Gormley, and Bruce Alan Kimbrew

Summary

Three-hundred-sixty degree (360-degree) feedback is one of the most important ways HRD professionals help leaders more accurately assess their behavior, skills, and influence in today's turbulent organizations. This full-circle feedback synthesizes information from a leader's major constituents in one package. This article discusses the steps of the 360-degree feedback process and shows how the 360-degree toolkit can be used. While 360-degree feedback can be useful at all levels of an organization, this article only examines its use at the highest levels of the organization: CEOs and their teams or their boards of directors. In this article, we refer to those we work with, clients or senior managers, as "leaders."

Facts About 360-Degree Feedback

The feedback process should be a voluntary program focused on development rather than on performance assessment. Leaders in today's organizations have many sources of evaluation of their performance; however, feedback for development is not as readily available. Our goal is to help leaders understand how they are perceived by their superiors, peers, staff, and sometimes customers. Leaders can choose to use those perceptions to change and become even more effective in their organizations. Information is collected from all of the key players who interact with the leader. Thus the name "360-degree feedback" derives from the full circle of constituents working with the person. It is a confidential and data-driven process. Confidentiality is important for eliciting accurate and complete information.

A critical element of 360-degree feedback is when the report is presented and a dialogue begins with the leader. The feedback session is best facilitated by an expert, neutral third party. As an HRD professional, you may want to consider whether you are the best person to administer this process. In organizations in which trust levels between HR and management are low, it is best to have a neutral third party deliver the feedback. In situations in which the paranoia is high in an organization or the organization's competition is fierce, leaders may only want to discuss their feedback with their internal HRD practitioners. Companies sometimes try to save money by doing the 360-degree process by themselves with the help of the internal HR and/or HRD group. Using only the internal staff may not be very productive if the internal team has little experience with 360-degree feedback. In this situation, it would be better to hire a consultant to the HRD team who can "shadow consult" with the team and assist them.

Three-hundred-sixty-degree feedback is best administered as part of a complete leadership development process. We use the coaching model illustrated in Figure 1 to explain the process to leadership. The phases of the leadership coaching model are followed in the feedback process, even if ongoing coaching is not the desired goal. The phases are contracting, assessment, feedback, planning, ongoing coaching, and evaluation.

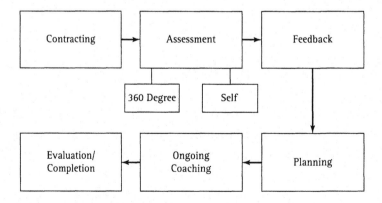

Figure 1. Leadership Coaching Model

Tom J. Ucko and Jan M. Schmuckler developed this coaching model in 2005.

The 360-Degree Feedback Process

Phase 1: Contracting

Contracting is the first step in the process. It establishes a foundation for the total engagement. It's the phase during which all the factors of the project will be discussed and decided on. During the contracting meeting, it is important to cover what the leader wants and expects from the process. It is equally important to tell the leader what you, the HRD professional or consultant, can offer and what you want from a leader for the project to be successful.

After contracting with the leader of the team and clarifying the process, the consultant meets with the leader to plan a kickoff or launch meeting with the whole team. Samples of some handouts that could be used at the kickoff meeting are at the end of this article. They include:

- A list of facts about 360-degree feedback in general;

- An outline of the process;

- A sample agenda for a feedback meeting;

- How to choose raters;

- Sample interview questions; and

- A letter to the client's team.

Phase 2: Assessment

After the contract is signed, the consultant conducts the assessment phase. This phase includes determining what tool will be used and collecting the feedback. Consultants are looking for themes and patterns in the data that will significantly impact the individual and the whole organization.

A great number of assessment tools are available for examining skills, styles, and behaviors. Because of the amount of data involved in 360-degree feedback, it is usually best to use an online tool for collecting and compiling data. It is also important to consider your overall purpose in conducting the survey. You may want to use a leadership tool that covers multiple competencies or a more focused tool if seeking to improve a specific leadership competency. You should also consider ease of use; your leader's style (Does he or she prefer more data-driven instruments?); the validity and reliability of the instrument; and any requirements for training and certification.

Other options include conducting interviews in conjunction with or at the completion of the survey instrument. If you are interviewing after completion of a survey, Exhibit 5 has some sample questions. If you are just interviewing and not doing an online assessment, then the following questions are typically asked:

- What does the leader do really well?

- What are the leader's greatest strengths?

- What could the leader do better?

- How would you characterize the leader's ability to articulate a clear and compelling vision?

- How does the leader provide directions to others? Please give an example.

- If you had one piece of advice for this person to be a more effective leader, what would it be?

Once the survey tool is decided on, meet with participants so they can choose their feedback raters. If you conduct a kickoff or launch meeting, the raters can be chosen at that time. The final recommendations for raters should be reviewed by the participants and their managers.

Phase 3: Feedback

After the assessment data is collected, review and analyze the data for the feedback phase. In this phase, a consultant presents the findings of the assessment to the leader, drawing a clear picture of the leader's current behaviors and/or skills and areas for improvement.

The following example at a large nonprofit demonstrates some of the ways that 360-degree feedback can fail at the feedback stage.

> Suzanne, executive director of a youth program in Berkeley, had already been through one 360-degree process with an external consultant during a previous CEO's leadership. A new CEO asked that all of his leadership team go through another 360-degree process. All seven of them agreed. The HR director was picked to lead the process, even though she was part of the leadership team and would be receiving feedback herself. The CEO decided that he would deliver the feedback to each member of his team. This put Suzanne in a very ambiguous position. She was not told whether the survey was performance based or development based. No action plan was asked for at the end of the feedback session. Although Suzanne disagreed with some of the feedback remarks and data, she felt that it would be impolitic to challenge them, since the CEO and head of HR were both involved.

Whether an HRD practitioner, organizational consultant, or full-time coach, anyone can easily fall into some of the pitfalls of the feedback phase. According to

Edie and Charlie Seashore and Gerald Weinberg (1991) in *What Did You Say? The Art of Giving and Receiving Feedback*, the myth is that "If feedback has all the correct ingredients in its delivery—clear, specific, timed right, non-judgmental, and speaks only to behavior—it will be accepted as given." However, we know that leaders actually choose what they will accept and what, if anything, they will do about the information. Preparing the leader ahead of time will increase the chances of acceptance. It is the responsibility of consultants to make the feedback process known and visible. Preparation may include discussing the feedback process using pictures or models.

For the process to be effective, leaders must accept the feedback and use it to benefit both themselves and their organizations. Consultants working with leaders must help them create action plans and provide to them in executing their plans so that organizations are successful.

Phase 4: Planning

The result of a 360-degree feedback session is a plan with two or three objectives or goals that the leader is interested in and committed to working on. The success of any program hinges on follow-up. The consultant's role during this phase is to help leaders clarify and prioritize their development objectives and assist in the creation of a plan for achieving them. Development activities can include on-the-job training, mentoring, education, workshops, coaching, and so forth. At leadership levels, we find that the most successful activity is ongoing coaching. Although the process may only consist of phases 1 through 4 of our leadership coaching model, we highly recommend that Phase 5, Ongoing Coaching, and Phase 6, Evaluation, be included to maximize results. For more information on all phases of the leadership coaching model, refer to Leadership Coaching: Avoiding the Traps (Schmuckler & Ucko, 2006).

Conclusion

Considering the pace of change in business today, leaders continually need to develop new capabilities and build capacity on their teams. The 360-degree feedback process helps leaders prioritize their own development needs and those of their teams while tracking the progress of both.

HRD practitioners play a key role in implementing such programs, whether they do it by themselves or bring in external consultants. Either way, organizations can benefit immensely from the proper use of this flexible and powerful tool.

References

Schmuckler, J.M., & Ucko, T.J. (2006). Leadership coaching: Avoiding the traps. In E. Biech (Ed.), *The 2006 Pfeiffer annual: Consulting* (pp. 241–247). San Francisco, CA: Pfeiffer.

Seashore, C., Seashore, E., & Weinberg, G. (1991). *What did you say? The art of giving and receiving feedback*. North Attleborough, MA: Douglas Charles Press.

Jan M. Schmuckler, Ph.D., *is an organizational psychologist and leadership coach who works with leaders to achieve outstanding business results. Her more than thirty years of experience with leading global companies in high technology, biotechnology, and the financial sectors brings unique perspectives for competing more effectively. Dr. Schmuckler was director, Graduate Coaching Certificate Program, John F. Kennedy University. Currently she spends most of her time on her own consulting practice.*

Ann M. Gormley, *senior organization development consultant, has more than fifteen years of experience as an internal and external consultant specializing in organization, leadership, management, and employee development. She has a master's in HR and organization development from the University of San Francisco and a B.S. in business administration from Stonehill College. Gormley has facilitated workshops, conferences, and 360-degree feedback surveys throughout the United States, Europe, and Asia for Applied Materials, SanDisk Corporation, Juniper Networks, Palm Inc., and 3Com.*

Bruce Alan Kimbrew *is a student at John F. Kennedy University. He completed his graduate certificate in coaching in 2007 and his master's in organizational psychology in 2009. Kimbrew is a managing director at Jones Lang LaSalle.*

Facts About 360-Degree Feedback

- 360-degree feedback is a voluntary program focused on development and not on assessment of performance.

- The goal is to help people understand how they are perceived by their managers, peers, direct reports, and sometimes customers.

- Information is collected from the person's manager, peers, and staff. The name "360-degree feedback" describes the full circle of people working with the person.

- 360-degree feedback is a confidential process.

- 360-degree feedback is usually facilitated by an expert neutral third party.

- 360-degree feedback is a data-driven process.

Outline of the 360-Degree Feedback Process

Contracting

- Leader contacts HRD practitioner, coach, or consultant.

- HRD practitioner launches process with leader.

Assessment

- Participants actively choose their feedback raters in partnership with their managers and the consultant.

- Raters and participants complete online or paper-and-pencil survey.

- Data is collected.

- Feedback report is prepared.

Feedback

- One-on-one feedback session conducted by consultant.

- Team feedback meeting is held.

Planning

- Consultant helps create action plan.

- Action plans are implemented.

Ongoing Coaching (optional)
Evaluating

- Review implementation plans with consultant.

- Redo 360-degree instrument and/or interview raters (optional).

- Consultant and leader decide on next steps for leader and his or her team members.

Sample Agenda for Launch Meeting

Date:

Welcome (from CEO or senior vice president, if not client)   15 to 30 min.

Set tone (from leader of client team)   30 min.

Meeting with whole team   45 to 60 min

- What is 360-degree process?
- Leadership Coaching Model
- Purpose of 360-degree feedback
- Benefits of this method
- Choosing raters (optional)
- Q&A
- Summary and next steps

How to Choose Your Raters*

- Choose a balanced point of view, in other words, not just people who see only your positive contributions.

- Selection should include your manager, three or more peers, three staff people who report to you, and two to three clients.

- People who have known you at least one year and not more than five years are the ideal candidates for obtaining accurate feedback for development and/or performance.

---

* Adapted from 1998 audio tape of Robert (Bob) W. Eichinger.

Sample Questions for Interviews After Completion of Survey

- What are strengths or opportunities of the client for growth?

- With whom and in what situations/circumstances does growth occur?

- What is the impact (positive or negative) of this growth?

- What could client do differently in the future to leverage strengths or address opportunities for growth?

- What positive things can result if the client leverages or addresses this growth?

Sample Letter to Client's Team

Dear Colleagues,

For our 360-degree feedback process and coaching program, we have some work to do before we start. [Insert consultant name] will be our consultant and giver of feedback. [He/She] is going to have all of us take the [name or description of assessment]. [He/She] will send you the information that you need to rate yourself.

[He/She] will generate an individual report for each of you based on your own rating and those of the seven to ten raters you and I choose. My administrator will set up a two-hour interview for [insert name of consultant] to go over the feedback with you. You will be asked to complete an action plan based on your strengths and challenges as reported in the feedback.

Please respond promptly when [insert name of consultant] gives us the information to complete the online version of the 360-degree survey. It only takes fifteen minutes to complete.

We will start the process on [insert start date]. Please submit names of raters that you want to use to me and to [insert name of consultant and email address]. This is a great opportunity to learn more about ourselves and about our team.

Thank you for your continued support and commitment.

[Insert leader's name]

Building Support and Engagement for Technology Initiatives

Kris Taylor

Summary

Large-scale technology implementations are complex, multi-year projects that involve several distinct phases. Robust communication is essential for successful implementation and ongoing adoption of the new tools and processes. Due to the complexity, depth, and length of these projects, communication to end-users can be fragmented and primarily focused on technology and IT process. The result is often confusion and disenfranchisement.

Implementing a communication approach that is end-user focused and sensitive to the needs of each stage of the project results in end-users who are more likely to support the change, be engaged in the implementation, and understand the importance of the initiative and their roles in each stage.

ERP, UAT, CRM, ITLT, SOS, BPR, ABAP, ASAP. . . . The list goes on and on. These and other acronyms and technical terms are the dreaded "geek speak" to the majority of the individuals in your organization, yet these are the same people for whom you are building and designing IT solutions and on whom your ultimate success depends. They are the end-users for the newest technology initiatives in your company—the ones who will either embrace the technology or doggedly hold on to your legacy systems. How you communicate with these same individuals can mean the difference between support and adoption versus resistance and stonewalling. But we all know that successful communication only happens when the receiver understands the message—a challenging task when it comes to technology.

In addition to speaking different languages, large-scale technology initiatives typically have an excruciating long ramp up curve—years in many cases. During that time, others in the organization might see it only as a project that consumes time and talent with a project team that is disengaged from the mainstream organization. Little information is forthcoming, and, when it is, it may be an incomprehensible jumble of project reports, IT details, and vague (and often changing) schedules and timelines.

When the solution is unveiled, we expect people to learn, support, and embrace new tools, processes, and ways of doing their jobs. Just as switching the system on is no easy task, neither is turning end-users on. We expect that they will be supportive, engaged, and excited to learn—even though they have not been informed, involved, and engaged in the process until the last minute. Is it any wonder that this can be a formula for failure, with resultant behaviors of stalling, confusion, lack of enthusiasm, and resistance?

The Keys to Support and Engagement

Informing, engaging, and involving end-users along the way can help bridge this gap between ignorant and informed, ambivalent and anticipating, and rejecting and accepting. Doing so requires the intention and ability to think and communicate like an end-user rather than an IT professional.

Remember the country-western song by Toby Keith that was popular a few years ago: "I Want to Talk About Me"? The lyrics hold the key. When communicating to end-users about a technology project, focus the conversation on them.

It is natural that the project people want to talk about themselves—the project, the process, the hardware, the software, the testing process, coding and transports—all the things that are vitally important to them, their world, their value, and their focus. The problem is not only that this information is incomprehensible to most end-users but that it fails to serve the purpose of engagement.

Those messages are neither heard nor understood. End-users want to talk about themselves! They want to know about what this means to them, how they will be trained, when their desktops will change, whether their jobs will still be there, and, if they are, will they be better or worse. Engagement is about considering the other point of view, reaching out, and showing others how and when they will become a part of this project. It is about showing how things fit—how this project will shape their work world in the near future.

The challenge is to think less like a geek and more like an end-user. This requires an understanding of the end-users' specific concerns and needs. One must consider the project from an outsider's view in light of timing, impact, and outcomes. Let's look at typical phases in a technology project and how to shift the focus from "us" to "them."

Building User Engagement into the Plan

In the *Planning* stage, the project team is in its infancy, weighing hefty decisions, long-term implications, and big-dollar spending requests. While we might want to talk about our selection factors, the various solutions evaluated, and the nuances of system architecture and performance, others in the organization just want the basics—why this is a good choice and what the advantages are.

Keep communication in this stage brief and to the point. Let others in the organization know why are you making this change and how will it help everyone in the future. Share the compelling reason, the business purpose of the change, and the value for them. Do it in terms that are easily understood.

While you may not have specific implementation dates at this point, laying the groundwork in terms of number of years and amount of effort helps to set appropriate expectations.

Fostering Support at Every Step

In the *blueprint* or *design* stage, the project team is almost singularly focused on processes—the exhaustive effort to capture as-is, to-be, and the gap between them. Those not involved in the process are often stunned at how long this stage takes and perplexed that there is not much to show for it other than reams of documentation and technical specs.

Communication efforts at this stage of the project can build an overview of the process to create a level of understanding about the project team's work and what the future will hold. Engagement at this stage can be built by connecting a broader audience to the work of defining as-is and to-be states with a focus on the expected benefits. Involve key opinion leaders in a meaningful way, especially those who will go into the work environment and spread the word credibly. Think carefully about the opportunities for input and pulling in key individuals during the review process.

A note of caution—be especially clear about roles and expectations at this stage. If your goal is to expose others to foster learning and understanding, be very clear that you are NOT looking for input and revisions. If they have an ability to change or shape the solution, let them know. If you would like them to understand the new processes and begin to prepare their work areas for the changes, ensure that is communicated clearly. Care taken here can avoid confusion, potential disengagement, and misunderstanding.

Moving into the *build* or *configure* step is an exciting milestone. The challenges here include the fact that initially the system is truly an ugly duckling—it's not very stable, has lots of bugs and issues to be resolved, and is fairly skeletal as it begins to take shape.

Rather than confusing folks with talk of test scripts, test plans, and test documents and unit, integration, and UAT, consider communicating the end result of all this testing. The message that "We are testing the system in a number of different ways so that once you begin to use it, it is robust, thoroughly tested, and will perform as expected" is really what end-users want and need to hear. Drop the geek speak about testing and get right to the result in clear and plain English that reassures and builds confidence.

This is also the time at which "pre-go-live jitters" begin to occur. End-users see the solution is taking shape and that it will be impacting their world in the near term. At this time, they again want to know about "me," specifically how they will learn this new system and be supported during the cut over. The more detail you can provide about how they will be trained, when they will be trained, who will do the instruction, what type of support materials are being created, and what type of help system will be available to them, the better.

Setting the Stage for a Successful Launch

Go live prep is when, from an end-user's perspective, the reality that the solution is coming and that they will need to do something different sets in. The challenge here is that the project team is involved in a flurry of deadline-driven activity, yet the communication needs are greater than ever.

Communication in this stage is specific and direct. It involves providing direction and guidance in how to prepare, learn, and cut over. It requires person-to-person and eyeball-to-eyeball interaction. You have to balance the end-user audience demands for time and attention with the internal needs of the team members to have time and space to complete their work.

Being intentional about communication channels helps ensure communication follow-through. Designate a point (or points) of contact and a person (or persons) whom users can reach out to and connect with. As the training effort is well underway, the training team can perform much of this role. And of course, the individuals responsible for organizational change management, Super Users (a small cadre of users who have received early, extensive training) and subject-matter experts (SMEs) can be invaluable.

You can also be intentional about planning for robust communication at specific times and pre-plan ways in which two-way communication can happen. Town halls, road shows, updates at regular meetings, podcasts, and information booths in high-traffic areas or at company events can be scheduled, replicated, and done either face-to-face or virtually. The keys are that they are planned, the information is relevant, and, once the format and materials are in place, they are easily replicated. An internal website, share point site, or other electronic document sharing tool can also help by providing standard information to the broader organization. This can include cut over instructions, pre-implementation checklists, frequently asked questions, and a way to contact the team via email with questions.

Finishing Touches to Enable Sustainability

In *post go live*, we tend to think the work is over, but now it really is about "them." Finally, we are talking the same language and living the same reality.

Communication here can serve two purposes. One is to ensure that end-users know where to go for support and help so that they can use the system as intended and develop competence and confidence. The second is to build a dialogue about the system that encourages continuous improvement.

For the first, find multiple ways to let end-users know how they will be supported. If there is a help desk number, provide it to them in a way in which it is easy to remember and access (on mouse pads, magnets, or other visible means). If project team members or SMEs are going to be in the work area following go live for support, ensure that end-users know how to contact them and that you are sincere about wanting to help. If there is online help, explain how to use it in your training sessions. Over and over again, send the message that the goal is to support end-users so that they can learn to use the system as painlessly as possible.

To encourage continuous improvement of the system, the underlying business processes, and the skills of the end-users, find a group of interested and able employees you can pull together for regular communication sessions. Here they can share their experiences and their discoveries and, as a result, learn from one another. This is a powerful way to build a connected base of end-users and to ratchet the utilization of the system to a higher level across the enterprise. You can also designate these individuals as the "go to" people for new information—so that they become a channel outward for key messages that need dissemination into the field. The two-way nature of these groups makes for robust learning and improvement and builds ownership along the way.

Communication is never easy, and communication of broad-based, mammoth IT projects is even more challenging. The imperative is to do it well, or the cost is disengagement, confusion, and failure to successfully launch the new system. Be intentional about building a communication plan that considers the various stakeholders in the audience and what is needed from their perspectives. Change the key messages and delivery methods at various times in the project based on the needs of the end-user. Always remember to talk about "them" when communicating with them.

Conclusion

Enhance end-user engagement and buy-in by delivering messages with the end-user in mind and asking what they want to know. Encourage two-way dialogue, which is not only more powerful but also helps you to gauge what their informational needs are. Find ways to simplify the message—by omitting complex, technical jargon and focusing instead on talking about what is real and meaningful to your audience. Check along the way for understanding and then for impact. Use this information to shift and adapt your message as you go to ensure understanding, relevance, and clarity.

Beauty is in the eye of the beholder. Ultimately, solid, clear, and timely communication about IT initiatives that is meaningful and beneficial to the end-user can greatly improve the support, acceptance, and usage of your new IT system.

Kris Taylor, CPLP, SPHR, *is the president of K. Taylor & Associates, a consulting group that helps organizations successfully navigate the human side of strategically oriented change. She has twenty-eight years of experience in organizational change and development, learning, training, and human resources. K. Taylor & Associates provides change management services for large-scale organizational changes, including ERP and technology implementations, cultural changes, and enhancing the learning and development function.*

Consulting Opportunities in the Nonprofit Sector

Phil Van Horn

Summary

Nonprofit organizations represent a growing market that is in need of organization development consultants. The nonprofit sector has grown substantially in the past decade, as has competition among nonprofits for fundraising. Executive officers of nonprofit organizations don't believe their boards are as engaged in the planning and governance of organizations as they ought to be. Such inattention not only creates an unhealthy relationship between the executive and certain board members, but it prevents organizations from fully serving their communities. While the number of nonprofit organizations continues to increase, many boards are not fully cognizant of their responsibilities and, hence, liabilities, as directors.

The Nonprofit Sector

With approximately 1.4 million organizations registered with the Internal Revenue Service accounting for roughly 5.2 percent of the U.S. gross domestic product, nonprofits represent an increasingly influential sector of our local, state, regional, and national economies (The Urban Institute, 2006). Equally important to note is that the Urban Institute estimates that 29 percent of Americans serve as volunteers for nonprofits. Nonprofits fill a vital role in providing human and environmental services; physical and mental health resources; and art, historical, and cultural opportunities and are substantially funded by fee income and charitable gifts.

With nearly one-third of Americans volunteering time for nonprofits, and given the amount of assets managed by foundations, charities, and other nonprofits, it is critical that the leaders of nonprofit organizations understand their responsibilities as executives and directors of these organizations.

Survey of Nonprofits

Align™, an organization development and training consultancy, recently conducted a survey of executive directors of various small nonprofits, ranging in size of annual operating budgets from less than $25,000 to greater than $5,000,000. The results indicate that nonprofit organizations face similar challenges, regardless of their size. Selected survey responses:

- The areas that the executives reported their organizations struggle with the most are strategic planning (36.5 percent) and board training (35.1 percent). Recruiting board members and recruiting qualified paid staff tied for third among their concerns at 32.4 percent.

- Asked to rate the top three areas in which their boards could benefit from facilitation and training, "fundraising" received an 82 percent response; "effective governance," 55 percent; and "strategic planning," 54 percent.

- Forty-six percent of executives report increased competition for fundraising.

- Forty percent of executives responded that more than two-thirds of their respective boards' membership do not understand and accept responsibility for financial stewardship of the organization.

- Sixty-three percent of respondents believe they are doing a successful job in recruiting and retaining competent and productive staff, yet at the same time 45 percent believe they are only fair to extremely deficient in human resource development and succession planning.

- Forty-three percent of executives plan to leave their organizations in two to five years.

- Sixty percent believe their organizations are only fair to extremely deficient in setting clear priorities and documenting goals and objectives.

- Fifty-seven percent believe their organizations are successful to extremely successful in having an organizational structure in place to accomplish goals and serve clients.

- Forty-eight percent believe their organizations are fair to extremely deficient in leadership's communication of goals, strategies, and values.

- Fifty-nine percent believe their organizations have the ability to meet changing community needs and build additional capacity.

Discussion

Conventional wisdom would have us believe that fundraising is the number one struggle for nonprofits. In this survey, it was rated fourth (24.3 percent). While fundraising is *the* critical objective for most nonprofits, executives are relatively comfortable in *their own* abilities to raise funds, but not in the abilities of their respective board members. It is significant that, rather than fundraising, *what concerns executives most is their boards' lack of commitment to planning and training in how to be an effective organization.* The message from executives to boards is clear: before we can do any substantial fundraising, we must have our house in order. That means strategic planning to include clearly articulated vision, mission, and goals with consistent communication of these to all stakeholders.

These are the overriding functions of leadership at any organization. Nonprofit boards are comprised of volunteers who steal time from their families and careers to serve. And while they typically receive no compensation, they are every bit as accountable to the public as their peers who sit on the boards of publicly traded companies or hold elective office.

Documenting goals and objectives is integral to holding the organization (and, hence, the board itself) accountable. Documentation is also critical to the communication process.

It is somewhat incongruent that most executives believe they successfully recruit and retain staff, yet 45 percent recognize they are lacking in human resource development and succession planning. Further analysis of the survey reveals that 60 percent of those executives who plan to leave within two years have no succession plans in place.

And, while executives have reservations about their respective boards' engagement in planning, training, organizational governance, and communication, a significant percentage nonetheless believe their organizations have the ability to meet changing community needs and build additional capacity. The inconsistency here is glaring.

An organization that neglects regular strategic planning and board training will either be drawn into trying to be all things to all people, or will remain mired in an outdated paradigm. Either way, it most certainly will not effectively adapt nor build additional capacity.

Conclusion

Nonprofit organizations are in need of consulting help in developing plans for long-range goals, leadership succession, and governance.

Too often, nonprofit board members don't attend to their stewardship roles as they should. While executive directors of nonprofits recognize the issues, they are frustrated in their attempts to get board members to commit to planning and training. What too many board members don't understand is that *the board is the legal entity.* It is not the staff, the facilities, nor the clients or donors. The board is the entity legally responsible for all activities of the organization. The consequences of poor stewardship by a board can be catastrophic for individual directors, the organization, and the community it purports to serve.

In addition, executive directors must recognize that they may unwittingly be enabling board behavior. To function without human resource development and succession planning, combined with the belief that their organizations will remain viable and relevant despite the lack of strategic planning, is akin to denial.

Reference

The Urban Institute. (2006). *The nonprofit sector in brief: Facts and figures from the Nonprofit Almanac 2007 prepared by the National Center for Charitable Statistics.* Washington, DC: Urban Institute Press.

Phil Van Horn *is president and CEO of Western States Learning Corporation, a non-profit corporation that provides life-long learning opportunities through a variety of consulting and training services, and a principal at Align™, an organization development and training consultancy. Throughout his professional career of more than thirty years, Van Horn has developed and delivered adult leadership and team-building courses for numerous organizations. He has served on numerous local, state, and national boards of directors. Van Horn received his M.Ed. from the University of Missouri-Columbia.*

Forming TIGERS®-Hearted Teams

Dianne Crampton

Summary

Collaborative work cultures that pay attention to behaviors such as trust, interdependence, genuineness, empathy, risk, and success (TIGERS) in the workplace are important in today's economy. In February 2007, the U.S. Small Business Administration reported that small businesses comprised of five hundred or fewer employees are the largest employment segment in the country. They are the backbone of the U.S. economy. Yet many of these companies, some strikingly fast-growing, find themselves struggling with issues such as attracting talented team members and sustaining growth. A survey conducted by TIGERS Success Series in 2007 concluded that the number-one reason talented employees leave companies is because they will not accept a poor company culture or attitudes that violate values such as trust when other work opportunities are present. TIGERS is a leadership model that provides a foundation for success.

Forming TIGERS-Hearted Teams

Ask any entrepreneur what it was like to build a team-based organization by paying attention to workplace culture and core values, and the stories you hear are wonderful. Their memories—even through difficult at times—are good.

Consider the founding members of a company that made digital flat-screen technology possible. The founders spent much time contemplating how to create a team-based, values-based workplace environment. They evaluated how certain behaviors and attitudes would impact employees—team members—and make a difference both inside and outside of the company. They concluded that:

- As a team-based company, we are about creating wealth and health in a holistic way.

- As a team-based company, we have fun and enjoy our work.

- As a team-based company, we are building a legacy through value-based decisions with results sustainable over a long period of time.

- As a team-based company, we take care of each other.

Core value and cultural decisions like these breathe life into a team-based organization and allow leaders to chart an ethical course. And in taking care of one another, leaders and team members build kindness into their work communities.

Any entrepreneur who fails to pay attention to culture and values when forming a team-based organization is committing a serious mistake. This is especially true in situations in which it's clear a team-based organization makes the most sense for promoting innovation.

Staying on course during growth phases is difficult without an inner compass that guides the way. Team member conflict, communication problems, and predictable human relationship issues are more manageable once culture and values are integrated into the strategic planning process.

Over the years, in fact, many business writers have argued in favor of teams as an organizing principle. They concluded that decision making through collective intelligence is far superior to decisions made by individual leaders isolated in boardrooms and removed from front-line operations.

These business philosophers have hammered home that even a skilled and informed leader makes the right decision less than 50 percent of the time when relying solely on his or her own information to solve problems never encountered before (Forrest, 1974; Senge, 1990; Surowiecki, 2004; Yukl, 1989).

During the 1980s, as the notion of team-based workplaces began to gain ground, the question was posed: "What is required to not only build teams, but to build *effective* teams?"

In 1987, a study was conducted at Gonzaga University to discover what builds an ethical, quality-focused, successful, and committed group of people (Crampton, 1987). The study looked at education, psychology, and business group dynamic research and models. Instead of discovering management techniques and business equations, the researchers found that six collaborative values or core principles directly impact collaborative group behavior. These six values are trust, interdependence, genuineness, empathy, risk, and success—TIGERS.

At the same time, the researchers concluded that certain work cultures support these behaviors, while others do not. Over the years, TIGERS served both work groups and community groups. Consulting results produced an interesting insight— that work cultures divide into two distinct cultural work categories. The first, the Individualistic Culture, supports individual achievement. Social psychologists have named numerous subsets of this culture, which favors competition among employees and the advancement of individual achievers. The other, the Collaborative Culture, supports true teamwork, principles of interdependence, and collective achievement that benefit from the TIGERS collaborative values and directly impact group behavior.

Table 1 breaks out the differences into greater detail.

Table 1. Individualist and Collaborative Group-Centered Culture Indicators

INDIVIDUALIST CULTURE LEADERSHIP FOCUS	COLLABORATIVE AND GROUP-CENTERED CULTURE LEADERSHIP FOCUS
Leadership is earned by being more skilled than others. Advancement is a competitive process.	Leadership is expected of everyone. Advancement comes from the group's achievements and peer recommendations.
Power is held by few.	Power is held by many.
Goals are achieved through others.	Goals are achieved with others.
Success is achieved through management direction and employees following orders.	Success is achieved through team achievement and team coaching and facilitation.
Strong individual personalities influence the culture.	The culture is value-centered with transparent norms, rules, and procedures that apply to everyone.
Leaders hold power and autonomy in their positions, resulting in power over others.	Leaders hold power in direct proportion to the number of people they serve.
Organizational input is controlled by few.	Organizational input is controlled by many.
Organizational direction is driven by few.	Organizational direction is driven by many.
ADVANCEMENT AND LEARNING	**ADVANCEMENT AND LEARNING**
Individuals are skilled and compete with their skills for promotion.	Individuals are skilled and learn additional skills to be more cross-functional.
Upward promotion is based on individual achievement.	Upward promotion is based on team skills and endorsement from team members.
Competition for advancement is based on individual achievement.	Advancement is based on team achievement, relational skills, team skills, and the respect one receives from the group
Training benefits upward promotion.	Training benefits cross-functional achievement and upward promotion.
Opportunity for achievement is directed by others.	Opportunity for achievement is self-directed.
Opportunity for advancement is directed by others.	Opportunity for advancement is self-directed.
Freedom and authority increase though promotion.	Freedom and authority are collective and benefit group achievement.

INDIVIDUALIST CULTURE LEADERSHIP FOCUS	COLLABORATIVE AND GROUP-CENTERED CULTURE LEADERSHIP FOCUS
A pool of employees with limited job scope and little opportunity for upward mobility is required.	All employees have opportunities for advancement horizontally, through cross-functional team roles, and vertically based on their problem-solving and group-leadership skills.
Feedback is infrequent and benefits upward advancement.	Feedback is frequent and benefits work quality and employee motivation.
Key positions are filled from outside the organization.	Key positions are filled from within the organization.
The environment promotes work skill development.	The environment promotes personal growth, leadership skills, and work skill development.

COMPENSATION	COMPENSATION
Large differences in pay scale mark upward advancement.	Small differences in pay scale mark upward achievement.
No pay increase for knowledge obtained unless promoted.	Good increases in pay for knowledge obtained for cross-functional application.

COMPETITION AND TEAM WORK	COMPETITION AND TEAM WORK
Emotional connection to work is subordinate to being told what to do.	Team members have an emotional connection to work and will often take on additional tasks to help the organization succeed.
Internal competition is directed toward people, departments, resources, and power.	Internal competition is directed toward work processes and procedures that contribute to improved quality and cost savings.
External competition is for market share.	External competition is for market superiority with the best products and services for the best price.
Problems are explained as being caused by people.	Problems are investigated for procedural and process solutions first and people last.
Working with others benefits self-promotion.	Working with others is how work is done.
High commitment exists for following directions and doing a job correctly.	High commitment exists for contributing to the organization's success on multiple levels.

PROBLEM SOLVING AND OTHER INDICATORS	PROBLEM SOLVING AND OTHER INDICATORS
Problem solving is achieved by management direction.	Problem solving is achieved through team direction.
Management tells employees what to do.	Employees do not need to be told what to do. They need to be guided to a direction.
An element of uncertainty exists in the workplace.	Transparency exists in the workplace.
The culture benefits work.	The culture benefits work and gives people the opportunity to achieve transcendent needs.

Reprinted by permission of TIGERS Success Series, Copyright ©1987 TIGERS Success Series, Bend, Oregon.

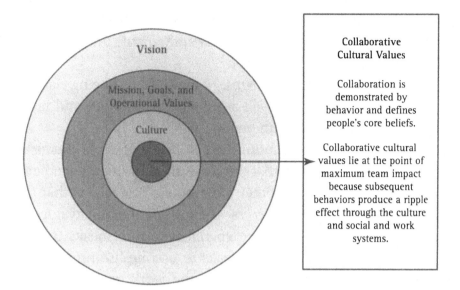

Figure 1. Collaborative Cultural Values

Reprinted by permission of TIGERS Success Series, Copyright © 1988 TIGERS Success Series, Bend, Oregon.

In the same way, the most complex issues facing organizations undergoing transformational change from an individualistic culture to a collaborative and team-based culture involve keeping many of the principles that reinforce individualistic cultures. The failure to fully transform creates a cultural split, which results in confusion and conflict among employees and ethical dilemmas in governing the organization.

The diagram in Figure 1 explains how culture and values affect a collaborative team dynamic. Collaborative or competitive values often disappear from view in mature cultures. However, their impact is always felt and is visible by how people treat one another and how work is achieved on a daily basis.

Over the past twenty years, based on my work with large, medium, and small organizations in both the private and public sectors and with community groups, I have concluded that the most efficient time to establish a collaborative core value culture is when the organization is in the start-up phase and rapidly growing. However, merging organizations and organizations undergoing cultural change are also successful when committed leaders and their boards of directors pledge their allegiance to sustainable collaborative values that will withstand changes in leadership over the course of time.

The TIGERS Validation Process

Once the six TIGERS collaborative values—trust, interdependence, genuineness, empathy, risk, and success—surfaced from education, business, and psychology group dynamic studies, I developed a survey containing fifty-seven questions to determine whether the values were measurable and reliable indicators of collaborative team development (Crampton, 1987).

Teams from seventeen intact groups, including a Boeing facility, participated in the survey. The teams received a pre- and post-survey and team-building interventions over an eighteen-month period.

The results were independently monitored by heads of departments at Gonzaga University. One finding concluded that the core values or interdependence and success are highly correlated with the other four values. This means that an improvement in either interdependence or success will increase the other values, too.

It was also interesting that the interdependence value speaks to building collaborative relationships, while success speaks to accomplishing quality work and achieving goals. Therefore, balances between the work people do and the well-being and relationship quality of people doing the work is critical for long-term team success.

Another finding was that the six values predict group behavior either by their inclusion or omission. This means that group dynamics are measurable and that corrective action can be taken to shorten the time new teams spend in confusion ("storming").

Another finding indicated that certain understandings that people have about effective team behavior line up with individual values. Therefore, the survey could measure with a good degree of reliability where teams are strong and areas for improvement.

One year later, another study was conducted by school districts through the Washington State Education Association (WEA) (Dater, 1988). Officials from the teacher's union wanted to identify specific training to offer teachers to improve team skills for school site councils. The concept of school site councils—teams— was a new concept in Washington State.

The trend toward site councils—composed of teachers, parents, and a principal— indicated a belief that a site council was better-suited to make decisions, solve the school's problems, and create and monitor improvement programs than were school administrators who had little knowledge of the school's daily operations and service area. This was a transformational shift from school administrators making all the decisions to localized, team decision making.

Unfortunately, training and development days for teachers were seriously limited. WEA wanted to know where they would receive the best return on their training investment on a school-by-school basis.

WEA concluded that the TIGERS survey was highly predictive and gave the school a good team opinion snapshot for strategic training and development purposes. And because the six values are demonstrated by behaviors that are readily visible, WEA officials concluded that TIGERS was basic, simple, and made good common sense.

As a result, officials further concluded that the quality of the values can also be measured and monitored over time as a site council changes or grows. This is an important feature for any team that gains and loses team members and for leaders who want to know what to look for in new employee candidates. TIGERS offered a way to track and monitor a strategic team development process on a school-by-school basis.

From the time the studies were concluded in 1993, work with merging organizations and newly emerging teams cultures concluded that the six TIGERS values—trust, interdependence, genuineness, empathy, risk, and success—reinforce the vision, mission, goals, and operational values of team-driven organizations.

The values and supporting behaviors limit the time teams spend in conflict and are powerful predictors for selecting successful new employment candidates to fill positions on existing teams (Loy-Ferri, 1993).

Behaviors That Support TIGERS

Successful small business owners with a stable workforce learn early how important it is to hire the right candidates for existing teams. Consequences are steep for hiring the wrong person. Job turnover creates workforce gaps, with substantial hidden costs, making forward progress difficult in a fast-paced, rapidly changing economy.

Also, leaders of larger organizations who embrace group-centered practices also realize that more than job descriptions come into play when teams are empowered to achieve company goals. How team leaders interact with team members; how team members relate daily to one another; how team members resolve conflict and solve problems; and how team members and leaders commit through all phases of a project are key to how well a project gets off the ground and whether it is completed satisfactorily.

Identifying team relational criteria the organization holds to be important and identifying behaviors and communications that support group efforts are critical. Taking an additional step beyond traditional strategic planning processes—which identify vision, mission, goals, and operational values—is necessary. Drilling down to identify collaborative team behaviors that are embraced by employees gives organizations and teams a platform from which to operate. It also sets the criteria for leadership development and the expectations of newly hired employees.

Over the past twenty years, different teams have contributed insight into what behaviors support trust, interdependence, genuineness, empathy, risk, and success in their organizations. These behaviors are easily observed in how team members treat one another, how different departments relate with one another, and how customers are cared for on a daily basis. A brief summary and listing of behaviors follows (Crampton, 2007).

Trust

Trust is confidence in the integrity, reliability, and fairness of a person or organization. Trust is an essential human value. Like fine oil, trust is the lubrication that keeps teams functional when conflict arises. It is difficult to acquire and, if abused, harder to salvage. If destroyed, people will often be asked or choose to leave the organization.

What Behaviors Damage Trust?

- Unhealthy competition between workers

- Lack of follow-through

- Not walking the talk

- Falsifying information

- Withholding praise and feedback

- Inconsistency and lack of predictability

What Behaviors Build Trust?

- Sharing information

- Openly discussing disappointments

- Collaborative problem solving

- Soliciting and implementing others' ideas when appropriate

- Establishing and communicating expectations, standards, and ground rules

- Giving employees timely performance reviews

Interdependence

Interdependence relies on behaviors founded on sharing, openness, acceptance, support, and personal introspection, leading to mental and emotional growth and psychological wholeness. It is contrasted to dependence, which requires someone more proficient or powerful to take care of another person. In contrast with the competitive work culture, wherein someone with more power ultimately wins and another loses, interdependence is based on the idea that *if we win, I win*. Interdependence, therefore, means that two or more people appreciate and rely on each other's strengths and are mutually responsible for their own limitations. Because interdependence requires self-awareness and appreciation for others, it demands high levels of emotional maturity, self-esteem, and commitment to excellence.

What Behaviors Damage Interdependence?

- The belief that a person has the power to change someone else

- The belief that leaders hold all the answers

- The belief that leaders must solve all the problems without input from others

- Allowing employees to blame co-workers for system problems

- Allowing an *us and them* attitude to thrive in the workplace

What Behaviors Build Interdependence?

- Win-win problem solving and the reduction in win-lose and lose-lose conflict solutions

- When procedural and communication errors occur, apologize and forgive

- Team-building activities that build understanding between people

- Facilitative and coaching leadership styles

- Allowing workers to change ineffective work procedures that directly affect them

- Building a sense of responsibility and accountability among managers, team leaders, and workers

- Helping employees understand the value of differences

Genuineness

Genuineness is a personal quality each person brings to the team. It promotes sincere, honest, respectful, and direct communication in an open and responsible way.

Obstacles that most often impede genuine behavior stem from both internal and external sources. Internal obstacles are caused by fear. Examples include fear of change, fear of not belonging or being viewed by others as not being a good person, fear of being inaccurate, fear of appearing disrespectful or contrary, and fear of appearing too vulnerable. This results in reality avoidance, dishonesty, rationalization, denial, and performance anxiety.

External obstacles may also give rise to fears, such as fear of repercussions and fear of betrayal. Ultimately, genuineness thrives in an environment of understanding and kindness in which fear is minimized and respect for differences is valued.

What Behaviors Damage Genuineness?

- Triangulation or allowing people to discuss concerns and complaints with co-workers who have no power to bring matters to closure

- Inferences made and not challenged about co-worker behavior and intentions

- Not sharing observations, facts, or intuitive hunches

- Belittling people with contrary opinions and concerns who express their ideas to ensure that everyone thinks and behaves in the same way

What Behaviors Build Genuineness?

- Respect for self and others

- Sharing information and discussing concerns without fear of repercussion

- Critical thinking skill development

- Confrontation and feedback skill development

- Self-awareness

- Mentorship programs

- Coaching and facilitative management styles

Empathy

Empathy is the ability to understand or imagine the feelings and ideas of another person. It does not imply agreement.

Empathy is essential for resolving conflict in ways by which everyone is satisfied with the outcome. Empathy is important for collaborative negotiations and is essential for identifying behaviors that harm another person's reputation or emotional, psychological, and physical safety.

Each employee has certain rights that are linked to empathy. These include the rights of respect, safety, and opportunity for fulfillment. Empathy, therefore, has a powerful influence on organizational learning, conflict resolution, team harmony, and embracing diversity.

What Behaviors Damage Empathy?

- Narcissism and self-obsession

- Opportunism

- Rationalizing that the end justifies the means

- Aggressive competition among employees and departments that damages the self-worth or safety of another person

- Passive-aggressive conflict strategies among employees and departments that results in harm to another

What Behaviors Build Empathy?

- Care for self and others

- Kindness

- Desire to understand others

- Collaboration

- Excellent listening skills

- Good personal boundaries

Risk

Risk is the potential exposure to loss or injury resulting in fear of the unknown. On the downside, fear of risk results in stagnation, because if people are penalized for calculated risk taking, they become fearful of new ideas. On the upside, risk is the fuel behind change and quality improvements.

Therefore, organizations that fail to look at errors as learning tools lose a valuable market edge. They tend to be more backward and unable to change or learn from mistakes. As a result, they are not as responsive to market competition as organizations that embrace risk and put into place problem-solving methodologies and post-project debriefing sessions that minimize it.

What Behaviors Damage Risk?

- Retaliation against people who make thoughtful decisions that result in an error

- Failure to clarify goals, procedures, and expectations

- Criticism

- Fear of failure

- Perfectionism and over-analysis

- Making it difficult to bring errors to light

- Viewing mistakes as failures rather than opportunities

What Behaviors Build Risk?

- Performance feedback and coaching

- Establishing accountability and commitment at all levels of the organization

- Debriefing completed projects and developing improvement processes

- Recognizing that honest mistakes are learning opportunities

- Establishing problem-solving methodologies

- Viewing problems as opportunities

Success

Success means effectively achieving what an organization has set out to do. It is a fundamental rationality for why teams are formed. For this reason, it is essential that team members clearly understand and commit to organizational change and to the organization's mission, values, and goals. If people resolutely feel that a change or a goal won't be successful, they will often demand a change in leadership or quit.

Similarly, if people do not understand how their work efforts contribute to success, they often do not give their best. Some, on the other hand, will continue to excel based on the notion that their good efforts will result in personal rather than group gain. If the promotion does not occur, their efforts and attitudes often turn sour.

The TIGERS values establish a balance between goals being achieved through excellence and the psychological satisfaction of people doing the work. If people resolutely know how to succeed, and if the principle *if we win, I win* holds true, then the balanced equation spreads success throughout the team in the form of bonus, profit sharing, or some other non-monetary reward that is valued by people accomplishing goals. For example, TIGERS experience has shown that working four ten-hour shifts is often more highly prized than money among younger workers who want to spend extra time with their families.

What Behaviors Damage Success?

- Lack of personal commitment and accountability for organization goals

- Withholding information caused by unhealthy competition among work groups

- Poor morale

- Lack of direction

- Short-term problem solving

What Behaviors Build Success?

- Building understanding, commitment, and ownership of company goals at all levels of organization

- Involving as many workers' ideas into goal implementation as appropriate

- Establishing and communicating quality standards, planning, work design, and system refinement strategies for all levels of operation

- Celebrating successes

- Giving credit to employees

- Evaluating and removing operational barriers

- Training to improve both work and relational skills

- Helping employees understand how important their job performance is to achieving company goals

Conclusion

TIGERS is a research-based, collaborative team and leadership model that has served both the public and private sectors since 1987. The values are supported by behaviors that predictably build an effective team. Also, core value-based behaviors strike a balance between how work is done and the people doing the work. When collaborative values are recognized and held as important, the resulting behaviors produce greater harmony and communication among people, which results in less strife. The payoff is increased creativity and improved morale.

In those organizations in which behavior standards are spelled out and expectations of how people are to treat one another are commonly known and evaluated, both group harmony and increased productivity follow.

References

Crampton, D. (1987). Unpublished master's dissertation. Spokane, WA: Gonzaga University.

Crampton, D. (2007, February). Core values for functional teams: Understanding how to improve employee relations and communications with measurable results. *HR Reports*.

Dater, L. (1988). Unpublished study. Spokane, WA: Washington Education Association.

Forrest, D.W. (1974). *Francis Galton: The life and work of a Victorian genius*. London: Elek.

Loy-Ferri, D. (1993). Mt. Adams Furniture Yakima Indian Nation case summary: Together for Tomorrow Intergenerational Conference diversity recommendations to the White House. Spokane, WA: TIGERS Success Series.

Senge, P. (1990). *The fifth discipline: The art and practice of the learning organization*. New York: Doubleday.

Surowiecki, J. (2004). *The wisdom of crowds: Why the many are smarter than the few and how collective wisdom shapes business, economies, societies, and nations*. New York: Doubleday.

Yukl, B. (1989, November). Managerial leadership: A review of theory and research. *Journal of Management, 15*.

Dianne Crampton *developed the TIGERS team development model in 1987. TIGERS supports both public and private leaders and their teams with onsite and web-based services. Crampton has published in a business anthology endorsed by Stephen Covey and written for trade magazines. Merrill Lynch nominated her for* Inc. *magazine's regional small business and entrepreneurial awards. Her work with Native Americans was recognized at a United Nations–sponsored conference in 1994.*

Effective Executive Coaching
An Illustrative Case Study*

Leonard D. Goodstein

Summary

I have used a case study to identify what I regard as the critical ingredients of effective executive coaching. After describing in broad strokes my coaching engagement in this case, I extract eight basic principles that enhance the probability that an executive coaching process will be effective. The case study is used to provide an illustration of how each specific principle facilitated a successful outcome in that specific instance and how each of these principles can be used in effective executive coaching.

The Case

Tom had been the managing partner of a large, national law firm for almost a year. John, a senior partner in the firm who himself once had played Tom's role, had became concerned about Tom's reluctance to execute some important decisions. John contacted me and arranged a lunch meeting for the three of us to discuss the situation.

At the lunch, John was very candid about his concerns about Tom and strongly recommended that Tom engage me to be his coach, a decision with which Tom hesitantly agreed. We initially agreed to meet weekly to discuss the issues the firm faced and to determine whether working together would be helpful to him. Over a period of several months, Tom and I met regularly and reviewed in detail a variety of situations that faced the law firm, including the merging of several practice areas, retiring a troubled senior partner with performance problems, managing cultural differences between the firm and a recent acquisition, and the like.

---

*The names and some descriptive details of this case have been altered to protect the identity of the client.

The 2010 Pfeiffer Annual: Consulting.

During this time, we gradually built a relationship of openness and trust and Tom became more and more willing to confide in me. While he understood that a variety of situations required prompt action, he found it difficult to promptly address them, even though he had thoroughly discussed each of them with the executive committee, the firm's decision-making body. Thus the question arose of what prevented Tom from doing what he knew needed to be done and had endorsed doing.

As we discussed each of these necessary actions in detail, it became clear that most of these situations required some kind of confrontation, often with hardnosed, difficult people; after all, they were all lawyers. He found these confrontations exceedingly unpleasant and upsetting, and it became obvious that he had been avoiding them, hoping that the situation would be resolved without any action on his part.

Once this pattern of avoidance and the underlying reasons for the pattern became clear, the contract between Tom and me needed to be renegotiated. Rather than getting to know each other, the relationship needed to be focused on giving Tom the support he needed to tackle unpleasant situations. Our sessions now involved developing a detailed plan on how to approach each situation, rehearsing how Tom would handle objections, role playing various scenarios that might develop, and generally providing Tom with the courage he needed to handle confrontation. Further, he agreed to seek feedback regularly from John, the senior partner who had initiated the coaching process, to assess how he was doing and obtain additional support for his behavior change.

Over time, Tom became more and more confident and needed less and less preparation for doing what needed to be done, so I slowly began to disengage from the relationship. It had become clear that, while Tom would never enjoy confrontation, he now knew that he had the skills and emotional resilience to better fulfill the demands his role as managing partner of a large, complex organization required. We terminated our relationship with Tom stating his appreciation for my having coached him to be successful when it otherwise might not have occurred. Several years afterward, Tom called to inform me that he had decided to step down as managing partner to return full-time to the practice of his legal specialty, appellate law.

The Principles

The example of Tom illustrates the principles that I regard as essential to an effective executive coaching relationship. These include:

- The client must have clear evidence that a definable problem exists.

- The client must agree that the problem is solvable.

- The client must agree that coaching might help resolve the problem.

- There must be a clear contract between the coach and the client.

- The contract has to be renegotiated as the goals become clearer.

- The goals must be specific and limited.

- There has to be organizational support for the client's change.

- Once the refined goals are reached, the coaching relationship should end.

Let us now examine each of the points in greater detail.

The Client Must Have Clear Evidence That a Definable Problem Exists

All of us resist negative feedback. Each of us likes to believe that he or she is being the best that we can be. It usually takes hard evidence to convince someone that he or she has a problem, especially if you're "from management" and "here to help." Feedback from a single individual, although supported by strong evidence, is extremely likely to be discounted, even if that individual is the boss. "That's your opinion" may not be voiced, but it almost always lurks in the back of the recipient's mind.

Perhaps the most powerful evidence about the need for behavioral change comes from a 360-degree feedback instrument, especially when a skilled facilitator works to help the recipient understand, digest, and accept the feedback. Denying that ten to twelve other people all see you in a certain unflattering way is difficult, even for the most resistant person. When such negative feedback is coupled with an invitation to obtain coaching to work on improving certain negative aspects of one's behavior, it is difficult to reject such an opportunity.

Another useful approach involves using a well-validated psychological assessment, especially one that compares the client's responses with a large group of senior managers and executives. I have found the Hogan Development Survey (HDS) (Hogan & Hogan, 1998) to be very useful in executive coaching. The HDS is based on research conducted at the Center for Creative Leadership on why managers and executives get derailed. Derailment occurs when a manager or executive who has had a history of rather continual success suddenly goes off the track and is seen as failing. The HDS profile compares the client's responses to a database of over 2,000 managers and executives on eleven scales, each of which involves a specific pattern of behavior that has been identified as leading to derailment. Among the scales are Excitable, Skeptical, and Cautious. Reviewing the HDS profile with a client usually provides hard data that is quite difficult for the client to deny or refute.

In the case of Tom, no 360-degree feedback was obtained, nor was any psychological test administered. Rather, a well-respected and well-liked authority, John, was willing to confront Tom with a good deal of anecdotal evidence about negative behavior that needed to be addressed. John's status, his long-time relationship with Tom, and his skill in addressing issues made it impossible for Tom to reject John's feedback. Unfortunately, there are too few Johns in our society, persons willing and able to identify problem behavior and to recommend positive steps to address such behavior.

The Client Must Agree That the Problem Is Solvable

The second step in effective executive coaching requires a positive view that behavioral change is possible. A belief in the immutability of human behavior is unlikely to lead to successful coaching. Far too often, under these circumstances, potential clients will argue that this is the way that they're made and it's useless to try to change. They often provide examples of their prior unsuccessful attempts at changing their behavior and conclude, "What's the use?"

Given such attitudes, I have found that attempting to change this belief system is difficult, if not impossible, to accomplish and suggest that withdrawal from any effort at coaching is the best alternative. It should be noted that, during these early negotiations, it can become apparent that other problems in the potential client's life, such as a pending divorce, alcoholism, long-standing neurosis, or even psychosis, make coaching inadvisable. Coaching is not psychotherapy!

Tom clearly understood that his behavior was not meeting the expectations of his organization and strongly believed that he could change it. He initially pointed out that he had never failed at anything in his life and that he was not planning to begin now.

The Client Must Agree That Coaching Might Help Resolve the Problem

The client must be helped to understand the nature of the coaching process and what positive outcomes are possible from such a process. It is the responsibility of the prospective coach to describe clearly the coaching process, what he or she would expect from the client, and what the client, in turn, could expect from the coach.

Coaches differ in their approaches, both from one another and in how they would approach different clients. For example, some coaches require that they be allowed to observe the client performing at his or her work site; others ask to interview peers and subordinates. I have used these and other approaches, depending on the nature of the client situation. My point here is that the approach in any particular case must be made clear to the client, even if that approach may later be changed. In describing the process, the coach needs to make clear to the client how the agreed-on process is likely to help the client resolve the presenting situation.

Tom quickly understood that he had been procrastinating in implementing a variety of decisions, but was not clear as to why this was occurring. The initial coaching contract was to help Tom figure out why he was blocked from implementing decisions that he himself had participated in making, as this understanding might enable him to become a better implementer. Tom agreed that these steps were necessary if he was to succeed in his role as managing director.

There Must Be a Clear Contract Between the Coach and the Client

A contract is an agreement between two willing parties about what each will do in the future. Nowhere is this more important than in coaching. The client and the coach must commit to what each will do to make the coaching process successful. The frequency and location of the sessions should be made specific, and both parties must agree that these sessions will be of high priority. If there are financial considerations involved in the process, these have to be spelled out. Some coaches prefer to have all of these details memorialized in a written contract. While I rarely find this necessary, I understand that such written contracts can be used as powerful weapons in the coaching process.

The coaching contract, written or oral, should include the requirement for the client to be open and candid, for the coach to listen closely and ask hard questions, and for both parties to maintain strict confidentiality about what transpires in the process. Most importantly, the contract should spell out the goals of the coaching process in clear, behavioral terms. These goals should be trackable, and, where possible, mileposts for achieving the goals should be included. Almost invariably, the initial contract should be to explore the client's understanding of his or her situation and to develop a working relationship. Once the client and the coach can agree on the problem behavior and how it might be addressed in coaching, a new contract is required—one that clearly identifies the behavior to be changed and how coaching will facilitate that change.

With Tom, all of these specifications were met. The law firm would pay for my services when invoiced and approved by Tom. There was clarity about when and where we would meet, and only on one occasion did he cancel a coaching session because of an internal emergency. It was made quite explicit that the initial goal was to understand how Tom delayed implementing decisions and why this occurred. An important point to recognize is that the cause of Tom's problem was never part of the contract, nor should it have been. Such an inquiry changes the coaching process to psychotherapy, which should never be part of the contract.

The Contract Has to Be Renegotiated as the Goals Become Clearer

As we noted in the previous section, the initial contract involves having the client and coach get to know one another, establish trust, and develop a joint understanding of the problem behavior. Such an exploration involves identifying when the problem behavior exhibits itself, the cues that engender the behavior, and how much awareness the client has that the behavior is about to occur and his or her awareness of the reactions of others to that behavior.

When there is a clear, joint understanding of the circumstances under which the behavior occurs and when the client shows awareness of the behavior and its consequences, the coach can begin to suggest ways that coaching can help remedy the situation. These include rehearsing situations, role playing, involving peers in signaling that the client is beginning to behave in the inappropriate fashion, and so on. This approach to coaching assumes that awareness and a conscious decision to modify one's behavior, coupled with external support, can result in behavioral change.

One important element of the contract is making it explicit that this coaching relationship is time limited. In the best of all possible worlds, this would occur when there is clear evidence that the changes that have been contracted for have been achieved and stabilized. But there needs to be clarity about how this relationship will end, regardless of whether or not the desired changes have been realized. We will return to this topic later.

As was noted in Tom's case, the contract dictated that Tom would identify situations with a high potential for confrontation, discern how that confrontation might occur, and develop a set of plans for effectively dealing with that situation. The contract also stipulated that Tom agree to rehearse how he would respond, to engage in role playing, and to figure out how he might involve his peers in order of the degree of potential confrontation, beginning with the easy ones and working his way up the list.

The Goals Must Be Specific and Limited

Effective coaching requires that the coach and the client set realistic, specific behavioral changes as the goal of the process. These goals should be set as the client and the coach gain an in-depth understanding of the non-functional behaviors that led to the initiation of the coaching relationship. Moreover, the goals should be modest, achievable, and capable of being tracked.

The goals of effective coaching should be modest, as behavior change is difficult to accomplish. Experienced psychotherapists recognize that even long-term, intensive psychotherapy usually produces only limited results. To assume that a more limited coaching process can produce a personality transplant is a snare and a delusion. An effective coaching process involves setting modest goals, goals that are achievable.

My experience is that most clients referred for coaching are not high fliers, but rather persons who have been derailed and need remediation for the behaviors that led to the derailment. It is rare that clients are referred for coaching to enhance nascent leadership abilities or to develop a high-potential executive for the future. Even in such cases, clear behavioral goals have to be set and tracked. Without such agreed-on goals, it would not be possible to develop a coaching strategy and a plan of action.

It should be clear from our analysis of the case of Tom that clear, specific, and achievable goals were set. These goals led to a plan of action that, when implemented, resulted in the goals being met. Tom was quite satisfied with the outcome of the coaching process, and as a by-product of this process, it became clear to Tom that filling the role of the managing partner of a large, complex organization was a poor fit for him and enabled him to return later to his true love, the practice of law.

There Has to Be Organizational Support for the Client's Change

Behavior change never occurs in a vacuum. The behaviors that are the target of the change always are demonstrated in an organizational setting. Over time the people in this setting have developed ways of responding to the expected behavior. These responses often have the effect of sustaining the problem behavior and, in some cases, even eliciting it. This vicious cycle needs to be broken. While the coach can help identify these responses, positive behavior change is more likely to occur when there is institutional support for this change. As Goldsmith (2009) has noted, involving key stakeholders in the change process is critically important.

Goldsmith goes on to point out that these stakeholders need to do three important things to facilitate positive change. One is to "give up on the past," that is, do not remind the client of how bad things used to be. Two, "be helpful and supportive" of the observed changes, even when they are incomplete and awkward. And three, "tell the truth," that is, do not either minimize or exaggerate the observed changes. Provide honest feedback; simply tell it as it is!

In Tom's case, we were able to enlist John, who made the initial referral, as a stakeholder who could and would monitor Tom's attempts at change. His wealth of experience and his stature, coupled with his commitment to Tom's success, provided the necessary organizational support that resulted in positive change.

Once the Refined Goals Are Reached, the Coaching Relationship Should End

Coaching is a time-limited phenomenon. As we noted above, how the coaching relationship will be terminated should be part of the ongoing contractual process. Ideally, as signs appear that the desired changes are now part of the client's behavioral repertoire, the coach should begin to reduce the frequency of coaching contacts, specifying how the relationship will end. While many clients desire some continuing relationship with the coach, these should be minimized and brief.

More than a few clients do not seem to profit from coaching, even with competent experienced coaches. The dysfunctional behaviors that led to the referral may be too deeply rooted in psychological issues that are beyond access by a coaching intervention. As the coach begins to recognize that little change is occurring and the client seems "stuck" in his or her existing pattern, this lack of movement must be addressed regularly in the coaching sessions. If such feedback does not unfreeze the client, termination has to be the focus of the relationship, together with suggestions about seeking more intensive help.

Termination of a coaching relationship is often difficult for both parties. Often the client has become dependent on the coach for advice and support. The client wonders whether he or she can sustain these changes without this help. Thus, weaning the client by gradually reducing both the frequency and length of contacts is a useful strategy, coupled with encouraging the client to rely more and more on the institutional support systems that he or she has used to effect the changes.

But termination can also be difficult for the coach. Coaches form emotional attachments to their clients and have a genuine commitment to the clients' success, making termination troublesome for the coach. And the fact that a client is a source of revenue for the coach is not an insignificant factor. Coaches have to manage the termination process actively and sort out their own motivation for wanting to maintain a relationship with a client. Discussing this issue with a senior colleague is a useful strategy, helping the coach to develop greater self-understanding and to facilitate the termination process.

My relationship with Tom ended with a reduction in the frequency of contacts. Because I had to travel some distance for our meetings, shorter sessions seemed inappropriate, and we therefore agreed to talk by telephone on a set schedule less and less frequently. And our final contact was when he called years later to announce that he was returning to the full-time practice of law.

Conclusion

Effective executive coaching requires planning. Since most referrals to coaches are for persons who have either derailed or are seen as highly likely to derail, the reasons for the derailment must serve as the focus of the coaching process. The initial phase of the plan involves the client and the coach developing a joint understanding of the reason for the referral—what is the real problem—and its impact on the client's career. The next stage of the plan is helping the client understand that these behaviors are changeable, coupled with an agreement to work on reducing or altering the behaviors involved in creating the problem.

Throughout this process, there must be a clear contract between the client and the coach about the nature of their relationship and its goals, and any changes in that contract and its goals must be made explicit. Any successful plan has to have explicit, modest, and achievable goals for changing the client's behavior, and there must be institutional support for the client and these goals. Finally, the plan requires a clear understanding about how termination of the coaching relationship will occur.

While the nature of the client's problems necessarily will determine how the coach will apply these principles, and acknowledging that there will be variations as a function of the coach's background of training and experience, I believe that following these broad principles is necessary for effective executive coaching.

References

Goldsmith, M. (2009). Coaching for behavioral change. In E. Biech (Ed.), *The 2009 Pfeiffer annual: Consulting*. San Francisco: Pfeiffer.

Hogan, R., & Hogan, J. (1998). *Hogan development survey manual*. Tulsa, OK: Hogan Assessment Systems.

Leonard D. Goodstein, Ph.D., *is a Washington, D.C.-based consulting psychologist who specializes in executive coaching, strategic planning, and strategic management—the implementation of the strategic plan. He is also a principal with Psichometrics International, LLC, an online, pre-employment assessment organization. His latest book,* A Practical Guide to Job Analysis, *was published in 2009 by Pfeiffer.*

Assessments and Coaching
An Incongruent Pair
Teri-E Belf and Rafael Rivera

Summary

In this controversial paper, the authors, representing different cultures, educational backgrounds, and professional fields, share how they came to the same conclusion that assessments do not belong in the coaching profession. For this article, assessment refers to an instrument given to a client for the purpose of giving the client data about him- or herself. Assessment does not refer to the measurement of successful achievement of the client's goals. The authors explore how the philosophy behind external assessments is inconsistent with the internal assessment philosophy of coaching.

Many coaching professionals think that the process of coaching includes, even requires, that assessments be done. When we established the foundation for coaching, we did not include any formal assessments. The purpose of coaching was, and still is, to help clients increase their awareness and increase their responsibility, that is to say, their ability to respond to the awareness. To gain awareness, clients go inside. A core belief of coaching is that clients have their own answers and, through the application of the coaching process, clients have the opportunity to discover that internal wisdom.

Belf's Perspective

A book that significantly influenced me in college was *One Little Boy* by Dorothy Baruch. After a school assessment, a young boy was told he was a slow learner; this result earmarked him for slow learner classes. Several years later, someone reversed this label and began working with him as if he were a smart student. Guess what? This little boy became a smart student. The earlier assessment was incorrect;

we become who we are told we are. Our identity is often formed by sometimes incorrect external feedback.

Lest you think my bias against using assessments in coaching is unfounded, my background and dissertation were all about assessments. My academic background includes a master's degree and sixty credits beyond (C.A.G.S.) in education research, evaluation, and learning. I chose this field because I wanted to explore how people learn, and measuring learning involves assessments and evaluation instruments. I was steeped in assessments.

In that decade of my work life, I was certified to do almost every achievement and IQ test that existed in English as well as those that were pictorially and kinesthetically based so they could be administered cross-culturally.

My distaste began when I encountered many experiences during which people adopted the test results as so legitimate that they stopped being open to self-evaluation and self-validation. Test-takers would consistently report that the results of the test were already known to them; the test results merely validated what they intuitively knew. Now they had labels, someone else's labels. Inappropriately, they would lock in their identity based on the test results; for example, someone who took the Myers-Briggs Type Indicator (MBTI) might say, "I am an ESTJ." Those trained to administer assessments are taught that the assessment is merely an indication, not the truth, whole truth, and nothing but the truth. However, when people receive results, they forget that and assume the identity of the label given to them. They forget that they have their own wisdom internally and proceed to rely on the external assessment as proof of who they are.

The Origins of Coaching: No Assessments

When I entered the field of coaching in 1987, there were very few coaches, and none of us were using assessments. A few years later, in a leadership capacity as chair of the Credentials Committee for the International Coach Federation, my committee formulated the Accreditation, Credentialing, and Continuing platform for the profession. Our core assumption was that clients have their own answers and inner wisdom, and that they can access, assess, and interpret their answers through the guidance of the coaching process.

Confusion has arisen in the public mind because other professions such as organization development, career management, and management consulting do use assessments. For their purposes, assessments are important tools. As coaching has risen in popularity, many of these professionals are now referring to themselves as coaches, although they continue to do the same thing they were doing before. The public then assumes incorrectly that coaches are supposed to use assessments. This inaccurate conclusion is especially prevalent in the business and executive side of coaching.

For example, organization development is a profession that has introduced assessments such as DiSC, FIRO-B, and MBTI, as well as 360-degree feedback. The intention of an assessment is to allow clients to learn more about self through the gathering of data deemed valid by the research done by test developers. Accurate interpretations must be done by those trained to do them. Often coaches are brought in to take the results of the interpretations and create a development plan or coach an existing development plan.

Whereas coaching and organization development may be complementary processes and procedures, they are not the same profession, and each profession needs to be honored for the contributions and value it offers. Coaching does not include assessments. Organization development does.

Coaching in Business Without Using Assessments

I have had experiences with corporate clients who ask me to do executive coaching and ask which assessment I use. I explain that I do not use assessments as a part of coaching. They can reallocate the money for something else. My work with clients helps them reveal their own assessments and interpretations. Most of the time, even though the sponsors are surprised, they allow me to proceed. If feedback from others is needed, such as from staff, peers, or the boss, the client learns how to ask for (and receive) the feedback directly. There is no need to administer confidential instruments so that the source of the feedback is anonymous. Do we want clandestine communication or open dialogue in organizations? In our lives?

Rivera's Perspective

Coming from a different culture and perspective, I learned early on that my answers to some of the questions in established personality assessment tools corresponded to my unique and unaccounted-for views or interpretations. My cultural background and speaking English as a second language meant also that how I perceived or interpreted an assessment questionnaire could lead to assessment results that were on average less representative of who I was and how I thought. I will always remember a dialogue with a colleague following a Myers-Briggs assessment of all the employees in the unit. We were discussing a particular question for which the response choices included the words "just" and "fair." It turns out that, even though we had the same preference, we responded differently based on those words. For this colleague, her choice was clearly based on the definitions of the words. For me, the choice was based on my personal experience with these two words as a minority living in the United States.

I use a number of assessment tools and techniques in organization development interventions. These provide some baseline data and spark the dialogue among team members. They help increase awareness among team members of overt and covert behaviors and processes that impact the organizational environment and how individuals relate to each other. The focus of these interventions, even when the consultant focuses on individuals as part of the plan, is still the organization and how can individuals work better together.

I was introduced to coaching while I was finishing my master's degree in OD. What appealed to me the most about coaching was the client-centered approach and the core premise that the client has all the answers. Coaching as I experienced it engaged the whole person. I was already familiar with humanistic psychology and the work of Maslow and Rogers, among others. Coaching appealed to me as the next logical step, engaging the client at a deeper level in a non-therapeutic or prescriptive client-coach relationship. In this newly defined context, I found personality assessment tools limiting. There is no single assessment tool or combination of tools yet that can capture the whole person and his or her being. In my practice, I find that focusing the client early on the results and categories of personality assessment tools can serve a specific purpose in an OD intervention. Yet using an assessment as a starting point in coaching is contrary to the ultimate goal in coaching practice, which is to help clients understand their deeper potential by helping them access their own best answers. In most cases, in order for clients in a coaching relationship to be able to reach their own best answers, clients must let go of categories that limit their self-images and how they perceive their current environments.

When I use an assessment tool in an intervention, I see myself as a consultant. I am gathering data, analyzing it, and sharing it with the client. This is usually followed by a number of recommendations based on the goals and how the data analysis impacts the client system. On the other hand, using assessment tools in coaching limits my grasp of the whole person because of the use of prescribed categories. In my experience, there is a flawed presumption that we can use the same personality assessment tool on different individuals with similarly applicable results. Every time I am approached by a client or colleague who identifies him- or herself by a four-letter MBTI profile ("I'm an ENTJ"), I respond, "I have news for you. You are much more than that."

As a coach, I understand that part of my role is to provide clients the opportunity to come up with their own holistic assessment, focusing on who they are and coming to terms with the depth of their unlimited potential. Coaching at its best opens up a path to self-discovery, awareness, and a desired future.

Conclusion

In summary, coaches Rivera and Belf, representing different cultures, educational backgrounds, and professional fields, shared how they came to the same conclusion: that assessments do not belong in the profession of coaching.

Whereas assessments do offer caution that the data is not meant to be absolute, people often rely on assessments because they have been validated through research, cost a lot of money, and require expertise to deliver and interpret. Some developers of assessment instruments remind us that data are intended to identify preferences and leanings and are based in probabilities. Even so, this is all external data. When we rely exclusively on external data, it hampers our ability to access our own internal information.

Do we not have the ability and inner wisdom to interpret who we are? Coaching says we do have that capability. Coaching challenges clients to access their *own* information.

One big difference between assessment and coaching is that assessment presumes that external instruments are necessary to access data. Coaching is based on the premise that one can access that data directly.

As one client put it, "I learned to trust I have the knowledge I didn't know I had, and I learned how to access that knowledge I didn't know I could access."

In true coaching form, we leave the reader with questions and challenges that open up considerations for using, or not using, assessments in coaching. Can you assume that all the information you have ever received from an assessment is correct? How do you know which elements of an assessment feedback are accurate and which are not? To what extent do you need an assessor to tell you whether an assessment is accurate or not? Bring to mind a time when you received assessment feedback that you perceived was accurate. What were the implications for your behavior and choices? Now, bring to mind a time when you received assessment feedback that you perceived was inaccurate. What were the implications for your behavior and choices? And the most important question: What might happen if you began to trust your own internal wisdom?

Our ability to trust and access our inner wisdom through self-discovery is one of the best outcomes (gifts) a client can obtain from being coached.

Teri-E Belf, MA, CAGS, MCC, *is a purposeful and inspiring coaching leader, coach trainer, coach, and author with twenty years in the coaching field and eighteen years of HRD and T&D management experience. Her current passions include serving on the ICF Ethics Committee and developing DVDs to train managers in coaching competencies. She is the founder of Success Unlimited Network®, LLC, an international coaching community, and director of an ICF-accredited coach training program.*

Rafael Rivera, B.A., M.S.O.D., *is an organizational specialist at the National Education Association in Washington, D.C., with twenty-one years of experience in training and education, organization development, community and membership organizing.*

Communicating with Professional Savvy

Karen A. Travis

Summary

In the beginning, consultants were valued primarily for their technical expertise. Today, the pressure for consultants to have technical competency *and* good people skills is unquestionable.

Knowing how to create and maintain meaningful relationships while providing superior solutions is not natural for everyone. However, just as we can learn our technical skills, consultants can also learn how to communicate, specifically to manage a client conversation.

Providing experts with a tool that can help them manage client conversations will go a long way toward ensuring professional success.

Have you ever ridden a unicycle? For most of us, that is not a pretty picture. We spin, we twist, we wobble back and forth, and then fall off! Few of us ever master a unicycle. Perhaps we achieve some degree of balance or, if we work at it, ride around for a few feet before we hit the first bump and fall off again.

Although most of us won't ever master a unicycle, many of us can ride a bike (even if we won't be winning the Tour de France). Having two wheels instead of one makes a lot of difference.

So what do a unicycle and a bicycle have to do with your consulting skills? Let me explain.

The bicycle's back wheel represents your expertise. Its front wheel corresponds to the conversation you're having with a client or a co-worker. Your back-wheel expertise gives you power to propel things forward, but just as important is your front-wheel skill to steer the conversation in the right direction.

Why Master the Conversation

When you master a conversational process, you significantly improve your client relationships by making the ride go as smooth as riding a bicycle. Using proven methodology to manage your conversations, you'll be better able to:

- *Figure out what someone really needs*—steering in the right direction.

- *Maintain good communication*—keeping all pathways clear.

- *Achieve cooperation* — maintaining balance when you ride through the rough spots.

You can also proactively manage the relationship by:

- Modeling productive behaviors;

- Reflecting back a client's behavior; and

- Turning around a client's uncooperative, resistant attitude.

Background

For those who have been in the consulting business for quite some time, we know that it has changed a lot. Technical competence is still necessary, but it's not enough to ensure success anymore. Many consultants rightfully claim to be technical experts in their respective fields, but when choices abound, people select their consultants (or their computers) based on other factors that appeal to them. For example, people have been known to buy a computer because it came in a cow-spotted box or because the laptop's casing is sparkling fuchsia.

In the early 1990s when software innovations first allowed more businesses and individuals to file their own tax returns, progressive firms realized they needed to focus more on clients' concerns about managing their investments or running a business, rather than figuring out what was left over and how much to pay the government. Even if you are a techie or an accountant, knowing how to deal with people is critical. Those who can't deal effectively with others are squeezed out or kept in the back room.

Building your conversation management expertise (CME) provides a structured, practical process for clarifying client needs, identifying solutions and opportunities, and resolving conflict. And it ensures you are front and center. Having productive conversations is crucial. When anyone—client, colleague, or family member—walks away dissatisfied, it will hurt you.

Take Charge of Your Client Interactions

So how do you assume responsibility for the client relationship and lead the way to productive conversations, optimal solutions, and mutually satisfactory relationships? Remember, satisfaction depends primarily on that front bicycle wheel being properly inflated. It's not good enough to react to clients, so we must take charge on their behalf—that's what they're paying for. They appreciate having one less thing to worry about, because we're doing it (or anticipating) it for them.

Defining Reciprocal Behavior

One way to build positive momentum in our client work takes advantage of a natural inclination to reflect back another person's behavior. This tendency plays a significant part in our interactions with clients and others. It's easiest to "go with the flow" and let things happen. The client acts; we react. Assuming that the client sets a productive tone and direction, this approach can work. Otherwise, we end up reflecting negative behaviors and working to our own disadvantage.

Great consultants are proactive, not reactive.

Because people tend to act toward us like we act toward them, the practice of reflecting behavior has been elevated to the status of a psychological law called the "Law of Reciprocity." How we react to a person can depend on how that person first acts toward us. For example, if the other person speaks loudly, we tend to react by speaking loudly, too. If the other person acts anxious, we're inclined to become anxious, too.

The question is: Who reacts to whom? Whose behavior determines the tone and course of an interaction?

Usually the tone is set by the person who first communicates something beyond a neutral attitude. Person A "acts" and Person B "reacts." If, however, Person B instead acts in a manner of his or her own choosing, then Person B usually sets the tone for that interaction.

We role model behaviors we want our clients to reciprocate rather than automatically reacting to what they say or do. We act deliberately to achieve professional, productive momentum in our interactions.

Initiating Desired Behaviors

How do we develop productive momentum in each interaction? By demonstrating desired behaviors such as:

- Respect for that person and his or her organization;

- Attentiveness;

- Understanding; and

- Helpfulness.

This influences the client to reciprocate by:

- Respecting us and our company;

- Paying attention to us;

- Understanding our "needs" (e.g., a schedule conflict with another client, a need to charge for services rendered);

- Supporting us; and

- Having confidence in our ability.

When we influence clients to reciprocate the positive behaviors we role model, we establish rapport. For example, little things such as using the client's name, listening attentively, and even dressing appropriately demonstrate our respect for the client and help us earn respect in return. By making even small adjustments in what we say and do, we can achieve big results.

When to Reciprocate Behavior

Just as clients can reflect back our behaviors, we can also reciprocate some of their behaviors. First, it's good to accommodate another person's preferences. When we deal with someone who talks more slowly than we do, it's natural to slow down, too. If the other person acts more formally, we show our regard by becoming more formal ourselves.

This accommodation, known as consideration, is called selective reaction. Ideally, we don't want to be so set in our ways that we fail to be responsive and considerate. Say a client is discussing vacation plans and greets us in a relaxed, open manner. We respond by acting in a casual way. But another speaks abruptly when telling us he or she is in the midst of budget planning. We can respond appropriately by being brief, but not by being abrupt in return.

Reciprocating a person's behavior also gives us a way to encourage more of that behavior. We gain by responding in kind to desirable behaviors such as:

- Friendliness

- Reasonableness

- Cooperativeness

- Enthusiasm

If you want to learn more about behavioral tendencies and human behavior, assessments such as the DiSC® Personality Profile and Myers-Briggs Type Indicator® focus on helping us understand our own behavior and style preferences and how to adapt to the behavior of others.

Mitigating Unproductive Behaviors

We also need to minimize the harm done by clients' unproductive behaviors. If the person acts uncooperatively, it's important to maintain a cooperative tone while exploring what has bothered him or her. If a person is upset and vents angry accusations, we don't react with anger. Instead, we demonstrate calmness, respect, and self-control. This counteracts the anger by influencing the person to reciprocate productive behaviors.

If someone is angry or upset, first calm him or her down before trying to have a rational conversation; we don't want to totally ignore unproductive behaviors.

Other unproductive behaviors that are important to counteract include:

- *Resistance*—by being cooperative;

- *Argumentative behavior*—by being agreeable;

- *Blaming behavior*—by being understanding; and

- *Demanding behavior*—by being helpful.

Occasionally, difficult or angry people won't turn around completely when they see our behavior. But although they may not reflect or immediately acknowledge it, at some level they recognize professionalism and respect us for it. Our next interaction with that person promises to be much better.

Consultants Are Human Too

No doubt, we probably express negative behaviors at some point, whether or not a client has provoked us. We're most likely to lapse into negative behaviors when we become tired, pressured, or bored. Having too little stress in our lives can be as dangerous as having too much. The relationship between negative behaviors and stress is shown in Figure 1. It's important to recognize this relationship so we can avoid falling into counterproductive work behaviors when our stress level is very low or, more likely, very high.

The three most common negative responses are insincerity, sarcasm, and what's known as "zero response." Typically, we just slightly edge into these negative behaviors so that it's an undercurrent in the relationship, rather than becoming flagrantly unprofessional.

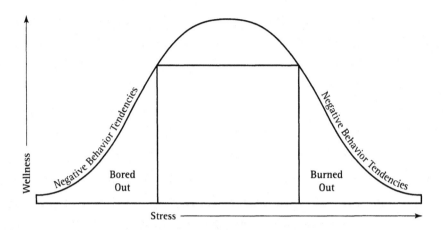

Figure 1. The Relationship Between Stress and Unprofessional Behavior Tendencies

For example, some consultants start sounding phony or automatic. They throw out sing-song, routine phrases that communicate their lack of regard for the other person.

The worst offense is a "zero response," which is a deliberate failure to respond to another person. By saying nothing, we show disregard. In fact, being silent when the person expects a response is insulting. And it's just as insulting to avoid acknowledging someone's feelings by changing the subject, as in this exchange:

Client: "This bill is outrageous. There's no way we used this many hours."

Response: "Can I have your account number?"

The ultimate "zero response" is cutting someone off or avoiding contact completely. Harold Ross, the first editor of *The New Yorker*, became legendary for dodging contact with his clients and colleagues. He even went so far as to install a mirror system in the hallway leading to the restroom so that he could make the trip only when he knew the coast was clear of anyone he might have to deal with.

Although this example might seem exaggerated, it happens. I recently had a consulting colleague admit to going to his client's office when he knew the key person was out of the office.

Simply put, we should act the way we want others to act—or continue acting—toward us. Some behaviors we initiate or reciprocate; others we counteract.

The Bicycle Analogy Revisited

Conversation management expertise is a fundamental part of the expertise we need to conduct our client interactions. This type of expertise has become as important in today's professional world as our technical expertise. Indeed, technical and conversation management expertise have become as interdependent as the two wheels of a bicycle (see Figure 2).

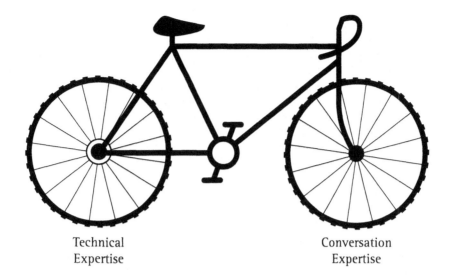

Technical
Expertise

Conversation
Expertise

Figure 2. Well–Balanced Conversational Expertise

We consultants typically have a technical and nontechnical (customer-facing) side to our jobs. Remember, the technical expertise is like the back wheel that propels the bike while the front wheel steers it. Technical expertise moves us forward, but we always need conversation management expertise to get to where we ought to go.

No matter how technically capable or experienced we are, we can't succeed in the consulting profession if we aren't good at working with people. Not only do we have to fix the client's problem, but as someone recently told me, we may have to "fix" the client, too!

Since most of us are not psychologists or counselors (and don't want to be), "fixing" the client means having the ability to communicate effectively. And not only is good communication sure to improve customer satisfaction, but it will be less frustrating for everyone involved.

Conversation Management Expertise (CME)

At my company, Sigma, we use and teach a four-step conversation management process called LIST® (see Figure 3). The steps in the process are designed to be used sequentially. They are:

1. *LEARN* the other person's perspective and needs.

2. *INDICATE* you understand the person's needs and perspective.

3. *SOLVE* the problem with an action plan that satisfies the needs.

4. *TELL* the person what to expect next as a result of the solution.

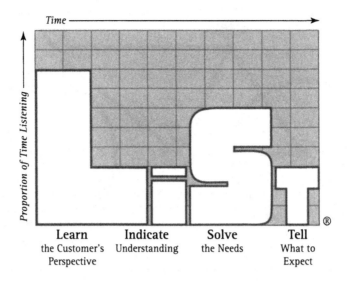

Figure 3. The Proportion of Time Spent Listening Versus Time Spent on Each Step in the LIST® Process

This article describes a simplified view of the LIST® process. Sometimes, as consultants, we are learning sequentially or simultaneously from individuals who are not only representing their needs, but are speaking for the organization too. For the sake of simplicity, we'll focus on managing one conversation at a time.

While the LIST approach works for many reasons, a paramount one is that *you never put the back wheel before the front.* Said another way, if you're already providing solutions, but you haven't learned what the client *really* needs, you're sure to get off track. It's never a good feeling seeing the client later and the conversation starts with, "Oh, by the way, I forgot to mention something." That could change everything. But when you get it right—the front wheel before the back wheel—you always move forward, and therefore more efficiently.

This approach is powerful because it allows others to meaningfully participate in the conversation, providing information that adds to the expertise you already have. In this way, it lets you guide the conversation like an expert cyclist.

LIST

Learn

As consultants, we are trained to glean only relevant information regarding a person's problem or opportunity and ask questions to sort fact from fiction. As a result of our training, we tend to "filter out" and discount what people say about their concerns, other related problems, or future plans. We focus on "just the facts."

But learning about the problem from the client's perspective and including a wide range of needs is wise. Again, to keep things simple, we assume that we learn primarily by listening. In fact, during the course of the conversation, it's best to listen in order to learn. But as one workshop participant recently told me, "I've spent years trying to be a better listener, but I didn't bother to learn what the person really meant."

Tip for the L-Step: Not sure if you have all the information? Simply ask: "Is there anything else?" and be quiet.

Indicate

In the second step—Indicate—take a moment to summarize what you heard from the other person's perspective. *Why* is the stated need important? You should paraphrase a person's concern, not repeat it back to him or her word for word. Once we've acknowledged the reason(s) for moving forward, we can put our technical expertise to work. Finally, this is what you wanted to do all along!

Tip for the I-Step: If a client keeps repeating his or her concerns, it's time to try an Indicate statement. The client is waiting for you to acknowledge him or her.

We don't suggest tabling your expertise; just hold off for a bit. Only offer solutions after (1) you have learned what's really going on from the client's perspective and (2) you have let the client know that you understand.

Solve

Depending on specific areas of expertise, we all have different ways of determining viable solutions. In the third step—Solve—ask fact-finding questions and do whatever else you need to do to recommend the best course of action. Given what you know, you're aiming for a solution that's both logical and comfortable for everyone concerned.

Let me emphasize the importance of suspending our desire to ask questions right away. When we begin by gathering information that's important to *us*, we may miss talking about what's important to our clients. Once we begin our questioning, the clients may not provide us with information that could be helpful because we disrupt their thought processes. Even if a problem or opportunity is urgent, going straight to solutions without letting them fully describe all their needs or concerns does not lay a sound foundation for a strong relationship.

Tip for the S-Step: Ask clarifying questions, in a logical order, based on what the client has shared with you. Use language the client understands and demonstrate your expertise.

Tell

In the last step, Tell, we explain what the person should know about the plan of action—the proposed solution. In this step, not only do we verify that the client understands the solution, but we verify that he or she *accepts* our solution. If it's not accepted, what should be done next? Repeat the LIST process. Go back to the L-step and repeat the process until you have an agreed-on plan of action.

Tip for the T-Step: Follow up with an email to confirm the details. Seeing the agreed-on action in writing can reinforce the conversation or uncover an objection that was missed earlier.

When to Use Your Conversation Management Expertise

There's no need to go through all the LIST steps when the person asks for something that you can easily provide. For a routine request, we suggest you simply "learn and confirm" to make sure your proposed solution meets the client's requirements. However, all too often, we assume that the client's request is routine. This is especially true the longer we have a relationship with the client.

A LIST conversation may take ninety seconds or it may take ninety minutes, but such a conversation can always help to probe a bit deeper, before assuming the request is routine. LIST is useful for consultants in dealing with people who:

- Need your advice or help;

- Are complaining, angry, or demanding; and/or

- Could use more of your products or services but don't know it yet!

While we have focused our conversation management expertise on consulting, trainers can also use LIST in managing participants who may have objections to your training class. Rather than taking them out to the hall and asking them to stop disrupting your class, with LIST you can have a respectful and understanding conversation in front of the entire class. As the old adage goes, if one person is thinking it, others probably are too.

Conclusion

With practice, you'll find using your conversation management expertise (in concert with your technical expertise) as smooth and easy as riding a bicycle. At first, it may seem like your conversations take longer, as you spend more time listening. However, with time, you'll reap the benefits. Your conversations will solve problems, maintain rapport, and achieve what you and your clients want—moving forward together. So take command of the people side of your job and steer your way to more productive, mutually satisfactory relationships with clients (and others, too!). Managing productive conversations is fundamental to successful (and enjoyable) client relations.

References

DiSC® is a registered trademark of Inscape Publishing.

LIST® is a registered trademark of Sigma Performance Solutions, Inc.

LIST® 1993–2008 Sigma Performance Solutions, Inc. LIST was originally published in *Take Charge! How to Manage Your Customer Relationships* by Grace Major, Sigma, 1994.

Myers-Briggs Type Indicator® is a registered trademark of Consulting Psychologists Press, Inc.

Karen A. Travis *is the president of Sigma Performance Solutions, Inc. A professional trainer, consultant, and frequent keynote speaker. Travis graduated from Cornell University with a bachelor's in business management and The Johns Hopkins University with a master's in applied behavioral science. Sigma provides training, coaching, and consulting for leading organizations worldwide in high-tech, healthcare, and financial services, using LIST® and other tools to leverage technical expertise with productive conversations to improve and sustain business results.*

Successful Organization Development and Growing Pains

Eric G. Flamholtz and Yvonne Randle

Summary

This article reviews a framework for understanding and managing the process of successful organization development in business enterprises. It also summarizes recent empirical research designed to test the framework. Finally, it examines some of the implications for practicing managers and leaders.

As used here, "organization development" refers to the process of developing the set of organizational capabilities or the "form" required by an enterprise as it grows in size and complexity. If the process is done well, a business enterprise will thrive and prosper. If done inadequately, the organization will suffer.

This article presents a specific organizational life cycle model (Flamholtz, 1986, 1995) that can be used to measure the point at which specific transitions in the development of an enterprise should occur. The article presents this model in conjunction with an organizational effectiveness or success model (Flamholtz, 1986, 1995) that has been and is being empirically tested (Flamholtz, 2003) to indicate what needs to be done for successful organization development as well as what happens when organization development is unsuccessful (that is, "growing pains").

The Continuous Challenge of Organization Development

Practicing managers are faced with the problem of building and sustaining successful business organizations. This is an extraordinarily complex process and requires the ability to make adjustments based on changes in the market (customer tastes and preferences), the competition, technological progress, market trends, and the size and complexity of the organizations themselves in response to prior growth.

One critical aspect of organization development concerns the problems that emerge as a result of "suboptimal" organization development. These problems have been termed "growing pains" (Flamholtz & Randle, 2007). These growing pains are symptoms that something has gone wrong in the growth and development of a business enterprise. They are symptoms of organizational distress and an early warning or leading indicator of future organizational difficulties, including financial difficulties.

In fact, organizations can literally "choke" on their own growth when they have not developed the internal capabilities to support it (Flamholtz & Randle, 1987). The challenge of organization development is a continuous rather than a one-time task. Life cycle models (Adizes, 1979; Churchill & Lewis, 1983; Flamholtz & Randle, 2000; Greiner, 1972; Quinn & Cameron, 1983) suggest that there are definable states in the growth of enterprises from birth to expansion to maturity and, ultimately, to decline. Each stage of growth after successful "birth" occurs at a specific point in an organization's life and brings with it a predictable set of organization development issues that must be successfully dealt with if the organization is to move on to the next stage effectively.

Accordingly, we define organization development in economic enterprises as "the extent to which an organization's design (systems, processes, and structures) fits with its stage of growth/development." When an organization's design (internal capabilities) effectively supports the challenges it faces at a given stage of growth/development, the organization is said to have "developed" effectively. When the organization has failed to develop and implement the systems, structures, and processes (or infrastructure) needed to support its stage of growth/development, it has not "developed" effectively, and, as a result, it will experience difficulties and might even be in jeopardy of failing.

Model for Organization Development

In order to develop successfully, an organization needs a model of what is required to be built. Flamholtz (1986, 1995) has developed a model for organizational growth, which identifies the key "building blocks of successful organizations." In this growth model, organizational "form" or structure consists of six key components or building blocks: (1) markets selected, (2) products (including services), (3) resources to support growth, (4) operational systems, (5) management systems, and (6) corporate culture. The first two relate to the particular business the organization is in, while the last four comprise what might be termed organizational infrastructure.

Under this growth model, the challenge of building an organization is to create the appropriate combination of these six key variables or building blocks for the stage of growth an organization is currently in. If the organization is able to achieve the necessary design and changes in structure, systems, and management focus before it reaches a particular stage (as indicated by its size), it will either not experience problems or, at least, the problems will be minimized. However, this seldom happens.

The lack of a "fit" between size and organizational design leads to problems, which, as we mentioned, Flamholtz (1986, 1995) refers to as organizational growing pains. These growing pains indicate that change is needed if the organization is to continue operating effectively and thus reduce the likelihood of failure. They are also an indication of a lack of successful organization development. If, for example, a company does not focus on developing the systems needed to support its operations at $10 to $100 million in annual revenues, it will in essence still be operating as a birth stage organization, even though its size is consistent with the growth stage. This will place it at risk of failure (Flamholtz, 1986; Flamholtz & Randle, 1987).

Life cycle theorists suggest that success depends on the ability of managers to recognize and make the necessary changes in organizational form at the appropriate time (Flamholtz & Randle, 2007). Operationally, the problem is to create the appropriate design for the organization, given its stage of growth. In other words, successful organization development depends, to a great extent, on the organization's ability to create the internal systems, structure, processes, and design needed to support the size that it has become.

Flamholtz (1986, 1995) embeds these six critical tasks in what he calls a "Pyramid of Organization Development" (shown in Figure 1), suggesting that these tasks must be performed in a stepwise fashion in order to build a successful organization. In fact, Flamholtz suggests that the six key tasks making up the pyramid must all be developed individually and as a system for the organization to function effectively and increase its chance of long-term success.

Empirical Research Support for the Model

During the past several years, Flamholtz and his colleagues have conducted a program of research designed to test this model. Their research has provided empirical support for the proposed six-variable model (Flamholtz, 2001; Flamholtz & Aksehirli, 2000; Flamholtz & Hua, 2002a, 2002b; Flamholtz & Kurland, 2005).

The emphasis that should be given to each task differs depending on the size of the organization, that is, the stage of growth. The stages of growth and their

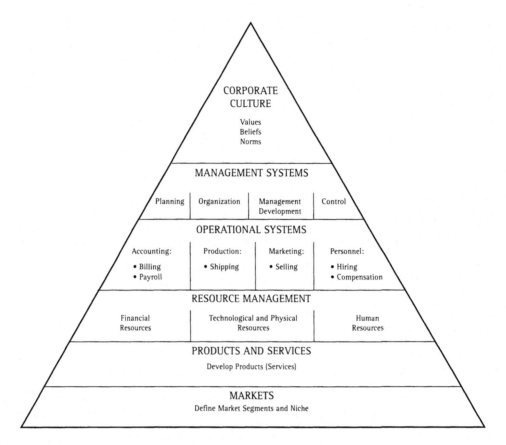

Figure 1. The Pyramid of Organization Development

related critical development areas, as well as the approximate size (measured in millions of dollars of sales revenues) at which an organization can be expected or should scale-up to the next stage is shown in Table 1.

Long-term success depends on the extent to which the organization's design (defined in terms of these six critical success factors) "fits" with its size. In other words, successful scale-up depends on the extent to which the organization has developed a design consistent with its size. When an organization has not effectively developed the systems, structures, and processes needed to support its size, it will begin to experience the aforementioned growing pains. This is indicative of the fact that the organization has not yet made the successful transition (defined in terms of having the appropriate organizational design) to its current stage of development (defined in terms of revenue). In brief, growing pains indicate that the organization has not successfully scaled up and that it is in need of doing so.

Table 1. Stages of Growth and Related Critical Development Areas

Growth Stage	Critical Development Areas	Approximate Organizational Size ($ in Millions of Sales)
I. New Venture	Markets and Products	Less than $1 million
II. Expansion	Resources and Operational Systems	$1 to $10 million
III. Professionalization	Management Systems	$10 to $100 million
IV. Consolidation	Corporate Culture	$100 to $500 million
V. Diversification	Markets and Products	$500 million to $1 billion
VI. Integration	Resources, Operational Systems, Management Systems, Culture	$1 billion +
VII. Decline	All Six Tasks	Any size organization

Flamholtz (1986, 1995) has identified ten common organizational growing pains:

- People feel that "there are not enough hours in the day."

- People are spending too much time "putting out fires."

- People are not aware of what others are doing.

- People lack an understanding about where the firm is headed.

- There are too few good managers.

- People feel that, "I have to do it myself if I want it done correctly."

- Most people feel that meetings are a waste of time.

- When plans are made, there is very little follow-up, so things just don't get done.

- Some people have begun to feel insecure about their places in the firm.

- The firm has continued to grow in sales, but not in profits.

Nature and Causes of Organizational Growing Pains

Growing pains indicate that the infrastructure of an enterprise (the resources, internal operational and management systems, and culture it needs at a given stage of growth) has not kept up with its size, as measured by its revenues. For example, a business with $200 million (U.S.) in revenues may only have an infrastructure to support the operations of a firm with $50 million in revenues, or one-fourth

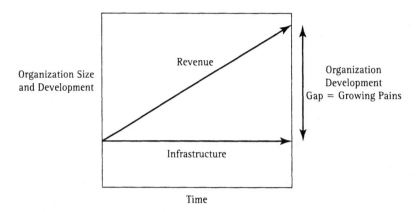

Figure 2. Organization Development Gap

its size. This type of situation typically occurs after a period of growth, sometimes quite rapid growth, where the infrastructure has not been developed to adjust to the new size and complexity of the organization. The result, as shown in Figure 2, is an organization development gap (that is, a gap between the organization's actual infrastructure and that required at its current size or stage of development), which produces the growing pains.

The severity with which an organization experiences these growing pains indicates the extent to which it is experiencing problems scaling up to the next stage of development. When these growing pains are extreme, the organization is in jeopardy of failing if it does not take the steps needed to develop the systems, processes, and design needed to take it fully into the next stage of growth (that is, it must have a design that fits with its size).

Empirical Research to Test the Framework

There is a growing body of empirical evidence that provides support for the proposed theoretical framework. This research is summarized below.

Organization Development and Financial Performance

Flamholtz and Aksehirli (2000) empirically tested the proposed link between the organization development model and the financial success of organizations. They analyzed financial and non-financial information relevant to the hypothesized model for eight pairs of companies in different industries and found a statistically significant relationship.

Flamholtz and Hua (2002a) provided additional empirical evidence of the hypothesized link between the organization development model and financial performance. They reported the results of a test within a single firm, using a set of fifteen relatively comparable divisions, and found a statistically significant relationship. They also identified thresholds of strategic organization development for profitability of individual companies or operating units.

Flamholtz (2001) provided empirical evidence of the hypothesized link between corporate culture and financial performance. He reported a test of this relationship within a single firm, using a set of eighteen comparable divisions. He found a statistically significant relationship between culture and financial performance.

Flamholtz and Kurland (2005) have replicated the study by Flamholtz and Hua (2002a). The prior research was replicated with similar results in an independent research site in a different industry (financial services). Using a set of seven relatively comparable divisions, Flamholtz and Kurland (2005) reported the results of a test within a single firm. They found a statistically significant relationship among the six key variables contained in the pyramid and financial performance. They also found that a statistically significant relationship exists between the variables that are hypothesized to comprise an organization's infrastructure (the top four variables in the pyramid) and financial performance.[1]

Stages of Growth

Randle (1990) provided empirical evidence that the stages of growth occur when predicted in terms of organizational size or revenues. She studied the evolution of the entire personal computer industry from the formation of new ventures until the industry "shakeout," and confirmed that the stages occurred when predicted.

Randle (1990) also provided evidence that firms with "organizational forms" that are adapted to the requirements of their size have a higher probability of success, and vice versa.

Growing Pains and Financial Performance

Flamholtz and Hua (2002b) presented an empirical test of the hypothesized relationship between organizational growing pains and financial performance. They found a statistically significant relationship. In addition, they identified evidence that there appear to be threshold levels of growing pains, which might be used to predict which organizations are likely to be profitable versus those that are unlikely to be profitable.

Flamholtz and Kurland (2005) replicated the study by Flamholtz and Hua (2002b). Their overall results were not statistically significant at the standard 0.05 level but were statistically significant at 0.07.[2] However, regressions of the individual

---

[1]The variables comprising infrastructure include resources, operational systems, management systems, and culture.
[2]Adjusted R2 was significant at 0.07. The sample size for this study was relatively small (n = 6); it was considerably larger in the prior Flamholtz and Hua (2002a) study. As a result, this relationship requires further investigation.

variables comprising the infrastructure indicated that there was a statistically significant relationship between the variable resources and growing pains. All of the divisions were experiencing rapid growth. This finding suggests that those that had greater resources (including people, financial, and other resources) were better able to manage their growing pains.

Additional Research Required

Taken together, this empirical research is supportive of the proposed theoretical framework. However, as noted in each of the prior studies (Flamholtz, 2001; Flamholtz & Aksehirli, 2000; Flamholtz & Hua, 2002a, 2002b), there is a need for additional research to replicate and confirm these findings. In addition, certain hypotheses remain untested.

Implications for Managers and Consultants

These results described in this article have some significant implications for practicing managers and consultants, as outlined below.

A Template for Strategic Planning and Organization Development

First, the article provides a "strategic lens" for viewing the process of developing a successful enterprise. It identifies the key areas that managers should be focusing on to build an organization (the variables comprising the pyramid of organization development). It also provides a template for organization development, the stepwise form of the pyramid itself. As such it provides an analytic framework for the process of organization development.

As consultants, we have used this strategic lens as a template for strategic planning with many companies (from new ventures to members of the Fortune 100) for almost thirty years. Our approach to strategic planning is to view it as a process of "strategic organization development," rather than just a process of creating "competitive strategy" per se. This is because of our research, which indicates that organizations are ultimately competing not only in products and markets but in organizational infrastructure as well. This is based on our notion of the sources of competitive advantage. Specifically, in contrast to the conventional view that products are the key source of competitive advantage, this framework suggests that the true sources of long-term sustainable competitive advantage are found in the organization's infrastructure, especially in its operational systems, management systems, and culture.

This framework has been supported by empirical research (Flamholtz & Hua, 2003; Flamholtz & Kurland, 2005). There also have been several published case studies describing this application of the pyramid framework to strategic planning and organization development in actual companies (Flamholtz & Randle, 2008; Kurland & Flamholtz, 2005; McGee & Flamholtz, 2005; Nayar & Flamholtz, 2005).

A Revised Balanced Scorecard

Another implication is that this framework provides the basis for an improved version of the so-called "Balanced Scorecard" (Kaplan & Norton, 1996). Although the balanced scorecard popularized by Kaplan and Norton is widely referenced, the variables contained in the scorecard have not received any empirical support; they are simply proposed, and the user is supposed to accept them as having face validity. Our framework offers an improved alternative to the four factors proposed in the balanced scorecard based on variables that have received empirical support. In effect, the current research leads to the next generation of the concept of the balance scorecard. The variables of focus in this revised version would be the six variables of the pyramid plus financial results: markets, products, resources, operational systems, management systems, culture, and financial results.

Conclusion

This article has provided a framework for understanding, measuring, and managing the process of organization development in economic enterprises. Organization development is viewed in terms of the movement from one stage of organizational growth to another over an enterprise's life cycle, after the stage of "birth" has been successfully completed. Specifically, "organization development" refers to the process of developing the set of "organizational capabilities" or "form" required by an enterprise as it increases in size and complexity.

Although there are pitfalls, it is possible to manage the process of organization development successfully. This article has provided a framework and summarized related research to help make a contribution to this process.

References

Adizes, I. (1979, Summer). Organizational passages: Diagnosing and treating life cycle problems in organizations. *Organizational Dynamics*, pp. 3–24.

Churchill, N.C., & Lewis, V.L. (1983, May/June). The five stages of small business growth. *Harvard Business Review*, pp. 30–50.

Flamholtz, E.G. (1986). *How to make the transition from entrepreneurship to a professionally managed firm*. San Francisco: Jossey-Bass.

Flamholtz, E. (1995). Managing organizational transitions: Implications for corporate and human resource management. *European Management Journal, 13*(1), 39–51.

Flamholtz, E. (2001). Corporate culture and the bottom line. *European Management Journal, 9*(3), 268–275.

Flamholtz, E.G. (2002/2003). Toward an integrative theory of organizational success and failure: Previous research and future issues. *International Journal of Entrepreneurship Education, 1*(3), 297–319.

Flamholtz, E.G., & Aksehirli, Z. (2000). Organizational success and failure: An empirical test of a holistic model. *European Management Journal, 18*(5), 488–498.

Flamholtz, E., & Hua, W. (2002a). Strategic organizational development and the bottom line: Further empirical evidence. *European Management Journal, 20*(1), 72–81.

Flamholtz, E., & Hua, W. (2002b). Strategic organizational development, growing pains, and corporate financial performance: An empirical test. *European Management Journal, 20*(5), 527–536.

Flamholtz, E., & Hua, W. (2003). Searching for competitive advantage in the black box. *European Management Journal, 21*(2), 222–236.

Flamholtz, E.G., & Kurland, S. (2005). Strategic organizational development, infrastructure, and financial performance: An empirical investigation. *International Journal of Entrepreneurial Education, 3*(1–3), 117–141.

Flamholtz, E.G., & Randle, Y. (1987, May). How to avoid choking on growth. *Management Review*, pp. 25–29.

Flamholtz, E.G., & Randle, Y. (1998). *Changing the game: Organizational transformations of the first, second and third kind.* New York: Oxford University Press.

Flamholtz, E.G., & Randle, Y. (2000). *Growing pains: How to make the transition from entrepreneurship to a professionally managed firm.* San Francisco: Jossey-Bass.

Flamholtz, E.G., & Randle, Y. (2007). *Growing pains* (4th ed.). San Francisco: Jossey-Bass.

Flamholtz, E.G., & Randle, Y. (2008). *Leading strategic change.* New York: Cambridge University Press.

Greiner, L.E. (1972, July/August). Evolution and revolution as organizations grow. *Harvard Business Review*, pp. 37–46.

Kaplan, R.S., & Norton, D.P. (1996). *The balanced scorecard.* Boston, MA: Harvard Business School Press.

Kurland, S., & Flamholtz, E. (2005). The transformation from entrepreneurship to professional management at Countrywide Financial Corporation. *International Journal of Entrepreneurial Education, 3*(1), 81–98.

McGee, M., & Flamholtz, E. (2005). The transformation from entrepreneurship to professional management at Pardee Homes. *International Journal of Entrepreneurial Education, 3*(2), 185–204.

Nayar, M., & Flamholtz, E. (2005). The transformation from entrepreneurship to professional management at Unitech Systems. *International Journal of Entrepreneurial Education, 3*(2), 169–184.

Quinn, R.E., & Cameron, K. (1983). Organizational life cycles and shifting criteria of effectiveness: Some preliminary evidence. *Management Science, 29*, 33–51.

Randle, Y. (1990). *Toward an ecological life cycle model of organizational success and failure.* Dissertation, University of California, Los Angeles.

Eric G. Flamholtz, Ph.D., *is president of Management Systems Consulting Corporation, which he co-founded in 1978. He is also Professor Emeritus at the Anderson School of Management, UCLA, and a member of the board of directors of 99 Cents Only Stores, a NYSE firm. He received his Ph.D. from the University of Michigan, where he worked as a researcher in the Institute for Social Research. He has also served on the faculties of the University of Michigan and Columbia University. His consulting clients have included Starbucks, Countrywide Financial Corporation, Amgen, American Century Investors, Neutrogena, and IBM.*

Yvonne Randle, Ph.D., *is vice president, Management Systems Consulting Corporation, and lecturer in the Anderson School of Management, UCLA, where she is a frequent instructor in executive education programs. She received her Ph.D. in management from UCLA's Anderson Graduate School of Management and a master's degree in public health from UCLA. Dr. Randle received her undergraduate degree from Stanford University.*

Team Building Without Time Wasting

Marshall Goldsmith and Howard Morgan

Summary

A common challenge faced by today's leaders is the necessity of building teams in an environment of rapid change with limited resources. Unfortunately, as the need to build effective teams is increasing, the available time to build these teams is often decreasing. The process of reengineering and streamlining, when coupled with increased demand for services, has lead to a situation in which most leaders feel they have more work to do and fewer staff members to help them do it.

Teams are becoming more and more common and important. Management theorists and organizations around the world are extolling the value of teamwork. As the traditional, hierarchical school of leadership begins to diminish in significance, a new focus on networked team leadership is emerging. Leaders are finding themselves as members of all kinds of teams, including virtual teams, autonomous teams, cross-functional teams, and action learning teams.

Research involving thousands of participants has shown how focused feedback and follow-up can increase leadership and customer service effectiveness (Hesselbein, Goldsmith, & Beckhard, 1996). A parallel approach to team building has been shown to help leaders build teamwork without wasting time. While the approach described here is simple, it is not easy. It requires that team members have the courage to regularly ask for feedback and the discipline to develop a behavioral change strategy, to follow up, and to "stick with it."

To successfully implement the team-building process described in this article, leaders will need to assume the role of coach or facilitator and fight the urge to be "boss" of the project. Greater improvement in teamwork will generally occur if the team members develop their own behavioral change strategy, rather than the leader imposes one on the team. This process should not be implemented if the leader has the present intention of firing or removing a team member.

Steps in the Process

The following process can be used to help teams assess themselves in a hurry. We've added some editorial commentary.

1. Begin by asking each member of the team to confidentially record his or her individual answers to two questions:

   - On a 1 to 10 scale (with 10 being ideal), how well are we doing in terms of working together as a team?

   - On a 1 to 10 scale, how well do we need to be doing in terms of working together as a team?

     Before beginning a team-building process, it is important to determine whether the team members feel that team building is needed. Some people report to the same manager, but legitimately may have very little reason to work interactively as a team. Other groups may believe that teamwork is important, but feel that the team is already functioning smoothly and that a team-building activity would be a waste of time.

2. Have a team member calculate the results. Discuss the results with the team. If the team members believe that the gap between current effectiveness and needed effectiveness indicates the need for team building, proceed to the next step.

   In most cases, team members do believe that improved teamwork is both important and needed. Recent interviews with members from several hundred teams in multinational corporations showed that the "average" team member believed that his or her team was currently at a 5.8 level of effectiveness, but needed to be at an 8.7.

3. Ask the team, "If every team member could change two key behaviors that would help us close the gap between where we are and where we want to be, which two behaviors should we all try to change?" Have each team member record his or her selected behaviors on a sheet of flip-chart paper.

4. Help team members prioritize all the behaviors on the charts (many will be the same or similar) and (using consensus) determine the two most important behaviors to change (for the benefit of the team).

5. Have each team member have a one-on-one dialogue with every other team member. During the dialogue, each member will request that his or her colleague suggest two areas for personal behavioral change (other than the two already agreed on for every team member) that will help the team close the gap between where it is and where it wants to be.

> *These dialogues occur simultaneously and take about five minutes each. For example, if there are seven team members, each team member will participate in six brief one-on-one dialogues.*

6. Let each team member review his or her list of suggested behavioral changes and choose the two that seem to be the most important. Have each team member then announce his or her two key behaviors for personal change to the team.

7. Encourage each team member to ask for a brief (five-minute), monthly "progress report" from every other team member on his or her effectiveness in demonstrating the two key behaviors common to all team members and the two key personal behaviors in need of change. Specific suggestions for improvement can be solicited in areas in which behavior does not match desired expectations.

8. Conduct a mini-survey follow-up process in approximately four months. In the mini-survey, each team member will receive confidential feedback from all other team members on his or her perceived change in effectiveness. This survey will include the two common items, the two personal items, and an item that assesses how much the individual has been following up with the other team members. The mini-surveys are simple enough to be put on a postcard and might look like the one shown in Exhibit 1.

9. Have someone outside of the organization calculate the results for each individual (on all items) and calculate the summary results for all team members (on the common team items). Each team member can then receive a confidential summary report indicating the degree to which colleagues see his or her increased effectiveness in demonstrating the desired behaviors. Each member can also receive a summary report on the team's progress on the items selected for all team members.

> *Before-and-after studies have clearly shown that if team members have regularly followed up with their colleagues, they will almost invariably be seen as increasing their effectiveness in their selected individual areas for improvement. The group summary will also tend to show that (overall) team members will have increased in effectiveness on the common team*

Exhibit 1. Sample Mini-Survey

Do you believe this person has become more (or less) effective in the past six months on the following items? (Please circle the number that best matches your estimate of any change in effectiveness.) **Team Items**	Less Effective		No Perceptible Change				More Effective	No Change Needed	Not Enough Information
Clarifies roles and expectations with fellow team members	−3	−2	−1	0	1	2	3	NCN	NI
Supports the final decision of the team (even if it was not his/her original idea)	−3	−2	−1	0	1	2	3	NCN	NI
Individual Items									
Genuinely listens to others	−3	−2	−1	0	1	2	3	NCN	NI
Strives to see the value of differing opinions	−3	−2	−1	0	1	2	3	NCN	NI

Has this person followed-up with you on areas that he/she has been trying to improve? (Check one)

❑ No Perceptible Follow-Up

❑ Little Follow-Up

❑ Some Follow-Up

❑ Frequent Follow-Up

❑ Consistent (Periodic) Follow-Up

What can this individual do to become a more effective team member?

_____

_____

_____

items. The mini-survey summary report will give tem members a chance to receive positive reinforcement for improvement (and to learn what has not improved) after a reasonably short period of time. The mini-survey will also help to validate the importance of sticking with it and following up.

10. In a team meeting, have each team member discuss key learnings from the mini-survey results and ask for further suggestions in a brief one-on-one dialogue with every other team member.

11. Review the summary results with the team. Facilitate a discussion on how the team (as a whole) is doing in terms of increasing its effectiveness in the two key behaviors that were selected for all team members. Provide the team with positive recognition for increased effectiveness in teamwork. Encourage team members to keep focused on increasing their effectiveness in demonstrating the behaviors that they are trying to improve.

12. Have team members continue to conduct their brief monthly "progress report" sessions with all other team members. Re-administer the mini-survey after eight months from the beginning of the process and again after one year.

13. Conduct a summary session with the team one year after the process has started. Review the results of the final mini-survey and ask the team members to rate the team's effectiveness on where it is versus where it needs to be in terms of working tighter as a team. Compare these ratings with the original ratings that were calculated one year earlier. Give the team positive recognition for improvement in teamwork and have each team member (in a brief one-on-one dialogue) recognize each of his or her colleagues for improvements in behavior that have occurred over the past twelve months.

    If team members followed the process in a reasonably disciplined fashion, the team will almost always see a dramatic improvement in teamwork.

14. Ask the team members whether they believe that more work on team building will be needed in the upcoming year. If the team believes that more work would be beneficial, continue the process. If the team believes that more work is not needed, declare "victory" and work on something else!

Why This Process Works

The process described above works because it is highly focused, includes disciplined feedback and follow-up, does not waste time, and causes participants to focus on self-improvement. Most survey feedback processes ask respondents to complete too many items. In such surveys, most of the items do not result in any behavioral change and participants feel they are wasting time. Participants almost never object to completing four-item surveys that are specifically designed to fit each team member's unique needs. The process also works because it provides ongoing feedback and reinforcement. Most survey processes provide participants with feedback every twelve to twenty-four months. Any research on behavioral change will show that feedback and reinforcement for new behavior needs to occur much more frequently than on a yearly or bi-yearly basis. A final reason that the process works is because it encourages participants to focus on self-improvement. Many team-building processes degenerate because team members are primarily focused on solving someone else's problems. This process works because it encourages team members to primarily focus on solving their own problems!

Let me close with a challenge to you (the reader) as a team leader. Try it! The down side is very low. The process takes very little time, and the first mini-survey will show very quickly whether progress is being made. The up side can be very high. As effective teamwork becomes more and more important, the brief amount of time that you invest in this process may produce a great return for your team and an even greater return for your organization.

Reference

Hesselbein, F., Goldsmith, M., & Beckhard, R. (1996). *The leader of the future*. San Francisco: Jossey-Bass.

Marshall Goldsmith *is a* New York Times *best-selling author and editor. His recent book,* What Got You Here Won't Get You There, *is a* Wall Street Journal *number one business best-seller and Harold Longman Award winner for Best Business Book of the Year. His newest book,* Succession: Are You Ready, *is part of the Harvard Business "Memo to the CEO" series. Dr. Goldsmith is one of the few executive advisors who has been asked to work with over one hundred CEOs and their management teams. He has been recognized as one of the world's top executive educators and coaches by the American Management Association,* Business Week, Fast Company, Forbes, Economist, *and* The Wall Street Journal. *His material is available online (for no charge) at www.MarshallGoldsmithLibrary.com, where visitors from 188 countries have viewed, downloaded, or shared over 2.5 million resources.*

Howard Morgan *is a top executive coach whose work with CEOs, senior leadership teams, and executive coach has earned him global recognition as an expert on optimizing individual and organizational performance. Morgan's practical understanding of executive leadership draws from seventeen years of line and senior executive experience. He was named as one of the world's top fifty coaches, recognized as one of five coaches with "a proven track record of success," and has authored numerous books and articles. He is managing director of Leadership Research Institute and, with Marshall Goldsmith, a founder of 50 Top Coaches.*

Effective Leader–Employee Relationships in the 21st Century

Edwin L. Mouriño-Ruiz

Summary

The workforce is changing, and the importance of relationships between leaders and employees will be crucial to the success of both and to the organizations they work in. The effects of leadership have been examined over the years, showing a variety of consequences, both good and bad, in numerous settings. One particular area of interest and study is the impact of relationships between leaders and employees, especially given that leaders develop different relationships with each of their respective subordinates.

This article will highlight the organizational implications of effective leader-employee relationships when there are differences within the workplace related to proximity (virtual versus co-located). In addition, the author will also explore how an employee's gender, ethnicity, and age might affect the leader-employee relationship. Last this article will review the results of study that looked at this phenomenon.

> "Unfortunately the 21st Century's turbulent knowledge economy with
> its non-traditional organizational forms and employment relationships
> renders the traditional study of how managers supervise subordinates
> largely irrelevant."
>
> George B. Graen, Ph.D., *New Frontiers of Leadership*, 2004

Leadership has been defined as the process of influencing others to understand and agree about what needs to be done and how to do it effectively (Yukl, 2002). Leadership has been studied extensively over the years and has given rise to numerous theories and perspectives. In discussing leadership and the role leaders play in organizations, it has been pointed out that leaders have always had some form of positive or negative effect on their employees' performance (Deluga & Perry, 1991). Leadership has been associated with affecting numerous employee factors such as motivation, loyalty, and communications. At the core of leadership is the development of relationships (Avolio & Kahai, 2004). The research highlights the need for leaders to effectively create and nurture relationships in order to achieve their objectives.

Qualities of Effective Leaders

In addition to having an effect on their employees, the leaders also influence the type of departmental and/or organizational culture they create and foster through their values, beliefs, and assumptions (Schein, 1992).

Culture has been defined as a pattern of beliefs and expectations shared by organizational members that produce norms that shape the behaviors of individuals and groups (Grantham, 2000). It is the organization or departmental environment that differentiates one organization from another. Culture consists of the unwritten rules that employees understand, accept, and abide by. Effective leaders in turn try to create a culture in which everyone can be heard and empowered (Collins, 2001), where employees feel valued, listened to, and appreciated.

When creating a positive environment or culture, trust has been identified as foundational. A study of one hundred student leaders in top undergraduate business programs found that leaders needed to create a culture that fosters teamwork that is supported through trust (Bennis, Spreitzer, & Cummings, 2001). In a similar study, the technically savvy readers of *Fast Company* identified social skills (72 percent) as more essential than Internet skills (28 percent) over the next five years (Kouzes & Posner, 2001). It appears that the relationships leaders establish with employees will be critical to the success of organizations.

Effective leaders also tend to exemplify the Pygmalion effect, or the self-fulfilling prophesy, by expecting the best of those around them (Bennis, 1989). By expecting the best from their employees, leaders can enhance loyalty and commitment from their employees. Good leaders know that it is important to make their subordinates believe in themselves and to feel special (Fox, 2002). By doing this, leaders continue to play a significant role in organizational or departmental culture and, in turn, this serves as a reflection of their leadership. Leaders who help their organizations outperform their competition through their people do so by surrounding themselves with competent people and creating a forum in which a dialogue can exist in order to resolve issues by establishing effective relationships.

Another trait that effective leaders demonstrate is positive emotional intelligence (EQ). Leaders with high EQ are aware of their behaviors and actions and how they can affect their subordinates, know how to effectively manage their behavior, are socially aware of how others feel in certain situations, and know how to effectively manage their relationships with those around them (Emmerling & Goleman, 2003). By managing their EQ, leaders enhance the positive effects of relationships with their subordinates by creating an engaging environment and culture.

The underlying theme throughout all of these aspects of leadership is the relationships leaders have with their employees and how trust and communications play a significant role in achieving success. How leaders treat their employees and maintain positive relationships with their employees will be one of the determining factors to retaining good employees. People tend to desire a sense of community where they work. Leaders who foster that sense of community benefit the bottom line of organizations (Grantham, 2000). Leaders have the responsibility of creating the right environment for their employees so that everyone can give his or her best in the pursuit of organizational objectives.

The Leader–Member Exchange

One perspective of leadership that has been studied and written about extensively is the leader-member exchange (LMX) theory. LMX has evolved over the last twenty-five years (Graen & Uhl-Bien, 1995). LMX's premise is that leaders differentiate on how they supervise their subordinates. Leaders treat some employees more positively than others, thus demonstrating favoritism and achieving different results. With some subordinates, the leader develops a closer, more trusting relationship and, in turn, expects better performance (Brower, Schoorman, & Hoon Tan, 2000). This behavior can lead to the self-fulfilling prophesy and in turn achieve what they expect.

In simple terms, LMX is defined as the quality of the exchange between a leader and his or her subordinates (Brower, Schoorman, & Hoon Tan, 2000). This exchange will affect the leader's expectations and behaviors. While both the leader and subordinate may enter the relationship expecting positive outcomes, things such as personality styles, background, communication styles, and other interpersonal and organizational factors can impact the ultimate exchange.

LMX is comprised of interrelated dimensions such as respect, trust, and mutual obligation (Graen & Uhl-Bien, 1995). The theory basically asserts that the relationship between a leader and his or her subordinates is predictive of the outcomes at the individual, group, and organizational level.

One study looked to demonstrate the influence of LMX on a safety climate (Hoffmann, Morgeson, & Gerras, 2003). The results indicated the importance of having effective working relationships with subordinates while creating a climate that emphasized employee safety. This research tends to highlight the satisfaction and commitment by employees when they believe their leaders are concerned with their livelihood. Another study looked into the effort expended toward the LMX relationship and how this effort affected the quality of the relationship (Maslyn & Uhl-Bien, 2001). This study pointed out that the more effort made toward developing and maintaining an effective relationship, the better the results for all the parties involved.

Lower satisfaction with leader-member relationships lead to lower job satisfaction, lower organizational commitment and increased turnover. Within ineffective relationships, managers need to become the catalyst for change and improve the relationships.

Positive LMX

Research has pointed out that high exchange relationships gain benefits for the leader through committed subordinates. However, high LMX requires attention, time, and responsiveness by the leader toward his or her subordinates (Yukl, 2002). Yukl goes on to point out that the relationship goes through three phases: (1) members test each other's motives, (2) mutual trust is developed, and (3) commitment becomes permanent. Once the commitment becomes permanent, the individuals involved and the organization gain benefits from the relationships.

LMX has also been studied in relation to the new employee. A newcomer to an organization enters with expectations, aspirations, and hopes of success in the new work environment. Met expectations are associated with commitment, job satisfaction, improved job performance, and motivation. Unmet expectations are associated with turnover and absenteeism. High LMX with new employees creates high commitment, turnover intention, and job satisfaction (Major, Kozlowski, & Chao, 1995). This research points out that, while a new employee's proactiveness is important, more important is the *supervisor's* proactiveness. Other studies have demonstrated that high LMX increases job satisfaction, satisfaction with one's supervisor, and commitment by the subordinate (Brower, Schoorman, & Hoon Tan, 2000). The important point made by this research is that it is necessary for leaders to maintain high LMX with all employees in order to gain full commitment and increased performance from all of their employees.

Negative LMX

A different perspective noted in the research is the effect of negative LMX or retaliation. Employees who perceive their relationships to be low with their immediate supervisors believe they receive less leader attention, support, consideration, and communication and suffer more work problems (Townsend, Phillips, & Elkins, 2000).

Leaders who conduct themselves in an ineffective manner that hinders their relationships with their subordinates tend to not only demonstrate a lack of leadership, but also minimize the positive effects of high LMX.

Challenges in the Current Environment

The work environment in the 1980s and 1990s caused leaders to change their expectations and behaviors. Organizations have evolved from the industrial age of command and control and conforming environment to the information age, wherein leaders have to create an empowering, participative, and trusting environment. Present and future organizations will be knowledge-based, and work will be done differently. However, for this to happen will require effective relationships and communications (Drucker, 1987).

Human capital is becoming a key ingredient and success factor for current and future information/knowledge-based organizations. An organization's human capital consists of the knowledge, skills, and experiences of its employees. Some organizations recognize that their human capital will be enhanced through employee satisfaction, which may lead to customer loyalty and, in turn, financial growth (Watson, 2003). When employees are less satisfied with their supervisors or organizations, they are less prone to recommend their organizations to customers. Because of this, employee relationships are an important indicator for leaders to track (Heskitt, Sasser Jr., & Schlesinger, 2003).

A study by the Human Resources Institute in 2004 highlighted a decline in employee loyalty. The study points out that 70 percent of organizations surveyed believe good worker-supervisor relationships mitigate this decline and that they are important for attracting and retaining motivated, loyal, and committed employees. In addition, it is also estimated that by 2010 there will be a ten-million-employee shortage in the workforce. There are numerous reasons for this, including the aging population, the changing attitudes of employees toward work, the changing of employee/employer relationships, and the changing relationship between leaders and their followers. This situation creates an interesting opportunity for leaders to create the type of culture and environment that attract and retain committed employees.

Clearly, the relationship between the employee and his or her immediate supervisor has a dramatic impact on how long an employee stays with an organization and continue to be productive. When a leader enables effective leader-employee relationships, regardless of whether his or her employees work virtually or are co-located, this positions the department and organization for success.

Communication

The theme throughout these different studies is that different factors influence the organizations of today and tomorrow. However, one fundamental ingredient for success that remains in place is effective communication. Communication is and will continue to be instrumental in enhancing the leader-employee relationship (Ulfielder, 2003). Communication will be increasingly difficult in a growing virtual environment in which technology forces a change in the communications process within organizations (Grantham, 2000). The true test of leadership will be communicating a compelling vision for the future (Collett, 2004).

Supervisor-employee relationships will continue to be important, as studies indicate that a perceived lack of fairness and trustworthiness has been cited as a key reason for employees rating their supervisors as poor over time (Mahan, 2004). In the organizations of the future, employees must work collaboratively *with* supervisors, not *for* them, as in the past.

The Virtual Workforce

The Virtual Employee

An interesting phenomenon in the workplace is the increased use of technology and the increase in virtual employees. One of the main reasons cited for the change of worker location is the cost reduction, such as the $550 million freed up by AT&T (Apgar, 1998). Another benefit is the increased productivity, as cited by 87 percent of surveyed employees. However, one key point highlighted in the research is that employees need coaching on the protocol of working in virtual environments. Regardless of the organizational structure, leader/employee distance, and the potential for failure, one can still have effective teams (Hoefling, 2001).

Technology provides the infrastructure for employees to communicate successfully in a virtual environment, to work together from separate places and at different times, and to not become socially isolated (Grantham, 2000). But working virtually requires an organizational culture that builds trust and values-sharing while focusing on achieving organizational results. To be successful in a virtual environment, leaders must build commitment, provide strong leadership and guidance, provide information through networking, manage results absent of physical sight of their subordinates, and enable dialogue (Hoefling, 2001). While leaders have to be able to use the technology, they need to be even more aware of and sensitive to the people issues.

Several studies have argued that physical distance decreases the opportunities for direct influence and decreases the effectiveness of the working relationship between the leader and follower (Howell & Hall-Merenda, 1999; Liden, Sparrowe, & Wayne, 1997). Clearly, leaders need to establish a regular pattern of communicating and a means to clarify work expectations while keeping employees informed. Leaders need to manage their relationships with virtual employees differently than those with co-located employees, while minimizing the perception of favoritism.

In the 1990s the number of virtual workers jumped tenfold from over one million to almost eleven million (Hill, Miller, Weiner, & Colihan, 1998). While expense reduction was a primary driver for this growth, improved productivity, morale, and work/life balance were some of the by-products. But in spite of these benefits, teamwork and communications have sometimes suffered. This may be partly due to the lack of understanding or acceptance by leaders of the need to improve their communications skills.

As noted previously, positive or negative LMX can affect the relationship between an employee and his or her immediate supervisor (Brower, Schoorman, & Hoon Tan, 2000). This relationship also has the potential to affect the broader dynamic of the virtual team (Graen & Uhl-Bien, 1995). How leaders treat one or more of their subordinates in their one-on-one relationships may affect how these individuals behave or perform on virtual teams (Graen, Hui, & Taylor, 2004).

The Virtual Team

A virtual team has been defined as a group of people who interact through interdependent tasks guided by a common purpose across time, space, and organizational boundaries (Maznevski & Chuedoba, 2000). In order for virtual teams to be successful, leaders need to provide clear and engaging directions with specific goals while delegating effectively.

The advantages that virtual teams provide, which include cost reductions, shorter cycle times, increased innovativeness, and a larger talent pool from which to hire (since an employee need not be near the organization), make them very attractive for organizations.

Two key disadvantages virtual team leaders need to address are communication and project management (Kossler & Prestridge, 2004). While technology may increase options for how information is communicated, it also increases opportunities to miscommunicate due to an absence of non-verbal cues; exclusive use of written communication ; and the fact that virtual teams are likely from different cultures. From a project management perspective, issues may arise around scheduling, coordinating efforts, and different subcultures. How leaders manage these will determine their own and their teams' success or failure.

As we said, how leaders lead and manage those employees they cannot see will determine their success (Handy, 1995). Some employees will continue to need some sense of purpose and place. Feeling left out will continue to be a side-effect of the virtual work environment.

Trust

Fundamental to the success of the virtual working environment is trust. In the absence of trust, some managers will use technology software to track and monitor employees. However, numerous studies have demonstrated the negative effects of monitoring on employees' morale and productivity (Arias, Nykodym, & Cole-Larramore, 2002). Another study has shown that telecommuters are more satisfied with communications than non-telecommuters (Watson-Fritz, Narasimhan, & Rhre, 1998). This may be partly due to the comfort of telecommuters with the use of technology or the initial relationship established by the leader, which reinforces trust, effective communications, and clarity of expectations.

In a different study, high LMX produced high follower performance, irrespective of distance between the leader and follower (Howell & Hall-Merenda, 1999). The researchers determined that success was partly due to the leader's frequent interaction with the followers and the support and encouragement felt by the followers. Finally, the quality of the leader/member relationship mediates the link between managerial trust and employee empowerment (Gomez & Rosen, 2001), whereas previous research pointed to the influence of organizational and social structural variables. Additional research has demonstrated that, the higher the LMX in a team, the better the team performed (Liden, Sparrowe, & Wayne, 1997).

e-Leadership

Avalio, Kahai, and Dodge (2001) outlined a concept titled "e-leadership" driven by the onslaught of technology. They define e-leadership as a social influence process mediated by technology to produce a change in attitudes, feelings, behavior, and performance by individuals. The authors state that, due to the virtuality of employees enabled by technology to work anywhere and any time, leaders will need to reframe their paradigm and mindset in order to ensure success for their organizations through their employees by establishing trust and practicing effective communications.

One way to visualize the integration of the concepts discussed to this point with the organizational benefits mentioned is through the model shown in Figure 1.

The Study

The author conducted a study to try to gain insight into the effects of the relationship between leaders and their subordinates when some subordinates were virtual

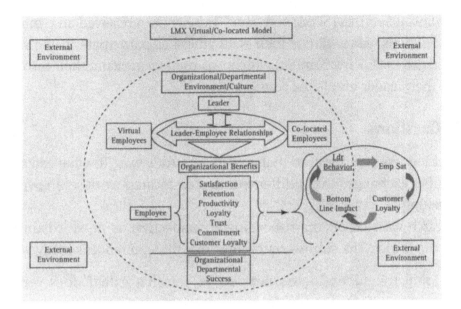

Figure 1. LMX Virtual/Co-Located Model

while others were co-located with the leader. In particular, the study compared leader-employee relationships from the subordinate's perspective in a co-located versus a virtual setting. In addition, the study assessed these differences, taking into consideration the subordinate's gender, age bracket, and ethnic background. The study added a new perspective, as most of the research has focused on the leader's perspective (Gerstner & Day, 1997) and not much research has been conducted on the virtual work environment.

The study assessed the effectiveness of LMX in an information technology (IT) organization, using the LMX 7 instrument, identified as one of the more psychometrically sound instruments to measure LMX (Gerstner & Day, 1997).

The organization consists of 4,000 employees who service 140,000 customers worldwide. The employees are located in the United States, from California to the Northeast; a small contingent is located in Canada. The major concentration of employees work in six major locations with many others working virtually. Approximately 7 percent telecommute. The employees vary in age, with women making up 33 percent; 80 percent are non-minority, 8 percent African American, 7 percent Asian, and 4 percent Hispanic. It is estimated that approximately 40 percent of the employees work at a distance from their immediate supervisors.

Selection of Participants

All organizational employees from director level down were considered to participate in the study. Ten percent of the employee population (or approximately four hundred employees) was randomly selected to participate, using the Statistical

Package for Social Services (SPSS) software. Those chosen received an e-mail requesting that individuals acknowledge their willingness to participate in the study; they also received the LMX 7 instrument, which was used to measure their respective perceptions of their leader-employee relationships.

Research Questions

The overarching research question that guided this study was: To what extent does the leader-member exchange (LMX) differ within a co-located work setting versus a virtual work setting?

The research focused on the subordinate perspective, as most existing research focuses on the leader. The sub-research questions that guided this study were:

> S-1: From the subordinate's perspective, to what extent does gender affect LMX within a virtual and co-located work setting?

> S-2: From the subordinate's perspective, to what extent does ethnic background affect LMX within a virtual and co-located work setting?

> S-3: From the subordinate's perspective, to what extent does the age range affect LMX within a virtual and co-located setting?

The research design was a factorial analysis of variance that included four factors, consisting of location, both virtual and co-located; gender; ethnicity, consisting of Caucasian, African American, Hispanic, Asian, American Indian, and other; and age level ranging from 18 to 29, 30 to 39, 40 to 49, 50 to 59, and 60 and above.

Results

Overarching Research Question. The overarching research question assessed the potential difference that LMX would have on employees working virtually and co-located. This study did not demonstrate any statistically significant difference. This means that, irrespective of where an employee worked, for this study in this organization, the results did not indicate any significant difference. This may be due to the heightened awareness of this organization's leadership of the importance of the employees and the expected effectiveness in managing in a virtual environment.

Sub-Research Question One. This question asked whether gender impacted LMX, whether an employee was virtual or co-located. The results did not provide any statistical significance. This seems to indicate that, at least in this organization, there were no perceived significant differences from a gender perspective in the relationships as seen by the employees. This organization appears to ensure equitable treatment in order to enhance productivity, regardless of gender.

Sub-Research Question Two. This question asked whether ethnicity impacted LMX, whether an employee was virtual or co-located. The analysis of this study did not provide sufficient evidence to indicate that ethnicity is a factor in employees' perception of leader-member exchanges or relationships. This might be due to the fact that this organization purposely worked to address diversity and inclusion issues, irrespective of an employee's location.

Sub-Research Question Three. This question asked whether age impacted LMX, regardless of where employees worked. Here the results did not provide any statistically significant information as to how the employees perceived their relationships with their leaders, irrespective of their age group. This may be due in part to this organization's leadership role in ensuring a continual open dialogue and effective communication with its employee population, regardless of their work location and age.

While the key research questions were not statistically substantiated, there were some interesting findings. Question 1 of the survey asked, "Do you know where you stand with your manager? Do you usually know how satisfied your manager is with what you do?" Here 18 percent of the respondents answered "rarely" or "occasionally," with 15 percent selecting "sometimes."

Question 2 asked, "How well does your manager understand your job problems and needs?" Here, 20 percent of the respondents selected "not a bit" or "a little." Question 3 asked, "How well does your manager recognize your potential?" To this question, 19 percent responded "not a bit" or "a little." Question 5 asked, "Again, regardless of the amount of the formal authority your manager has, what are the chances that he/she would support you no matter what the consequences?" Here, 25 percent responded "none or small," while 33 percent responded "moderate." Question 7 asked, "How would you characterize your working relationship with your manager?" Here, 33 percent of the study participants responded "average."

Overall, this information was not anything dramatically new or likely to hinder the organization, but it did provide some deeper insight into areas of improvement for the organization. When at least one-fifth of those surveyed do not know where they stand with their leaders or say that their leaders do not recognize their potential or understand their problems and needs, there is some room for improvement. When 25 percent do not believe and 33 percent are not sure that their leaders would support them, there is some room for improvement. Last, when 33 percent describe their working relationships with their respective managers as "average," there is also some room for improvement.

From the researcher's perspective, this deeper analysis of the data allows the organization an opportunity to continue to improve when it comes to leader-employee relationships whether co-located or virtual. The evolution of working co-located to virtually will require trust and clear communications. Managers will need to establish rapport by making themselves more available, being sensitive to the different time zones, and ensuring they understand what motivates each of their staff members (Jones, Oyung, & Pace-Shade, 2005).

In summary, the type of environment created within the organization by its leadership will drive employee behavior. Through effective and inclusive leader-employee relationships, leaders can enable employee commitment, loyalty, trust, improved customer service, and improved performance.

Conclusion

The LMX Virtual/Co-Located Model highlights the belief that the creation of a culture through effective leadership behaviors that support effective leader-employee relationships can lead to improved employee performance and enable organizational/departmental success.

Organizations of the future, particularly with the increasing virtual environment, will need to be collaborative. These organizations will require leadership that is clear, focused, and determined to achieve its goals with its virtual staff. They will require leaders who are constantly and effectively communicating the vision and goals of the organization (Bell, 2003). Clarity and constant communication will be fundamental in more complex virtual organizations.

Having all leaders foster an environment of continual learning (and thus employee development) will enhance an organization's capability to attract and retain employees (Corporate Leadership Council, 2003). This will better position an organization to create the type of environment that employees will want to remain a part of for a longer part of their careers.

A previous study highlighted five challenges for organizations with virtual employees and teams: building trust, cohesion, team identity, balancing interpersonal and technical skills, and recognizing the performance of the virtual team members (Kirkman, Rosen, Gibson, Tesluk, & McPherson, 2002). These challenges will provide leaders an opportunity to maximize the productivity of all of their employees, whether they work virtually or are co-located.

Implications for Human Resource Development (HRD)

> "We cannot lose sight of the fact that employee satisfaction, how you treat and deal with people, is the biggest lever in retaining and motivating a workforce. This means having the right environment and the right leadership in place."

Ed Taft, VP-HR, Lockheed Martin, 1960–2005

As the importance of strong, informed leadership and good relationships with employees continue to grow, organizations will need to ensure leaders are cognizant of and trained in these areas. As technology increases the possibilities for employees and leaders to have different work arrangements, this will create new challenges for organizations. These create some interesting perspectives and opportunities for further HRD research.

An addition, the changing demographics, especially changing age groups in the workplace, have meant that there are different expectations from employees regarding leadership. As expectations of leadership continue to evolve, there will be increased opportunities to research the implications of these changes.

While this study did not provide statistically significant results, the researcher believes there is more opportunity to study LMX in organizations that are not as mature in managing employees in a virtual environment. There is also the opportunity to conduct further research on LMX that assesses both the leaders' and employees' perspectives in a virtual environment. This type of research could add some interesting insights.

This research can also have implications for leadership development training. Identifying and developing the appropriate leadership competencies will be key for ensuring effective leader-employee relationships. Further research can address organizational culture and leadership's role in ensuring effective relationships, employee productivity, motivation, loyalty, and others.

Remember that leader-employee relationships will be even more crucial to the success of organizations in the 21st Century in the ever-increasing virtual/global and changing workforce.

References

Apgar IV, M. (1998, May/June). The alternative workplace: Changing where and how people work. *Harvard Business Review*.

Arias, S., Nykodym, N., & Cole-Larramore, A.A. (2002, Fall). Trust and technology in a virtual organization. *Advanced Management Journal*.

Avolio, B.J., & Kahai, S. (2004). Leadership: Current trends: Defining leadership. Available: www.hrinstitute.info/hri. Last accessed August 7, 2004.

Bell, M. (2003). Leading and managing in the virtual matrix. Paper presented at the Gartner Symposium ITXPO, Lake Buena Vista, Florida.

Bennis, W. (1989). On becoming a leader. Available: www.getAbstract.com. Last accessed July 11, 2003.

Bennis, W., Spreitzer, G.M., & Cummings, T.G. (Eds.). (2001). *The future of leadership: Today's top leadership thinkers speak to tomorrow's leaders*. San Francisco: Jossey-Bass.

Brower, H.H., Schoorman, F.D., & Hoon Tan, H. (2000). A model of relational leadership: The integration of trust and leader-member exchange. *Leadership Quarterly, 11*(2), 227–250.

Collett, S. (2004). Tests of leadership. Available: www.computerworld.com. Last accessed July 12, 2004.

Collins, J.C. (2001). *Good to great: Why some companies make the leap and others don't.* New York: HarperCollins.

Corporate Leadership Council. (2003). Literature review: Human capital management. Available: www.corporateleadershipcouncil.com. Last accessed August 10, 2004.

Deluga, R.J., & Perry, J.T. (1991). The relationship of subordinate upward influencing behaviour, satisfaction, and perceived superior effectiveness with leader-member exchange. *Journal of Occupational Psychology, 64*(3), 239–252.

Drucker, P.F. (1987, Jan/Feb). The coming of the new organization. *Harvard Business Review.*

Emmerling, R.J., & Goleman, D. (2003). Emotional intelligence: Issues and common misunderstandings. Available: www.EIConsortium.com. Last accessed February 16, 2004.

Fox, J.J. (2002). How to become a great boss: The rules for getting and keeping the best employees. Available: www.getAbstract.com. Last accessed April 23, 2004.

Gerstner, C.R., & Day, D.V. (1997). Meta-analytic review of leader-member exchange theory: Correlates and construct issues. *Journal of Applied Psychology, 82*(6), 827–844.

Gomez, C., & Rosen, B. (2001). The leader-member exchange as a link between managerial trust and employee empowerment. *Group and Organization Management, 26*(1), 53–69.

Graen, G.B., Hui, C., & Taylor, E.T. (2004). A new approach to team leadership: Upward, downward, and horizontal differentiation. In G.B. Graen (Ed.), *New frontiers of leadership.* Greenwich, CT: Information Age Publishing.

Graen, G.B., & Uhl-Bien, M. (1995). Relationship-based approach to leadership: Development of leader-member exchange (LMX) theory of leadership over 25 years: Applying a multi-level multi-domain perspective. *Leadership Quarterly, 6*(2), 219–247.

Grantham, C. (2000). *The future of work: The promise of the new digital work society.* New York: McGraw-Hill.

Handy, C. (1995, May/June). Trust and the virtual organization. *Harvard Business Review.*

Heskitt, J.L., Sasser, Jr., W.E., & Schlesinger, L.A. (2003). *The value profit chain: Treat employees like customers and customers like employees.* New York: The Free Press.

Hill, E.J., Miller, B.C., Weiner, S.P., & Colihan, J. (1998). Influences of the virtual office on aspects of work and work-life balance. *Personnel Psychology, 51*, 667–683.

Hoefling, T. (2001). *Working virtually: Managing people for successful virtual teams and organizations.* Sterling, VA: Stylus Publishing.

Hoffmann, D.A., Morgeson, F.P., & Gerras, S.J. (2003). Climate as a moderator of the relationship between leader-member exchange and content specific citizenship: Safety climate as an exemplar. *Journal of Applied Psychology, 88*(1), 170–178.

Howell, J.M., & Hall-Merenda, K.E. (1999). The ties that bind: The impact of leader-member exchange, transformational and transactional leadership, and distance on predicting follower performance. *Journal of Applied Psychology, 84*(5), 680–694.

Human Resource Institute, Inc. (2004). The decline of employee loyalty and commitment. Available: www.hrinstitute.info.com. Last accessed March 29, 2004.

Jones, R.C., Oyung, R.L., & Pace-Shade, L. (2005). *Working virtually: Challenges of virtual teams.* Hershey, PA: Idea Group Publishing.

Kirkman, B.L., Rosen, B., Gibson, C.B., Tesluk, P.E., & McPherson, S.O. (2002). Five challenges to virtual team success: Lessons from Sabre, Inc. *Academy of Management Executive, 16*(3), 67–79.

Kossler, M.E., & Prestridge, S. (2004). Leading dispersed teams (CCL No. 423). Greensboro, NC: Center for Creative Leadership. Available: www.ccl.org/publications .com.

Kouzes, J.M., & Posner, B.Z. (2001). Bringing leadership lessons from the past into the future. In W. Bennis, G.M. Spreitzer, & T.G. Cummings (Eds.), *The future of leadership: Today's top leadership thinkers speak to tomorrow's leaders.* San Francisco: Jossey-Bass.

Liden, R.C., Sparrowe, R.T., & Wayne, S.J. (1997). Leader-member exchange theory: The past and potential for the future. *Research in Personnel and Human Resources Management, 15,* 47–119.

Mahan, T.F. (2004). Employee surveys: If we understand the workforce, we can compete. Available: www.workinstitute.com. Last accessed September 19, 2004.

Major, D., Kozlowski, S.W., & Chao, G.T. (1995). A longitudinal investigation of newcomer expectations, early socialization outcomes, and the moderating effects of role development factors. *Journal of Applied Psychology, 80*(3), 418–431.

Maslyn, J.M., & Uhl-Bien, M. (2001). Leader-member exchange and its dimensions: Effects of self-effort and other's effort on relationship quality. *Journal of Applied Psychology, 86*(4), 697–708.

Maznevski, M.L., & Chuedoba, K.M. (2000). Bridging space over time: Global virtual team dynamics and effectiveness. *Organization Science, 11*(5), 473–492.

Schein, E.H. (1992). *Organizational culture and leadership.* San Francisco: Jossey-Bass.

Townsend, J., Phillips, J.S., & Elkins, T.J. (2000). Employee retaliation: The neglected consequence of poor leader-member exchange relations. *Journal of Occupational Health Psychology, 5*(4), 457–463.

Ulfielder, S. (2003). Can this relationship be saved? Available: www.computerworld .com. Last accessed February 19, 2004.

Watson, T. (2003). People make profits. *Advertising Age, 74*(17), 24–27.

Watson-Fritz, M.B., Narasimhan, S., & Rhee, H.S. (1998). Communications and coordination in the virtual office. *Journal of Management Information Systems, 14*(4), 7–28.

Yukl, G. (2002). *Leadership in organizations.* Upper Saddle River, NJ: Prentice-Hall.

Edwin L. Mouriño-Ruiz *is a manager and internal consultant within a major aero-defense organization. He is a multi-industry seasoned HRD professional with over twenty-five years of experience in consulting, leadership development, diversity, and learning and development. He has also set up a virtual university, presented at a variety of conferences, and conducted adjunct teaching in the college setting.*

How Can You Develop Leaders?
Let Me Count the Ways!
Lois B. Hart

Summary

Extensive research was conducted during the development of the Courageous Leadership Consortium, the goal of which is to locate innovative leadership programs for women. We found several traditional strategies or components used in leadership development programs such as training, networking, and mentoring. However, many lesser-utilized components were also discovered so, combined with the above three, we now had a list of eighteen.

This article reviews these eighteen components, provides examples of how and how frequently they are used, and shows how three organizations combined several to design their leadership programs. The goal of this article is to encourage leadership development professionals to consider using additional components in their own leadership programs and thus to enhance participants' learning and advancement.

Background

For over thirty years, I have done extensive work and research on leadership development, starting with a doctorial dissertation on leadership training for women. At that time, Dr. Ken Blanchard was my advisor and he inspired me to follow a career path that included training, speaking, consulting, and writing.

This work naturally included reading, talking to thought leaders, reviewing research, consulting, and searching the Internet for proven leadership models, activities, and resources to use in my work and books.

In 1998, I founded and served as executive director of the Women's Leadership Institute (see Hart & Waisman, 2005). A year-long program incorporated coaches who worked with participants weekly and who also worked with their managers. We helped these participants find mentors who also worked with the coaches. Resource people were tapped as needed for short-term consulting. Every month, participants attended leadership training workshops. In addition, we provided consulting services to the sponsoring companies on best practices used in "women-friendly" organizations. This unique process utilized several leadership development components and produced both promotions for and retention of our graduates.

The Courageous Leadership Consortium

With that successful program established, in 2005 we moved from a local to a national focus and founded the Courageous Leadership Consortium. CLC's vision is to *identify and disseminate innovative leadership models and educational resources to develop women leaders.* The mission is to *disseminate information through the CLC website,* www.courageousleadership.org, *with links to other relevant sites.*

As the research delved more deeply into the identification of program models and resources for leadership development, we noted *how* leaders were developed. What we discovered went beyond our expectations.

On the Courageous Leadership Consortium website, we use the word *component* to describe any strategy used to develop leaders. Most organizations use more than one component, and we were looking for those programs that used five or more.

The more research we did to identify leadership programs for women, the more the original short list of components grew. We have currently identified eighteen components. No organization that we explored uses all eighteen.

Eighteen Essential Components for Leadership Development

The following list covers the eighteen components along with their definitions and examples. Keep in mind that every organization featured here uses multiple components.

1. Alumni Groups

Alumni groups are made up of graduates from leadership programs who continue to be involved and provide continued support through one or more of the following: meet regularly, periodically, or annually; communicate via the Internet; have newsletters; or volunteer with their original leadership program as advisors or mentors.

For example, graduates of the Commonwealth of Pennsylvania's program, called the Leadership Development Institute (LDI), participate in an active LDI Alumnae Association. Several serve on the LDI Advisory Board. They hold monthly meetings, maintain a database, hold a Leadership Book Discussion Club, publish an online newsletter, and sponsor educational seminars and the annual Leadership & Learn Conference.

2. Assessments and Feedback

Assessments fall into two categories: self and 360. Personal assessments provide insights into individuals' values, behaviors, styles, skills, and attitudes. A 360-degree feedback assessment is an assessment of a leader's performance from his or her colleagues, direct reports, boss, the boss's peers, or even customers and vendors.

The Center for Creative Leadership (CCL) is known for its assessments and feedback process. CCL's Women's Leadership Program uses an instrument called Benchmarks® to measure the skills learned through its development activities, as well as identifying possible career "derailers." In addition to Benchmarks®, participants learn from two other personality assessments.

3. Awards

Awards are given based on various criteria. Often organizations are selected in order to spotlight their achievements in developing women leaders. Individuals are given awards for their exemplary leadership or as champions of women's leadership.

The ATHENA Award is named after the goddess Athena, who was known for her strength, courage, wisdom, and enlightenment—qualities embodied in the ATHENA leadership model. This annual award is established through local host organizations in partnership with ATHENA International. One woman or man is selected for her or his professional excellence, community service, and assistance to women's attainment of leadership skills. Nominations are solicited and an ATHENA sculpture is awarded. Since the program's inception in 1982, more than 5,000 awards have been presented in over five hundred communities in the United States and abroad. By honoring exceptional leaders, the ATHENA Award® program seeks to inspire others to achieve excellence in their professional and personal lives.

4. Coaching

Coaching is a one-on-one real-time relationship with an objective person who helps the leader identify what the leader truly desires from work and/or life, set targets, and overcome obstacles. The coach listens and asks questions while the client poses a problem, and together they find solutions.

Accenture's Great Place to Work program has four goals, one of which is moving women into leadership roles. Accenture created and now shares its Visible Career Progression Model with each employee from day one. Each Accenture employee is assigned a career counselor (coach) who reviews the model so that participants know what it takes to advance at Accenture, every step of the way. The coach advises his or her assignee on career growth opportunities, areas for development, and future career goals and objectives.

5. Community Service

As part of the leadership program, participants are required to plan and deliver some program or service to their community. Often this is done in small groups, although individual service occurs too.

The National Hispana Leadership Institute's participants are taught to reflect on themselves so that they may look ahead with renewed and expanded perspectives. They examine how, as Hispanics and women, they have historically looked at community issues to prepare them to reach out and build bridges with other groups of society. Each graduate develops a leadership project that will benefit a minimum of twenty-five Hispanic girls and/or women in his or her community.

6. Conferences

A one or more day event with keynote speeches, workshops, an exhibit hall, and opportunities for networking is often part of the program.

Women in Cable Telecommunications (WICT) partners with cable and telecommunications industry leaders at both the national and local level to provide leadership programs and services and challenges these companies to create professional advancement opportunities for women.

Programs include the Executive Development Seminar, Betsy Magness Leadership Institute, WICT Cable Boot Camp, Rising Leaders Program, and The Chapter Leadership Conference. This annual conference brings together WICT chapter leaders for training designed to help fulfill WICT's mission. This is the leadership conference for the industry. Participants learn how business leaders thrive in challenging business situations and the trends they are seeing that affect their success.

7. Conference Calls

Calls are made regularly or periodically among participants, or between a coach and participants, with the opportunity for everyone to participate to keep them connected. Topics vary.

The American Association of University Women's Leadership and Training Institute is using a novel way to share the knowledge and tools necessary for effective community leadership: interactive teleseminars, also known as "webinars."

Participants join a telephone conference call while following along on the Internet as presenters share documents, web pages, and other visuals. Since these are interactive sessions, participants respond to poll questions and see immediate responses. They submit questions electronically to be answered as the presentation progresses. Covering the topics of communication, development, membership, and programming, teleseminars or webinars provide time-tested as well as new ideas and tools.

8. Job Assignments

Job assignments provide leaders opportunities in areas in which they need experience so they will be better qualified for promotions at higher levels.

Safeway's "Championing Change for Women: An Integrated Mission and Strategy" program features comprehensive career development. Safeway seeks to promote management talent from within, drawing from all levels, including entry-level store employees, to fill its leadership ranks.

Safeway's human resources department develops high-potential slates that are distributed to district managers and vice presidents. High-potentials know that they are on this list and can be explicitly tapped for developmental opportunities within stores. In addition, during regular store visits, division senior management meets with the high-potentials to gauge career interests and discuss potential opportunities. Furthermore, all qualified employees—and particularly women and people of color—are encouraged to self-apply for "stretch positions" by responding to formal job postings in every store. Employees working flextime or part-time are also encouraged to apply for these assignments.

9. Mentors

The mentee or protégé is matched up with a mentor, who is someone with more experience, wisdom, or knowledge, either in her own organization or with another in her industry or profession. The mentor opens doors of opportunity, acts as a sounding board, challenges thinking, provides candid feedback, and encourages and guides the individual toward her goals.

Each participant in Leadership DELTA is paired with a mentor who understands both her field and what it takes to be successful on a short- and long-term basis.

At different times during the program year, Leadership DELTA participants, with the guidance of their mentors, complete assignments that will continue to build their leadership skills and expose them to key leaders on their campuses and in their communities. The Leadership DELTA participants complete their training during the DELTA National Conference, plus spend quality time with their mentors.

10. Networking

Leaders have a networking plan in order to enhance their careers, find needed resources, or obtain information. They regularly meet people, individually or in groups, in their organization or their community.

The annual goals of General Electric Women's Network (GEWN) reflect the overall GE business goals. The GEWN is run like a GE business and follows the same operating cycle. Linking goals in this way ensures that women working with and through GEWN are being developed and exposed to the issues most critical to the organization. It also provides the company with a convenient mechanism for developing a pool of individuals who can meet broad organizational goals.

GEWN leaders are identified through the Session C process and obtain hands-on leadership experience through their GEWN activities. This experience prepares women for leadership roles within the organization. The GEWN leadership structure includes the Kitchen Cabinet, comprised of senior women leaders representing a variety of GE businesses, an executive board of thirty senior-level women who drive key initiatives, and regional leaders who are high-performing, mid-career women who facilitate best practice discussions at the local level. Local leaders, who are early- to mid-career women, also lead local activities.

GEWN activities include performance, networking, customer service, and work/life balance. A variety of forums are used, including speakers' seminars, workshops, and networking dinners.

11. Newsletters

A communication vehicle, print- or web-based, is often used to inform readers of upcoming events, review books and other media, spotlight individuals or organizational practices, and provide other information that enhances professional development.

Two organizations that provide excellent newsletters include the White House Project and the Center for Creative Leadership.

The White House Project (WHP) is a national, non-partisan organization dedicated to advancing women's leadership across sectors and fostering the entry of women into all positions of leadership, including the U.S. Presidency.

Their weekly email-based newsletter is filled with current news about women running for office, regional and state developments, results of their research, books and other resources, and upcoming events.

The Center for Creative Leadership's newsletter, *Leading Effectively*, provides "tips, tools, and advice to the practicing manager." This monthly newsletter, delivered via email, covers leadership topics based on CCL's work with thousands of leaders and its research. The newsletter also includes books related to the articles, polls, upcoming programs, and announcements of webinars.

12. Organization Development and Consulting

Organizations use many tools and processes to assess and improve their culture, practices, policies, and procedures; obtain upper management support; design and implement various initiatives, programs, policies, and procedures; and evaluate these periodically.

Catalyst's Advisory Services is a strategic global diversity consulting practice that works with leading companies and firms to create work cultures that attract and retain a diverse talent pool. They partner with their clients to assist them in reaping the bottom-line benefits from an inclusive work environment. These services range from comprehensive environmental assessments and diversity strategy development to targeted workshops and benchmarking projects.

13. Research

Accepted research methods are used to evaluate the effectiveness of initiatives; program goals; succession plans; the selection, promotion, and retention of target groups; and cultural factors, all of which affect women leaders. Three organizations do continuous research: The White House Project, Catalyst, and the Center for Creative Leadership.

The White House Project conducts groundbreaking research on female candidates for elective office, including studying how the press covers female candidates and how often female experts and leaders appear on the Sunday morning political talk shows. WHP's most recent research project studied the barriers and opportunities women face in being elected to office by analyzing a number of political advertisements by female candidates from the last decade to help them present themselves most effectively in ads.

Catalyst studies of women's leadership, development, and advancement represent the cornerstone of its research offerings and portray the state of the workplace for executive women. It complements the other areas it researches by going behind the scenes to assess women's paths to success, the barriers they have faced on their way to the top, their aspirations, their approaches to achieving work/life effectiveness, and much more. Catalyst uses metrics to track the status of women on boards and women corporate officers and top earners at the largest companies in the United States and Canada. Each census is a marker for women's accomplishment and highlights progress yet to be made.

The Center for Creative Leadership has built its portfolio of programs, products, and services on a solid foundation of behavioral science research. The research CCL does seeks to advance the understanding of leadership and includes a diverse array of designs and multiple methods. The Center continually works on research projects to develop knowledge and expertise through several research groups: Individual Leader Development; Global Leadership and Diversity; Groups, Teams, and Organizations; Design and Evaluation Center; and Knowledge and Innovation Resources.

14. Self-Paced Learning Resources

Many organizations provide resources for leaders to learn from books, magazines, audiotapes, CDs, videotapes, and self-scored assessments. Recommended resources are used within an ongoing leadership program, within a mentor or coaching relationship, or as utilized by individuals on their own.

The University of Minnesota's Women's Leadership Institute program design includes a retreat and eight monthly meetings with opportunities for participants to network as well as engage in self-reflection and personal growth. These meetings include a combination of guest speakers, self-reflection, and group discussion. Methodology used for self-reflection includes the Myers-Briggs Type Indicator, articles and books to read between monthly sessions followed by discussions, and learning from each other's skills and experiences.

15. Speakers, Seminars, and Symposiums

These are programs that utilize an expert or experts to present ideas, concepts, reports, and skills to enhance leaders. Most of the time, this type of program is structured as a lecture with a question-and-answer period.

The Leadership America program brings together one hundred women leaders for a year-long series of three- and four-day seminars. Using many methodologies and activities, participants learn about the successes and challenges of national and international significance. Many speakers provide their expertise about the latest issues.

16. Special Interest Groups

Called a "SIG," these small groups are created around a specific topic, issue, or interest by and for individuals who want or need this specialized information.

The Rochester Women's Network (RWN) was founded in 1978 and is the largest network of its kind in the country. Members represent 450 local employers and more than 150 women-owned businesses. RWN is a multifaceted forum through which women create connections, build relationships, and make their marks. They offer members, as well as the community-at-large, challenging, stimulating programs, a wealth of valuable benefits, and continuing support, both personal and professional.

RWN is one of five organizations that use special interest groups. Small groups are formed around a particular career focus or interest that provides members with a unique source of ongoing support. These SIGs also provide an opportunity for professional growth and learning in a supportive environment.

17. Training and Education

Often called "classroom" learning, this process uses trainers, facilitators, or teachers who design and develop learning modules using a variety of adult learning methodologies.

Mount Mary College seeks to develop women who are leaders in their profession, church, and community. The basis of their Women's Leadership Institute Program (WLI) includes their Leadership Model plus Characteristics and Skills of a Mount Mary Leader.

The model includes self-knowledge and competence, an entrepreneurial sense of vision, communication skills, and the ability to inspire and strengthen leadership in others. The characteristics of a Mount Mary leader are integral to their leadership design: integrity, confidence, open-mindedness, initiative, flexibility, perseverance, creativity, vision, social commitment, sense of humor, and empathy. The skills of a Mount Mary leader make up modules in their training: communication, analysis and synthesis, decision making, empowerment, delegation, conflict management, knowledge of field, balance, collaboration, constructive criticism, and appreciation of diversity.

The WLI training program is presented in cooperation with the Vorhees Transportation Center at Rutgers University in New Brunswick, New Jersey.

18. Web-Based Training and Resources

Computer-based training (CBT) uses learning modules on a website where individuals can learn at their own convenience and pace.

The Executive Women International's (EWI) Academy of Leadership Certified Professional Leaders' Program is an online professional development program. This suite of classes (fifteen hours total) includes sessions from Peter Drucker, Tom Peters, the Conference Board, and the American Management Association. This program is available not only to all EWI representatives, but also to all employees of their member firms.

How Often Components Are Used in Leadership Development

Currently, the CLC website hosts thirty leadership development programs for women, in both profit and not-for-profit organizations, offered in-house and for the public. We made a decision that any program selected for the CLC website must use a minimum of five of the eighteen components.

The components used most often were not a surprise to us and perhaps not to you. Of the programs on the CLC website, *Training and Education* was cited by twenty-six, *Networking* by twenty-three, *Speakers* by twenty-two, and *Conferences, Mentors,* and *Self-Paced Learning Resources* by seventeen organizations.

Components that were used the least included *Job Assignments, Special Interest Groups, Conference Calls,* and *Community Service.*

We were surprised that both *Coaching* (five) and *Assessments* (seven) were not used in more programs. Clearly, few developers of leadership development programs are recognizing the value of some of these components.

How Components Are Combined in Exemplary Programs

1. The Executive Women International's Academy of Leadership Program

This program offers its members an amazing twelve of the eighteen components— *Alumni Groups, Community Service, Conference Calls, Conferences, Networking, Newsletters, Research, Self-Paced Learning Resources, Speakers, Special Interest Groups, Training and Education,* and *Web-Based Training and Resources.*

Executive Women International (EWI) was established in 1938 when Lucille Johnson Perkins recognized the importance and potential of an association of key women working with their executives. Over 3,000 companies and 3,500 representatives are members of EWI today.

EWI recognizes that leadership today is as much a textural issue as a structural one, requiring new models of behaviors, not just systems models.

The Academy of Leadership embraces a philosophy that believes that (1) "leadership can and must be taught" and (2) "everyone possesses leadership potential."

The four leadership modules spread over the year include one held at the EWI Leadership Conference and Annual Meeting.

EWI also capitalizes on today's technology to offer "The Certified Professional Leaders' Program," as mentioned above. Bi-monthly activities include the *Pulse* newsletter, a teleseminar, and the online bookstore and resources that focus on different topics.

2. The Center for Creative Leadership's Women's Leadership Program

This program uses ten components—*Assessments and Feedback, Awards, Coaching, Conferences, Networking, Newsletters, Research, Self-Paced Learning Resources, Training and Education, and Web-Based Training and Resources.*

The inspiration for the Center for Creative Leadership (CCL), founded in 1970, came from the visionary and highly successful businessman, H. Smith Richardson Sr., who built the Vicks Chemical Co.

All of CCL's programs blend cutting-edge research with innovative training, coaching, assessments, and publishing to create a highly personal experience with lasting impact. CCL's educational approach is based on a development model of "Assessment, Challenge, and Support," preparing leaders to manage with confidence, creativity, and resilience.

CCL's Women's Leadership Program began in 1987 as a three-day program known as the Executive Women's Workshop. It expanded to five days in 1994 and became known as The Women's Leadership Program. The Women's Leadership Program is designed for mid- to senior-level women managers who want to become stronger leaders.

Interfacing with the training sessions is coaching that allows the individual to prepare for and build on individual assessment information, 360-degree feedback, specific program reflections, and goal setting. This coaching process provides the support and expertise that are important for the individual's goal attainment.

Participants network with and learn from other leaders from a wide variety of organizations, industries, and countries. Important and recommended resources are provided as well.

Three other programs on the CLC website use nine components—Catalyst, the Commonwealth of Pennsylvania's Leadership Development Institute, and the National Hispana Leadership Institute.

To learn more about these and other exceptional programs, go to the CLC website, www.courageousleadership.org, select the *Programs* link, then select the *Components* you want to learn more about and to see how they are used in other organizations.

Conclusion

The hope is that leadership development professionals will consider using additional components in their own leadership programs and thereby enhance participants' learning and advancement.

Take time now to check which of the following components your leadership programs currently use:

- ❏ Alumni Groups
- ❏ Assessments and Feedback
- ❏ Awards
- ❏ Coaching
- ❏ Community Service
- ❏ Conferences
- ❏ Conference Calls
- ❏ Job Assignments
- ❏ Mentors
- ❏ Networking
- ❏ Newsletters
- ❏ Organization Development and Consulting
- ❏ Research
- ❏ Self-Paced Learning Resources
- ❏ Speakers, Seminars, and Symposiums
- ❏ Special Interest Groups
- ❏ Training and Education
- ❏ Web-Based Training and Resources

To improve your leadership program, ask yourself these questions:

- How many components do you presently use?
- Which of the components could you add to your leadership development "mix"?
- What would be the benefits to your organization and to your leaders if you added these additional components?

How *can* you develop leaders? The answer? In so many ways and in so many combinations. The choice is yours.

Resources

Catalyst. (1998). *Advancing women in business: The Catalyst guide.* San Francisco: Jossey-Bass.

Charan, R., Drotter, S., & Noel, J. (2001). *The leadership pipeline: How to build the leadership-powered company.* San Francisco: Jossey-Bass.

Conger, J., & Benjamin, B. (1999). *Building leaders: How successful companies develop the next generation.* San Francisco: Jossey-Bass.

Downey, D., et al. (2001). *Assimilating new leaders: The key to executive retention.* New York: AMACOM.

Hart, L.B. (1994). *50 activities for developing leaders, Volume I.* Amherst, MA: HRD Press.

Hart, L.B., & Waisman, C. (2003). *50 activities for developing leaders, Volume II.* Amherst, MA: HRD Press.

Hart, L.B., & Waisman, C.S. (2005). A comprehensive, effective, proven model to develop leaders. In E. Biech (Ed.), *The 2005 Pfeiffer annual: Training* (pp. 231–254). San Francisco: Pfeiffer.

Ruderman, M.N., & Ohlott, P.J. (2002). *Standing at the crossroads: Next steps for high-achieving women.* San Francisco: Jossey-Bass.

Smart, B.D. (1999). *Top grading: How leading companies win by hiring, coaching, and keeping the best people.* New York: Penguin Press.

Lois B. Hart, Ed.D., *is the founder and past executive director of the Women's Leadership Institute, a unique, year-long program of mentoring, coaching, and training executive women. In 2005, she formed the Courageous Leadership Consortium that identifies, develops, and disseminates innovative leadership models and resources to advance women leaders.*

Dr. Hart has over thirty-three years of training, speaking, organizational consulting, coaching, non-profit, and public education experience. She has written twenty-three books and tapes, including 50 Activities for Developing Leaders, Volumes 1 & 2 *(co-authored with Dr. Charlotte Waisman),* Moving Up! Women and Leadership, *and* Faultless Facilitation: A Resource Guide and Instructor's Manual. *Dr. Hart received her bachelor's degree from the University of Rochester, her master's from Syracuse University, and her Ed.D. from the University of Massachusetts.*

Leveraging Business Data to Develop Strategic Learning Solutions

Ajay M. Pangarkar and Teresa Kirkwood

Summary

Smart organizations recognize early that leveraging their "people knowledge" helps them deliver superior business results and gain a strategic edge over the competition. With the significant volume of business data available, the complexity of data sources, and real-time information requirements, the challenge is having your people assimilate and be able to leverage the critical business data that will help you to respond to rapidly changing markets and evolving customer needs. Leveraging an organization's business data to develop a more focused learning strategy is an opportunity that lies before those responsible for workplace learning and performance. This is also the "secret" of those "smart" organizations—getting people to learn how to recognize relevant business data and using it to your advantage.

Over the last few years, companies have been trying to make strategic use of the vast amounts of business data and information they acquire. Business data is now an essential part of strategic and tactical business management. In fact, a recent survey by Gartner (2006), an independent IT research firm, of 1,400 CIOs reveals that business intelligence is a priority for their organizations. Business data is becoming a strategic tool to help people lead, measure, optimize, discover, and innovate in order to change the landscape of their organizations.

The ability to access, use, and share data and information in an efficient and relevant way helps improve business performance. Effectively utilizing business data can empower employees to:

- Align day-to-day operations with overall company strategy and objectives;

- Identify and understand the relationship between business processes and their impact on performance;

- Access information relevant to specific user roles and responsibilities;

- Gain contextual insight into business drivers; and

- Monitor the vital business indicators that are needed to move an organization forward such as:

  - Current status and trends of the company's financial performance;

  - Organizational effectiveness and profitability; and

  - Critical operational metrics and key performance measures.

In short, every type of business data helps companies gain a comprehensive and integrated view of their business and facilitate better and more effective decision making. This is why learning professionals need to begin using the available business data to help them develop more focused learning strategies and initiatives.

The biggest challenge is that business is not a subject that often comes up when you think about workplace learning and performance (WLP). For the longest time, business managers did not see the relevance of "training and development" within an industrial environment, and learning and performance often were seen only as a cost center (or money pit). Fortunately, this is changing, mainly due to the increasingly significant role of information and knowledge for businesses. Organizational leaders who require their employees to act on the business data to gain an "edge" over the competition or develop internal efficiencies or build market share support this shift. The goal is to recognize, learn, solve, and act on the business intelligence at hand.

So what does this have to do with learning and performance? Business data is information the company obtains through various sources. This data must become knowledge employees can use. Without this knowledge, the chances of making poor business decisions increase, possibly resulting in missed opportunities or, worse, disaster. Identifying potential business opportunities such as increasing profitability, rigorously cutting costs, and calculating precisely where to spend resources for optimal impact are key issues not only for top management but also for business managers and employees at all levels.

Learning and performance professionals must be proactive in interpreting the business data to deliver targeted and results-driven solutions. Although the old adage states that knowledge is power, business knowledge is only useful (powerful) to an organization if it is relevant, learned, and applied. Simply possessing business data in itself means nothing. Because the business data is information leading to knowledge, learning plays a pivotal role not only as a conduit but also as a catalyst in leveraging that business data.

Connecting Data and Learning

Traditionally, those responsible for the learning needs of an organization focused on ensuring new skills and capabilities were effectively acquired, assimilated, and applied by employees. These are the core competencies of WLP professionals. On the other hand, the organization's senior management is focused on business outcomes. Closing the gap between what management wants to see and what learning can deliver will build value for those involved in WLP. Filling this gap by using the business data to develop learning solutions will deliver lasting and tangible business results for an organization.

Economic uncertainties and rapid market changes make planning and decision making more difficult, but more critical than ever. Learning and performance's revised role is to provide managers with the information to quickly adapt to new business scenarios and changing business conditions. Companies must constantly improve their ability to identify, organize, and analyze all the information (business data) available to them. WLP can help make this happen.

First, let's dispense with the idea that the business leadership of any organization will ever recognize the importance of learning. Their focus is solely on improved business performance; learning and performance (L&P) is only one of many tools to help them go where they need to be. They will listen to and utilize any catalyst that helps them get results. Learning and performance must demonstrate that it can link the business data to performance-oriented learning initiatives.

Just as you would learn about the culture and language when visiting another country, not only do you have to speak the language of business and performance, but you have to interpret the information and provide learning solutions that best apply to the environment (culture) and directly lead to better organizational results. Interpreting business data is a proactive role for L&P and will allow it to enable improved business performance.

What L&P Needs to Know

Learning professionals must understand managers' decision-making process and how they can leverage an organization's business data to be able to develop effective learning solutions. In effect, there are three types of decisions that an organization can make:

- *Strategic decisions:* These are the major decisions that companies make to achieve their corporate mission and strategic objectives. These types of decisions are crucial to the overall success of the organization and often impact every part of an organization when implemented (for example, should we acquire another company; should we enter a new market; should we develop a new product; and so forth). There are not typically many decisions of this type, but their value is large.

- *Tactical decisions:* These types of decisions usually utilize business data the most and are implemented in a relatively short period of time. They are tactical in that they help to achieve strategic goals by leveraging the intelligence at hand. Examples include a product manager deciding what discount schedule to put in place, a pricing decision for a new product, or the marketing strategy required to build market presence and brand awareness.

- *Operational decisions:* These types of decisions occur on a daily basis and, individually, do not pose a threat to the organization. When taken in aggregate, however, operational decisions can play a major role at the tactical and even the strategic level of the decision process. These types of decisions are usually made by employees who are not knowledgeable about or too concerned with business data. There is an opportunity to collect these types of decisions to drive improved business performance.

Every business decision can be categorized into one of these three areas along with its relevant and corresponding business data (see Figure 1). Arriving at a proper decision depends on the information available to the decision-maker, which

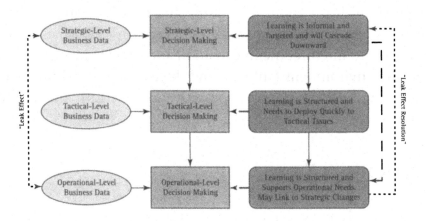

Figure 1. Data and Decision Making

determines the outcome and level of impact the decision will have on the organization. Business data not only facilitates the decision-making process but often dictates that some type of decision must be made. So what is the role of learning and performance?

The Role of Learning and Performance

Business data usually spur organizational leaders to make critical decisions. Business data incite change, and whenever change takes place, learning solutions are sure to follow. Learning and performance professionals can support managers by helping them to understand the data and thus arrive at an informed decision. Recognizing and acting on the data will add credibility and value for L&P, providing for more targeted and results-driven learning solutions.

Leveraging business data to develop more effective learning solutions can drive better business decisions. Let's look at how L&P can positively affect each decision category.

Learning Based on Strategic Data

The business data available for this type of decision is usually more complex and involved. The data itself involves many factors and requires deciphering. The decision-making process is more intense, affecting the organization as a whole. Learning and performance solutions at this level are primarily informal and targeted. The learning solutions developed to support and help resolve the decision-making process are tied directly to the overall learning strategy and key performance indicators. This means that a proposed learning solution at this level must cascade down through the organization and support the changes as they occur at the tactical and operational levels. For example, if some business data demonstrate that a primary competitor is finding success with a new feature on one of its products, then your organization needs to evaluate how to act on this critical information. A change or modification in the business direction will impact your organization's strategy, and your learning strategy will have to address the requisite changes and provide new learning initiatives at all levels of the organization. Furthermore, the outcomes of the learning initiatives you develop must be directly correlated to key performance indicators, usually through some type of strategic scorecard (see Pangarkar & Kirkwood, 2007).

Learning Based on Tactical Data

As mentioned earlier, tactical decisions tend to have direct implications for business and strategic objectives, especially in the short term. Tactical data indicates how aligned with or deviated from the business objectives the organization is. Learning solutions based on tactical data should demonstrate tangible results and be aligned to key performance measures cascaded down from the strategic level. For example, let's say your company strategic goal is to be the most customer-responsive and supportive organization in its market space. This would mean that the tactical business issues associated with this mission, such as customer service, employee product knowledge, and any other customer-oriented task, are in line with the company mission. The resulting tactical data must also be positive and be aligned with the strategic mission. If the tactical data, such as customer satisfaction measures, indicate any deviation from the mission, then learning and performance must act immediately. Preferably, as a learning professional, you would simulate scenarios for possible deviations before they happen and continually monitor and control the knowledge and skills development of the staff and act on a just-in-time basis.

Learning Based on Operational Data

Even though this type of data does not normally indicate any immediate threats to the organization, it may, like a small crack in a dam, provide early indications of larger business problems. Learning initiatives at this level are more in line with maintenance and support of employee skills, and the earlier you are able to interpret the data as it relates to the daily activities of the organization, the more effective employees can become. Using our previous tactical example, introducing customer relationship management software would facilitate a customer service representative's addressing the needs of a customer. If the customer rep, however, does not leverage the capabilities of the new system, then the "small crack" begins. The learning solution did not address the need adequately. Learning and performance should work in close partnership with other business units (or, as we like to say, become the business unit's learning department) to learn what the operational issues are and to deliver effective learning solutions. At this level, each learning strategy should be tailored to the needs of the business unit and its specific operational requirements that cascade up to and align with the tactical and strategic concerns of the organization as a whole.

Conclusion

Times have changed significantly for organizations of all sizes. Gaining an advantage in increasingly competitive environments is essential to simply survive, let alone thrive. Whether or not a company has access to relevant business data can mean the difference between real success and mediocre performance. Every piece of business data available provides companies with evidence and an early indication of how well the organization is meeting its business and strategic objectives. Companies that can exploit their own data and information to make smarter decisions will have a clear competitive advantage over their competitors. This is an opportunity for learning and performance professionals to gain prominence by helping to translate the data into useable knowledge.

As business data play a greater role and become a priority for senior management, companies will need flexible learning solutions that help them address and act on the business data in both the short and long term. As companies grow, the amount of complex business data will increase, and learning and performance will no longer be relegated to the "back seat," but viewed as an enabling force to leverage business data.

References

Gartner. (2006, January 23). *Gartner survey of 1,400 CIOS shows transformation of IT organization is accelerating* (press release). Available: www.gartner.com/press_release/asset_143678_11.html. Last accessed February 21, 2009.

Pangarkar, A., & Kirkwood, T. (2007, July). Linking learning strategy to the balanced scorecard. *CLO*.

Ajay M. Pangarkar, CTDP, *and* **Teresa Kirkwood, CTDP,** *are partners at CentralKnowledge.com. At CentralKnowledge, they align learning strategy and performance with business and strategic objectives. They are the authors of* The Trainer's Balanced Scorecard: A Complete Resource for Linking Learning to Organizational Strategy *(Pfeiffer) and* Building Business Acumen for Trainers: Skills to Empower the Learning Function *(Pfeiffer).*

Contributors

Elisabeth C. Ayres, PHR
1215 S. Clark Street
Arlington, VA 22202
(703) 859-6749
fax: (703) 647-1483
email: elisabeth.c.ayres@boeing.com

Teri-E Belf
2016 Lakebreeze Way
Reston, VA 20191-4021
(703) 716-8374
fax: (703) 264-7867
email: coach@belf.org

Beverly J. Bitterman
5307 Winhawk Way
Lutz, FL 33558
(813) 964-1260
fax: (813) 961-7062
email: beverly@beverlybitterman.com
URL: www.beverlybitterman.com

Jo-Ann C. Byrne, RN, BS, MHSA
Director, Education and Organizational
  Development
St. Vincent's Healthcare
1 Shircliff Way
Seton Hall, Room 4916
Jacksonville, FL 32204
(904) 308-3520
email: JoAnn.Byrne@stvincentshealth
.com

Catherine Cable
412 N Jordan Street, Number 201
Alexandria, VA 22304
(703) 967-2485
email: catherine.cable@
  thomsonreuters.com

Ann T. Chow
Metropolitan Detroit Bureau of
  School Studies, Inc.
391 Education
Wayne State University
Detroit, MI, 48202
(313) 577 1729
fax: (313) 577 8278
email: annchow@wayne.edu

Robert Clark
Educational Administration Program
California State University,
  Dominquez Hills
Carson, CA 90747
(717) 870-2840
email: rclark@csudh.edu

Dianne Crampton
19464 Summerwalk Place
Bend, OR 97702
(877) 538-2822
(541) 312-8869
email: tigers@uci.net
URL: http://www.corevalues.com

Alexander Crispo
Young Hall, Room 438
302 Wood Street
Purdue University
West Lafayette, IN 47907
(765) 494-5609
email: alwc@purdue.edu

Eric G. Flamholtz, Ph.D.
Management Systems Consulting
 Corporation
10990 Wilshire Boulevard, Suite 1420
Los Angeles, CA 90024
(310) 477-0444
email: ef@mgtsystems.com

Barbara Pate Glacel, Ph.D.
12103 Richland Lane
Oak Hill, VA 20171
(703) 262-9120
email: bpglacel@glacel.com
URL: www.glacel.com

Marshall Goldsmith
P.O. Box 9710
Rancho Santa Fe, CA 92067
(858) 759-0950
email: marshall@marshallgoldsmith
 .com
URL: www.marshallgoldsmithlibrary
 .com

Leonard D. Goodstein, Ph.D.
4815 Foxhall Crescent, NW
Washington DC, 20007
(202) 333-3134
fax: (202) 333-8519
email: Leng@aol.com

Ann M. Gormley
Gormley Consulting
2207 Castro Street, Number2
San Francisco, CA 94131
(415) 264-3973
email: anniegorm@aol.com

Lois B. Hart, Ed.D. President
Courageous Leadership Consortium
481 Claffey Road
Polson, MT 59860
(406) 250-9860
email: hart@montanasky.com
URL: www.courageousleadership
 .org

Amy Henderson
Henderson Training, Inc.
28770 Park Woodland Place
Santa Clarita, CA 91390
(661) 296-4490
email: amy@hendersontraining
 .com
URL: www.hendersontraining.com

Mahaveer Jain
V.V Giri National Labour Institute
Post Box No. 68
Sector - 24, NOIDA
U.P
India
0120- 2412524
email: mahaveerjain2007@gmail.com

Homer H. Johnson, Ph.D.
Professor of Management
School of Business Administration
Loyola University Chicago
820 N. Michigan Avenue
Chicago, IL 60611
   (312) 915-6682
   fax: (312) 915-6988
   email: hjohnso@luc.edu

Bruce Alan Kimbrew
2919 Burdeck Drive
Oakland, CA 94602
   (415) 385-3756
   email: Bruce.kimbrew@am.jll.com

Teresa Kirkwood
CentralKnowledge
214 Lamarche
Laval, Quebec H7X 3M7
Canada
   (450) 689-3895
   fax: (450) 689-3895

Lucille Maddalena, Ed.D.
Maddalena Transitions Management
P.O. Box 424
Belmar, NJ 07719
   (732) 280-6885
   URL: info@mtmanagement.net

Dawn J. Mahoney
N2827 N. Lake Point Drive
Lodi, WI 53555
   (608) 219-5785
   email: dawnjmahoney@charter.net

Linda S. Eck Mills, MBA
Dynamic Communication Services
20 Worman Lane
Bernville, PA 19506
   (610) 488-7010
   email: LSMillsRD@aol.com

Howard Morgan
P.O. Box 2468
Rancho Santa Fe, CA 92067
   (858) 756-6912
   email: howard@howardjmorgan.com

James L. Moseley
Administrative and Organizational
   Studies Division
Instructional Technology Program
College of Education
Wayne State University
395 Education
Detroit, MI 48202
   (313) 577 7948
   fax: (313) 577 1693
   email: moseley@wayne.edu

Edwin L. Mouriño-Ruiz
2400 Northampton Avenue
Orlando, FL 32828
   (407) 306-5218
   email: drmourino@hotmail.com
   email: Edwin.l.mourino@lmco.com

Mohandas Nair
A2 Kamdar Building
607, Gokhale Road (South)
Dadar, Mumbai–400 028
India
   (91 22) 2422 6307
   email: mknair@vsnl.net
   email: nair_mohandas@hotmail.com

Ajay M. Pangarkar
CentralKnowledge
214 Lamarche
Laval, Quebec H7X 3M7
Canada
  (450) 689-3895
  fax: (450) 689-3895
  email: ajayp@centralknowledge.com

Udai Pareek
IIHMR 1
Prabhu Dayal Marg,
Sanganer Airport
Jaipur, India 302011
  email: Udai@iihmr.org

Mona Lee Pearl
Executive Vice President and Chief
  Operating Officer
Western States Learning Corporation
1401 Airport Parkway, Suite 300
Cheyenne, WY 82001
  (307) 772-9001
  email: pearl@wslc.com
  URL: www.alignwslc.com

David Piltz
The Learning Key, Inc.
1093 General Washington Memorial
  Boulevard
Washington Crossing, PA 18977
  (215) 493-9641
  (800) 465-7005
  fax: (215) 493-9642
  email: dpiltz@thelearningkey.com
  URL: www.thelearningkey.com

Yvonne Randle, Ph.D.
Management Systems Consulting
  Corporation

10990 Wilshire Boulevard, Suite 1420
Los Angeles, CA 90024
  (310) 477-0444
  email: yr@mgtsystems.com

Harriet Rifkin
Rifkin & Associates, LLC
17 Roosevelt Street
Albany, NY 12206
  (518) 956-0511
  fax: (518) 514-1145
  email: harriet@rifkin-associates.com

Rafael Rivera
P.O. Box 17074
Arlington, VA 22216
  (202) 494-6335
  fax: (888) 217-7940
  email: rorivera@att.net

Travis L. Russ, Ph.D.
Assistant Professor
School of Business Administration
Fordham University
1790 Broadway, Office Number 1304
New York, NY 10019
  (212) 636-6354
  fax: (212) 586-0575
  email: russ@fordham.edu
  URL: http://faculty.fordham.edu/russ

Jan M. Schmuckler, Ph.D.
Consultation
3921 Burckhalter Avenue
Oakland, CA 94605
  (510) 562-0626
  email: jan@lignumvitae.com

Dr. Carol Ann Zulauf Sharicz
Associate Professor

Suffolk University
Boston, MA 02114
  (617) 573-8089
  email: csharicz@comcast.net

Karl E. Sharicz
SimplexGrinnell
50 Technology Drive
Westminster, MA 01441
  (978) 731-7551

Jody L. Shields
Consultant
Align Organizational Development and
  Training
A Division of Western States Learning
  Corporation
1401 Airport Parkway, Suite 300
Cheyenne, WY 82001
  (307) 772-9148

Kris Taylor
4710 South 100 East
Lafayette, IN 47909
  (765) 404-8950
  fax: (765) 448-9124
  email: kris@ktaylorandassoc.com

Sacip Toker
Administrative and Organizational
  Studies Division
Instructional Technology Program
College of Education
Wayne State University
369 Education
Detroit, MI 48202
  (313) 577 4648
  fax: (313) 577 1683
  email: saciptoker@wayne.edu
  email: saciptoker@gmail.com

Karen A. Travis
Sigma Performance Solutions, Inc.
660 Kenilworth Drive, Suite 104
Baltimore, MD 21204
  (410) 667-9055
  email: karen@sigmapsinc.com

Phil Van Horn, CEO
Western States Learning Corporation
1401 Airport Parkway, Suite 300
Cheyenne, WY 82001
  (307) 772-9000
  email: pvanhorn@wslc.com

Gary Wagenheim
5865 Wiltshire Street
Vancouver, British Columbia
V6M 3L7
Canada
  (604) 266-4866
  fax: (604) 266-4876
  email: wagenhei@sfu.ca

Devora Zack
President, Only Connect Consulting,
  Inc.
3 Bethesda Metro Center, Suite 700
Bethesda, MD 20854
  (301) 941-1800
  fax: (301) 765-2182
  email: dzack@onlyconnectconsulting
  .com

Sophia Zia
3000 Spout Run Parkway, B-510
Arlington, VA 22201
  (703) 528-8707
  fax: (703) 682-6135
  email: sophia.zia@aecom.com

Contents of the Companion Volume, *The 2010 Pfeiffer Annual: Training*

**Communication Topics

Editor's Choice

Inventories, Questionnaires, and Surveys

Articles and Discussion Resources